LF 2-03   8/03

P9-DHA-871

SPORT AND SOCIETY IN ANCIENT GREECE

This book provides a concise and readable introduction to ancient Greek sport. It covers such standard topics as the links between sport, religion and warfare, the origins and history of the Olympic games, and the spirit of competition among the Greeks. Its main focus, however, is on Greek sport as an arena for the creation and expression of difference among individuals and groups. Sport not only identified winners and losers. It also drew boundaries between groups (Greeks and barbarians, boys and men, males and females) and offered a field for debate on the relative worth of athletic and equestrian competition. The book includes guides to the ancient evidence and to modern scholarship on the subject.

Mark Golden is Professor of Classics in the University of Winnipeg. He is the author of *Children and Childhood in Classical Athens* (1990), and, with Peter Toohey, edited *Inventing Ancient Culture: Historicism, Periodization and the Ancient World* (1997).

SOUTHEASTERN COMMUNITY
COLLEGE LIBRARY
WHITEVILLE, NC 28472

KEY THEMES IN ANCIENT HISTORY

Editors

P. A. Cartledge
Clare College, Cambridge

P. D. A. Garnsey
Jesus College, Cambridge

Key Themes in Ancient History aims to provide readable, informed and original studies of various basic topics, designed in the first instance for students and teachers of Classics and Ancient History, but also for those engaged in related disciplines. Each volume is devoted to a general theme in Greek, Roman, or where appropriate, Graeco-Roman history, or to some salient aspect or aspects of it. Besides indicating the state of current research in the relevant area, authors seek to show how the theme is significant for our own as well as ancient culture and society. By providing books for courses that are oriented around themes it is hoped to encourage and stimulate promising new developments in teaching and research in ancient history.

Other books in the series:

Death-ritual and social structure in classical antiquity, by Ian Morris
0 521 37465 0 (hardback), 0 521 37611 4 (paperback)

Literacy and orality in ancient Greece, by Rosalind Thomas
0 521 37346 8 (hardback), 0 521 37742 0 (paperback)

Slavery and society at Rome, by Keith Bradley
0 521 37287 9 (hardback), 0 521 37887 7 (paperback)

Law, violence, and community in classical Athens, by David Cohen
0 521 38167 3 (hardback), 0 521 38837 6 (paperback)

Public order in ancient Rome, by Wilfried Nippel
0 521 38327 7 (hardback), 0 521 38749 3 (paperback)

Friendship in the classical world, by David Konstan
0 521 45402 6 (hardback), 0 521 45998 2 (paperback)

Food and society in classical antiquity, by Peter Garnsey
0 521 64182 9 (hardback, 0 521 64588 3 (paperback)

Religions of the Ancient Greeks, by Simon Price
0 521 38201 7 (hardback) 0 521 38867 8 (paperback)

Banking and business in the Roman world, by Jean Andreau
0521 38031 6 (hardback) 0 521 38932 1 (paperback)

Roman law in context, by David Johnston
0 521 63046 0 (hardback) 0 521 63961 1 (paperback)

GV
573
.G65
1998

SPORT AND SOCIETY IN ANCIENT GREECE

MARK GOLDEN

SOUTHEASTERN COMMUNITY
COLLEGE LIBRARY
WHITEVILLE, NC 28472

 CAMBRIDGE
UNIVERSITY PRESS

PUBLISHED BY THE PRESS SYNDICATE OF THE UNIVERSITY OF CAMBRIDGE
The Pitt Building, Trumpington Street, Cambridge CB2 1 RP, United Kingdom

CAMBRIDGE UNIVERSITY PRESS
The Edinburgh Building, Cambridge CB2 2RU, United Kingdom
40 West 20th Street, New York, NY 10011–4211, USA
10 Stamford Road, Oakleigh, Melbourne 3166, Australia

© Cambridge University Press 1998

This book is in copyright. Subject to statutory exception and to the provisions of relevant
collective licensing agreements, no reproduction of any part may take place without the
written permission of Cambridge University Press.

First published 1998
Reprinted 2000

Printed in the United Kingdom at the University Press, Cambridge

Typeset in 11/12.5pt Baskerville   [CE]

A catalogue record for this book is available from the British library

Library of Congress cataloguing in publication data
Golden, Mark, 1948–
Sport and society in ancient Greece / Mark Golden.
p.   cm. – (Key themes in ancient history)
Includes bibliographical references (p.) and index.
ISBN 0 521 49698 5 (hardback); 0 521 49790 6 (paperback)
1. Sports – Social aspects – Greece – History.
2. Olympic games (Ancient).
3. Greece – Civilization – To 146 B.C.
4. Greece – Social conditions – To 146 B.C.
I. Title.   II. Series.
GV573.G65   1998
306.4′83′0938–dc21   98–3004   CIP

ISBN 0 521 49698 5 hardback
ISBN 0 521 49790 6 paperback

Contents

List of plates	*page*	vi
List of figures and tables		viii
Preface		ix

1	Ways of seeing Greek sport	1
2	The evidence and its limits	46
3	Reflections of victory in literature and art	74
4	Divisions of age and sex	104
5	Class difference, dissent, democracy	141
	Conclusion	176
	Bibliographical essay	179
	Some important dates	183

List of works cited	186
Index and glossary	208

Plates

1   Two officials hold a rod (at knee level) to keep boxers at   *page* 53
    close quarters. Attic black-figure Panathenaic amphora,
    Cleophrades Painter, Taranto, Museo Nazionale
    115472, early fifth century. Photo: Ministero per i Beni
    Culturali e Ambientali, Soprintendenza Archeologica
    della Puglia, Taranto.

2   A fragment of a wrestling manual on papyrus. *P Oxy.*   56
    3.466, New York, Rare Book and Manuscript Library,
    Columbia University, first/second century CE. Photo:
    Rare Book and Manuscript Library, Columbia University.

3   Boxers bleed from the nose. Attic black-figure hydria,   59
    Leagrus Group, Vatican Museum 416, Beazley, *ABV* 365,
    no. 65, about 520. Photo: Direzione Generale Musei
    Vaticani, Vatican City.

4   Runners with loincloths. Attic black-figure stamnos,   67
    Michigan Painter, Oxford, Ashmolean Museum 1965.97,
    Beazley, *ABV* 343 no. 6, 510-500. Photo: Ashmolean
    Museum.

5   Orestes kills Aegisthus: the avenger as athletic victor. Attic 97
    red-figure calyx krater, Aegisthus Painter, Malibu,
    J. Paul Getty Museum 88.AE.66, about 470. Photo:
    J. Paul Getty Museum.

6   Female runner dressed as for the Heraea. Bronze   130
    statuette, probably from a Laconian workshop, London,
    British Museum inv. 208, about 560. Photo: British
    Museum.

7   Atalanta wrestles Peleus. Attic black-figure hydria,   135
    Atalanta Group, Manchester Museum 40085 (III H 5),
    Beazley, *ABV* 91 no. 3, about 560. Photo: The
    Manchester Museum, University of Manchester.

8   Heracles fights Antaeus: the hero as pancratiast. Attic 153
    black-figure eye cup, Leagrus Group, Paris, Bibliothèque
    Nationale 322, Beazley, *ABV* 380 no. 296, 515–500. Photo:
    Bibliothèque Nationale de France.

9   An official strikes a boxer for a foul. Attic black-figure 163
    Panathenaic amphora, Painter of Munich 1519, Rome,
    Villa Giulia 50680, Beazley, *ABV* 394 no. 10, about 510.
    Photo: Ministero per i Beni Culturali e Ambientali,
    Soprintendenza Archeologica per L'Etruria Meridionale,
    Rome.

Figures

1(a) Olympia. The Altis. (Reproduced with modifications   *page* 22
      and by permission of the author from Eric L. Brulotte,
      'The "Pillar of Oinomaos" and the location of Stadium I
      at Olympia', *American Journal of Archaeology* 98 (1994) 53–64,
      Fig. 1.)
1(b) Olympia. The Altis with Drees's Stadium I. (Ibid. Fig. 7.)   22
1(c) Olympia. The Altis with Brulotte's Stadium I. (Ibid.   22
      Fig. 6.)

Tables

1 The classical circuit (*periodos*)   11
2 The schedule of the Olympic festival, about 350 BCE   20
3 Geographical distribution of athletic victories in the games   36
   of the circuit, sixth century BCE–first century BCE
4 The Olympic programme and the traditional date when   41
   each event joined it
5 Ages of equestrian victors   121
6 Athenian equestrian competitors and victors, 600–300 BCE   172

Preface

This book stems from my teaching. The last fifteen years have witnessed an extraordinary upsurge of interest in Greek sport. This is perhaps best demonstrated by the appearance of the journal *Nikephoros*, devoted to ancient sport, and by the availability of no fewer than three collections of ancient literary sources on the subject in English translation (see the Bibliographical Essay). We may also point (among books in English only) to publications on the origin of Greek sport, its Near Eastern antecedents, its early cult environment, on important competitive festivals such as the Olympics and Panathenaea, on athletics at Athens, on combat sports, on the ideology of amateurism in ancient and modern sport. Yet there is no up-to-date survey of the place of sport in ancient Greek society. I myself order books by E.N. Gardiner and H.A. Harris for my students. But these, though informative and well illustrated, are inevitably misleading on many points of detail, especially those illuminated by ongoing archaeological investigations; and they are embarrassingly out of step with contemporary attitudes in respect to gender, social class and ethnicity. I hope that this book will go some way towards replacing them. It is meant to be accessible to classicists and ancient historians with no expertise in sport, to sport historians who know nothing of the ancient world, to those who watch and compete in events like the Greeks' and in events they never dreamed of. It may be within the considerable reach of Shaquille O'Neal. (Asked whether he had visited the Parthenon during a visit to Greece, the American basketball star responded, 'I can't really remember all the clubs we went to.') I have therefore translated all the Greek and Latin quotations from ancient sources; these translations are my own unless otherwise indicated. I also hope, however,

that there is something here for specialists too, both in the overall
approach I take and in its application to particular issues.[1]

This is *an* introduction to the study of ancient Greek sport and
society; it is not the only one possible. It reflects my own priorities as
a teacher: identifying different approaches, encouraging critical use
of evidence, tracing sport's links with attitudes and realities within
Greek culture as a whole. So, while I have aimed to include most of
the information I consider essential to an account of ancient Greek
sport, I have not always presented it in predictable ways. For
example, I have not provided a survey of the individual events most
commonly included in competitive festivals or of the ways in which
they were conducted – a feature of most introductions and sourcebooks. However, a list of the events on the Olympic programme
plays a part in an examination of the competing claims to pre-
eminence of equestrian and athletic competition; and I review
debates on the nature of the Greek jump and on the scoring of the
pentathlon in order to explore problems posed by the nature of our
evidence and the consequences which our solutions may entail for
our ideas about the Greeks. The index, which does double duty as a
glossary of terms, should reduce any inconvenience arising from this
strategy.

The first chapter outlines some current ways of seeing sport and
evaluates their applicability to ancient Greece. After an investigation
of three traditional topics still current today – sport and religion,
sport and warfare, the competitive culture of the Greeks and its
relationship to nearby nations – I turn to the approach which gives
this book its thematic unity. I argue that Greek sport is implicated in
what I call a discourse of difference. It served to express and
maintain distinctions between groups of many kinds (peoples, social
classes, genders, ages) as well as between individuals. It also afforded
a field for the Greek predilection to establish and dispute hierarchies
(as among festivals and events). I end the chapter with a demonstration of this understanding of Greek sport in action, examining
the motives for the real and imagined introduction of events at
Olympia. In the second chapter, I detour to survey our sources of
evidence and the challenges they impose; here the discussion
proceeds by case studies – of athletic nudity and the date of the first

---

[1] O'Neal: this book might also interest the baseball player Ben Oglivie, 'probably the first
home run champion since Lou Gehrig to carry around a volume of Plutarch' (Okrent and
Wulf 1989:334–5).

Olympics as well as the jump and the pentathlon. Chapter 3 returns to the discourse of difference *via* consideration of some consequences of victory and its representation in literature and art; the emphasis is on the praise poetry of Simonides, Pindar, Bacchylides and on the depiction of Orestes as a winner – and a loser – in Greek tragedy. Chapter 4 takes up gender and age. Women's success in equestrian competition against men might be used to demean such claims to distinction; their participation in athletics, though always (or nearly so) apart from men, revealed them nevertheless as inferior. As for age, horse-racing was generally the preserve of older owners, a means to prolong competition for the rich and increase their access to its rewards. This connection of wealth and equestrian competition crops up again in Chapter 5, on social class. Here I set out from reflections on the privileged position of the crown games in aristo-cratic ideology (as revealed through the myth of Heracles) to explore hostility to the athletic and equestrian elite in democratic Athens. A brief conclusion and a bibliographical essay on further reading round the book off.

Two preliminary cautions are in order. First, I refer to Greek *sport* and the Olympic (and other) *games*. Carrying as they do connotations of leisure and amusement, these terms are quite inappropriate (cf. Young 1984:171–6). Athletic and equestrian competition was serious business for the Greek: *agōn* (plural *agones*), the common word for contest, is the root of our 'agony'. I was puzzled as a student that my Ottawa high school had an English motto even though it taught five years of Latin. Now I realize that 'Play the game' is one of those modern ideas for which it is hard to find a Greek or Latin tag; the ideal of the 'good sport', while not utterly unknown, did not predominate among the Greeks. 'Nice guys finish last', 'Winning isn't the main thing, it's the only thing', 'Show me a good loser and I'll show you a loser' – these are slogans closer to the spirit of Greek sport. I use 'sport' and 'games' because the words have become established in this connection, and to avoid the awkwardness of 'athletic and equestrian competition'. This prompts my second warning. In confining my study to such contests alone, I omit other important areas of competition, the cultural *agones*, for musicians, singers, reciters of Homer and others, that shared the stage with them at many festivals and may even have overshadowed them at celebrations as significant as the Pythian games at Delphi. In part, this is because Greek writers too tended to group together athletic and equestrian events, in part because cultural competitions (for trumpeters and heralds) were late and of relatively little moment at Olympia, the most important festival of all (Crowther 1994b). But I must confess that I have let my own interests – especially in the rivalry between athletic and horse-racing – prevail over the temptation to write a comprehensive account of competition in ancient Greece, an ambition in any case doomed to failure in such a short book.[2]

It is pleasant to pass from my own shortcomings to those people who have done so much to make up for them. This book is dedicated to my students and co-workers at the University of Winnipeg, a pleasant and productive home away from home for the past fifteen years. Students have sometimes been guinea pigs, rarely parrots; on the contrary, much of the discussion of religion in Chapter 1 is indebted to the Honours thesis of Mark Matz, now a Rhodes Scholar at Corpus Christi College, Oxford. My colleagues in the Department of Classics (Jane Cahill, Craig Cooper, Bob Gold, Lou Lépine, Iain McDougall) have provided models of commitment and competence. Allison Sproul Dixon and her associates in the Interlending Department of the university library have worked tirelessly to decipher loan requests and still possessed energy enough to obtain the research materials I needed. What they could not find I was usually able to inspect on site due to the support of the office of the Associate Vice-President for Research and the members of the university's Research and Travel Committee.

I also owe thanks elsewhere. My editor, Paul Cartledge, commented on each chapter as it emerged; his own scholarship inspired me at the same time as his vigour put me to shame. Peter Garnsey, the co-editor of this series, urged readability with a clarity I can only hope to emulate. Don Kyle (my predecessor at Winnipeg) and Mac Wallace, friend and wise advisor for thirty years, read the whole typescript in draft; David Depew and Nancy Felson (-Rubin) commented on individual chapters. I am grateful for assistance of various kinds to Tim Barnes, Glenn Bugh, Douglas Cairns, Nigel Crowther, Richard Hamilton, Steve Hodkinson, Sandra Kirby, Hugh Lee, Harold Mattingly, Kathryn Morgan, Pauline Ripat, Jim Roy, Alan Sommerstein, Peter Toohey, Liz Warman, Ingomar

---

[2] Athletic and equestrian events: *gumnikoi kai hippikoi agones* (e.g. Hdt. 1.167, 6.38, 8.26, Xen. *Oec.* 7.9, Pl. *Resp.* 3.412b, [Dem.] 60.13).

Weiler. The Department of Classics, University of Toronto, provided me with an office, technical help and the best of company for the first half of the sabbatical year in which this project began. During the second half, I enjoyed the fellowship of Clare Hall, Cambridge and had the run of the resources of the library of the Faculty of Classics, Cambridge University. ('Greek sport', observed one of the locals, a specialist in Latin literary criticism, as I dusted off a copy of Moretti's list of Olympic victors. 'That's not very fashionable.') I was lucky enough to finish the book as a Summer Scholar at the Center for Hellenic Studies in Washington DC. To all these institutions, thanks for hospitality and help. I gratefully acknowledge the permission of *Aethlon* (formerly *Arete*): *The Journal of Sport Literature* to revise material originally published as 'Sport and wage-labour in the Heracles myth' (*Arete* 3.2 (1986) 145–58) for use in Chapter 5. My last debt is the oldest, to friends who played and talked sport with me before my interest became academic: Mike Beck, Bruce Burron, the late Paul Hoch, Bob Kellermann, Charlie Novogrodsky, Dave Whitson.

The focus of this book is on the classical period, roughly the fifth and fourth centuries before the current era. However, since I prefer to stress continuity within the ancient Greek world rather than change, the discussion frequently touches on events, institutions and evidence from periods before and after. Readers with a taste for paradox will note that this book about difference stresses similarities over time. On the other hand, the play of difference, itself a constant, might lead to innovations in some important areas, and I discuss these as circumstances require. Ancient dates without explicit indication of their era (as CE) are BCE. For ancient authors and works, I use the abbreviations of the *Oxford Classical Dictionary* or of H.G. Liddell, R. Scott and H. Stuart Jones, *A Greek-English Lexicon* (LSJ). Abbreviations of periodical titles follow *L'année philologique*.

CHAPTER I

Ways of seeing Greek sport

Sometime early in 400 BCE, the remnants of the '10,000', Greek mercenaries who had served under the Persian pretender Cyrus, reached Trapezus on the Black Sea. What happened next is recounted by one of their leaders, Xenophon, in his *Anabasis* (4.8.25–8). In the commentary which follows, I try to maintain a balance between historiographical and literary approaches, assuming that Xenophon reports events reliably while shaping the narrative for purposes of his own (cf. Moles 1994:70); the dialectic of fact and representation is made more complex in this instance by Xenophon's position of influence, which may have allowed him to pattern what actually occurred as well:

After this they set to preparing the sacrifice they had promised; they had enough oxen to sacrifice to Zeus in thanks for their salvation and to Heracles for his guidance as well as to conduct the sacrifices they had vowed to the other gods. They also held an athletic competition right on the mountain where they were camping. To see to the track and to preside over the competition they chose Dracontius, a Spartan who had been exiled from his home as a boy for accidentally killing another boy he had stabbed with a knife. After the sacrifice, they handed the hides of the slaughtered animals to Dracontius and began to encourage him to show them where he had made the track. He pointed to where they were in fact standing. 'This crest', he said, 'is a very good place to run wherever you please.' 'But how can men wrestle on ground as hard and overgrown as this?' they asked. 'The one who is thrown will get hurt a little more,' came the response. Boys – most of them from among the prisoners – competed in the sprint, more than sixty Cretans in the long race, others in wrestling, boxing, and *pankration* . . . ; it was good to see. For many entered the events and, since the female camp-followers were watching, there was a great deal of rivalry. There were horse races too. The riders had to drive the horses down the steep slope, turn them around in the sea and then lead them back to the altar. Many rolled down, and on the way up the slope was so steep that the horses proceeded only with difficulty at a walk. There was a lot of shouting and laughter and cheering.

There is more involved here than simply rest and recreation. Trapezus is the first Greek city the '10,000' have reached on their long and dangerous trek, and they celebrate in prototypically Greek fashion, recalling as they do an earlier competition, for Lycaean Zeus, at the expedition's outset (Xen. *An.* 1.2.10). Sacrifice is the central act in Greek religious observance, athletic and equestrian competition a mainstay of Greek male culture; it has recently been argued that the combination lies at the core of Greek sport – an idea to which I will return below (Sansone 1988). And yet this is a very unusual competition. Captives, slave booty, run against free Greeks. Cretans run alone. While some of the events familiar from Olympia and the other great festivals are included, others are not (unless they have dropped out of the text after the *pankration*), notably those which distinguish the pentathlon: the long jump, discus and javelin throw. This is all the more surprising in that soldiers on active duty might be expected to demonstrate their prowess with the javelin at least as a weapon of war. Oddest of all, perhaps, is the horse race. In one direction, it involves a laborious climb towards the altar. In the other, however, horses and riders run or roll downhill, like barbarian Persians or Odrysians instead of Greeks (Xen. *Eq.* 8.6); and their inevitable missteps call forth cheers and merriment. Compare this to the accounts of other equestrian accidents in some other literary texts, especially to the chariot disasters of tragedy, in which Hippolytus and the imaginary Orestes crash to the horror of their onlookers and the sorrow of all who hear.

Is this, then, a kind of comic travesty of an athletic competition, Xenophon's deadpan way of making us share the relief of his fun-loving fellows and also, it may be, of suggesting that their time among the barbarians has made them, for now at least, less than Greek? The Cretans may occur to us here. Famous as runners from Orsilochus, fleet of foot (Hom. *Od.* 13.258–70), to Sotades, twice Olympic champion in Xenophon's own lifetime (Moretti 1957: nos. 390, 398), they were no less well known as archers, the role they played in Cyrus's army (e.g., *An.* 1.2.9); their ability to fight from afar and lightly encumbered was ridiculed as well as respected, and their speed earns them a rather undignified special detail in a fake ambuscade a little later on (*An.* 5.2.29–32). And certainly comedy offers an approach to the figure of Dracontius, whose choice of a track is less considered, as well as less comfortable, than his colleagues had in mind. That's what you get when your organizer is not only a Spartan, a breed thought to be thick as well as tough, but a man polluted by bloodshed, accidental bloodshed at that – the Spartan who couldn't stab straight. This is an attractive reading, but I think a misleading one. The hides, presumably to be distributed as prizes, recall a famous passage of the *Iliad*, Achilles' pursuit of Hector: 'It was no sacrificial beast or oxhide they strove to win – the usual prizes that men gain in a foot-race; rather, they were running for the life of Hector, tamer of horses' (Hom. *Il.* 22.159–61). Dracontius' role is Achilles' of course, reintegrated into his equally temporary community to preside over the funeral games for Patroclus in *Iliad* 23; but there is something of Patroclus about Dracontius too, the Patroclus who accidentally killed a playmate as a boy in Opus and had to flee to Thessaly and exile (*Il.* 23.83–90). These Homeric echoes persuade me that Xenophon's tone is not altogether mocking after all. But that is not to deny something subversive in the spectacle.

Let us consider again the competition among boys. Nigel Crowther has recently suggested that slaves could compete in the Athenian Panathenaea (Crowther 1992c). This is hardly plausible, given the law (ascribed to Solon) which forbade slaves even to oil themselves let alone compete in Athenian palaestras, and is anyway not a necessary inference from the text Crowther adduces in its support (cf. Kyle 1992: 208 n. 127). The Demosthenic *Eroticus*, commenting on various distinctive marks of the *apobatēs* competition (probably at the Panathenaea), notes that 'in the other competitions (*athlematōn*), both slaves and foreigners take part (*metekhontas*), but the *apobatēs* contest is open only to citizens' ([Dem.] 61.23). Crowther takes this to indicate that 'slaves participated in all athletic events except the apobates' (37), but in fact the Greek need not imply this. The reference is most likely to the use of slave jockeys and charioteers in the equestrian events; these might well be said to 'take part' in competition, though there was no question of their winning prizes in their own right. The *apobatēs*, then, is unique among equestrian events. (Understandably, as it involved running as well as horsemanship.) Slaves were given access to gymnasia in some cities as early as the Hellenistic period, and a passage in Artemidorus's dream book may imply that they could compete in games with value prizes. But the only sure evidence for their competing against free Greeks (an inscription republished in Gardiner 1929) comes from an otherwise unusual local festival in Pisidia as late as the second century of the current era. This contributes to the shock – the intended effect – when Demosthenes describes Philip running the Pythian festival through slave managers of the games (Dem. 9.32).[1]

So this competition at Trapezus is very remarkable indeed. Xenophon and his comrades have maintained one of the usual distinctions in Greek athletics, the categorization of competitors as boys and men, while forgoing another. We may speculate as to why one distinction was maintained and the other abandoned in these specific circumstances. Boys, after all, were non-combatants, so it may well have seemed appropriate to mark them out in soldiers' games as well. But warfare had a way of enslaving the free, often suddenly and arbitrarily: the distinction so important at Olympia and elsewhere, between freeborn Greeks and all others, may have appeared less clear-cut on campaign. Whatever the explanation, this eccentric and little noticed competition is yet another indication of how varied the world of athletic and equestrian competition really was in ancient Greece; however, it also points towards one of its main constants, the production of difference. This must sound simple-minded. After all, creating difference is something competition, concerned as it is to establish winners and losers, is bound to do. I have in mind something more far reaching: Greek sport was enveloped in a series of hierarchies in which events, festivals, genders, nations and other groups were ranged and ranked no less than individuals. As elsewhere, it could be a vehicle 'of identity, providing people with a sense of difference and a way of classifying themselves and others, whether latitudinally or hierarchically' (MacClancy 1996:2).

That the games fostered unity among the Greeks is a cliché. An old cliché – Lysias in the early fourth century told his audience at Olympia that Heracles founded their festival in the hope of encouraging mutual amity among the Greeks – if still vibrant enough to inspire a new theory of the origin of Greek competitive festivals. The reality, of course, is that such amity was forged at the expense of other ties – or rather, through their rejection. Athletic exercise and competition marked Greeks off from their neighbours, and the great Greek festivals of athletic and equestrian competition excluded non-

---

[1] Solon: Aeschin. 1.138–9, Plut. *Sol.* 1.3; cf. the comments on the oil of the gymnasium as the smell of a free man in Xen. *Symp.* 2.4. Dream book: Artem. 1.62, second century CE; Langenfeld 1991:8.

Greek outsiders, *barbaroi*; at Olympia, the most prestigious, married women at least were barred from the site (see below, Chapter 4). Every competition involved a series of statements about various categories of humankind, some marked off, some masked. The likelihood that such a scheme of differentiation was working on the Greeks at Trapezus (or at least on Xenophon's representation of their activities) may lead to a resolution of a textual problem in the passage I have translated above. Where I translate 'female camp-followers', most manuscripts read *hetaírōn*, 'their companions'; some *hetérōn*, 'the others'. 'Camp-followers' renders *hetairõn*, an emendation ascribed to the sixteenth-century French scholar Brodaeus (Jean Brodeau), printed by Cobet in his school edition of 1859, defended by Löschhorn (1918, noting references to such camp-followers earlier at *An.* 4.3.19, 30), and accepted into (e.g.) the Teubner text of Hude (1931) and the selection edited by Antrich and Usher (1978). An account so concerned with distinctions of age, juridical status and national origin might well comment on gender too. With Brodaeus's conjecture, women are present and where they belong, watching from the sidelines.[2]

Another important distinction is not made explicit in Xenophon's account: social class. Nor was it marked in other competitions – no games included contests reserved expressly for the rich. But such contests there were all the same, the various equestrian events. At Trapezus, the soldiers ride their own horses, most of them, at this stage of their expedition, probably stolen. In general, however, the horse and chariot races of the Greeks were open only to those who could afford the extraordinary expense they required. In theory, they competed against allcomers; in fact, the pool of opponents was very limited, the chance of success correspondingly high, the probability of losing to a social inferior negligible. And the super-rich, or abnormally extravagant, could improve their odds through multiple entries, since they were not required to ride or drive for themselves or even attend the competition. One of the reasons horse races were an essential part of Greek athletic festivals was precisely to allow the elite to compete with each other without advertising the fact unduly, even after their communities (and to some extent other events) became more open to the participation of the poorer. And to compete longer

---

[2] Unity: Lys. 33.2, cf. Isoc. 4.43–6. New theory: Ulf 1991. Greeks and their neighbours: Pl. *Symp.* 182bc, Luc. *Anach.* 1–6.

than men who could only run, jump, throw and fight. (We may think of Pierre Bourdieu's distinction between popular sports, linked with youth, which are generally abandoned very early, and bourgeois sports, which are pursued much longer [Bourdieu 1984:212].) As Xenophon suggests, however, this privilege, or at least the response it was expected to evoke, might not always go unchallenged.

The discourse of difference in Greek sport and its consequences will be the main unifying theme of this book, revisited below in connection with victory and its rewards, age and gender categories and competitors' class origins. I should emphasize at the outset that this is just one approach to the subject. There are many others. The growth of the sport and leisure industries in the past twenty-five years has combined with the academy's new awareness of culture, ideology and representation to engender a profusion of studies and what one student of American sport calls a 'glorious disarray' of methods and models; brother, can you spare a paradigm? Totalizing theories – biological, environmental, psychological, sociological – vie with each other, while others affirm instead that sport takes its meaning from interrelations with other social institutions and practices in particular places and times.[3]

The unique nature of modern sport in the West is widely recognized, differently defined, disparately ascribed to modernization or industrial capitalism or Protestantism. In the most influential account, Allen Guttmann identifies seven intertwined features which work together to make modern sport (secularism, equality of opportunity to compete and in competition, bureaucratization, specialization, rationalization, quantification, the quest for records) and asserts that it arises from the scientific world view. Though some elements may appear in earlier cultures – 'we can turn to the Greeks for intimations of the modern . . . sports bureaucracy' (Guttmann 1978:45) – it is only today that they interact systematically. This accords with some anthropological approaches in which complex rules and competitions, elaborate equipment, the status of participants and spectator interest follow an evolutionary development from band to tribe to chiefdom and beyond (Blanchard and Cheska 1985:90–165). But though the author of another successful synthesis, Richard Mandell, agrees with Guttmann's characterization of

---

[3] 'Glorious disarray': Struna 1985; other surveys in Rader 1979, Rojek 1992. Particular places and times: e.g., Somers 1972, Adelman 1986.

modern sport, he insists more strongly on the cleavage between it and
what came before: 'European sports had no continuity with the
games and contests of the Greeks and Romans. They were . . .
natural adaptations that sprung anew out of local peasant culture and
from the need of the noble classes to demonstrate their ascendancy'
(Mandell 1984:3, 197). Similarly, for Eric Middleton parallels between
Greek and later European sport arise from like responses to urbaniza-
tion and the presence of a leisured elite; it is 'a question of analogy
rather than sequence, a matter of common denominators rather than
a progressive evolution' (Midwinter 1986:10).[4]

Attitudes towards the nature and role of modern sport (and so to
what preceded it) may vary as greatly even among those who concur
on its definition and singularity. Where the ideas of Norbert Elias
and his follower Eric Dunning have taken root, mainly in Britain,
students of sport history have concentrated on the body as a nexus of
power and on the gradual (and far from unilinear) growth of self-
and social control of bodily functions and physical impulses from the
Middle Ages on. Sport in this civilizing process is an appropriate and
regulated outlet for tension and aggressive behaviour (at acceptable
levels, against approved targets) and a source for the excitement
humans need. It is thus relatively benign. Marxists, however, stress a
darker reality. For them too the body is at the centre of analysis, but
it is a body reduced to a machine: according to one flamboyant
formulation, 'the intensive practice of sport is institutionalized
celebration of the mortification of the flesh', an ideological apparatus
of death, legitimating physical torture as politically neutral and
entertaining. Furthermore, commercialized and dominated as it is
by market forces, sport offers a new profit centre at the same time as
it delivers images, passions, myths and fantasies to reproduce the
dominant ideology on which capitalism feeds (Hoch 1972). Other
social critics single out and elaborate counts in this indictment, for
example, that mainstream sport imposes orthodox gender roles and
sexual practices (though it may also double as 'a covert world of
homoeroticism': Pronger 1990:178).[5]

All this work is unlikely to be of equal value for the student of

---

[4] Seven features: Guttmann 1978:15–89, cf. Guttmann 1988:5–8; critique in Blake
 1996:69–82.
[5] Elias's ideas: see Dunning and Rojek 1992 for this outlook and its critics. Flamboyant
 formulation: Brohm 1978:23–8, cf. Brohm 1986, 1992:75–89, and the comments of Gruneau
 1983:34–9, 1993.

Greek sport. It is undeniably interesting to reflect that the ability to walk upright has opened many paths for humankind and that our sense of smell, weak relative to dogs', and our comparatively keen eyesight have pushed us away from orienteering, say, and towards ball games and others dependent on hand–eye co-ordination (Cashmore 1990). But biology only influences history; it does not determine it. We must still account for the recent development of competitive orienteering in some parts of the world and the relative neglect of ball games in others (like ancient Greece). The role of climate and the environment is sometimes obvious – it is no accident that Canadians play ice hockey – but always mediated by other realities. (So the hypothesis that Greeks practised the long jump, not the high jump or hurdles or pole vault, because 'Greece was no land of fences and hedges; the chief obstacles were streams and ditches' may seem simplistic; Gardiner 1930:144.) Why has Sweden flourished as a hockey power while Norway, otherwise a dominant figure in winter sports, has not? Partly because in this instance money talked Swedish: the Swedes had more resources to invest in indoor arenas when the game began to grow popular in Scandinavia.

Some indication of the complex interplay between environmental and social factors may be gleaned from the case of leisure time activities in pre-contact Hawaii. Certainly Hawaiians surfed. The elite, however, preferred to race in sleds over ground they owned themselves, a cumbersome and costly form of competition which advertised their special status, not least in being able to transcend their natural surroundings (G. Krüger 1990). We may be reminded that there is very little evidence for swimming races among the Greeks (and this only in connection with the cult and myth of Dionysus) and that even boat races are rarer than one would expect among a maritime people, though found at such major competitions as the Panathenaea and (perhaps) at Isthmia. Against this background, the choice of the Greek elite to own and race horses (like that of their Hawaiian counterparts to sled) represents a claim to rise above the restrictions of the environment as much as financial constraints, since the rough terrain and lack of horseshoes, stirrups and effective harness made the horse inconvenient for travel and transport.[6]

At the local level, close study of individual communities will

---

[6] Swimming races: Paus. 2.35.1, Nonnus, *Dion.* 11.43–55, 400–30; Hall 1993:49–54. Boat races: Harris 1972a:112–16, 126–8.

always pay dividends, though of course a number of these is needed before general patterns emerge. One example: the fact that competition for teams of Athenian citizens at the Panathenaea (the boat race among them) were organized by tribe reflects the make-up of the tribe and its other functions in the democracy established by Cleisthenes in 508. These new and artificial constructs, corresponding to no previous kin or civic grouping and bringing together Athenians from widely separated neighbourhoods, were the basis of the committees vital to day-to-day administration at Athens and of the armed forces. Competitions provided tribesmen (in particular the boys and *ageneioi*, 'beardless youths', who took part) another venue to meet and to build the group solidarity essential in civic and, above all, military contexts. In addition, the distribution of the glory of victory, and its rewards, over a large group of contestants lessened the risk of exalting one individual over his fellow citizens – the aristocrat Cylon had tried to parlay a triumph at Olympia into a military coup in the late seventh century – while the agony of defeat was dissipated in the same way (Osborne 1993:30–2).

A second example of the resonance of local particularities: organized ball play was nowhere as important as at Sparta, where youths on five teams of about fourteen *sphaireis*, 'ball players', competed in an annual tournament in the city's theatre. The sport they played was probably a rough and tumble type of *episkuros*, in which teams tried to push each other past an end line by throwing a ball over their opponents' heads (Poll. 9.104). This is attested for ephebes, young men in military training, in many parts of the Greek world in later antiquity, but the Spartan version is best understood in the light of another local competition, this time unparalleled: an all-in battle between two companies of naked youths, again for possession of a field, an artificial island called Platanistas ('the Plane-tree Grove'), and of the city's geography (Kennell 1995:55–64). These competitors were somewhat younger, and Platanistas itself was not far inside Sparta's Hellenistic walls. The two group contests, then, much as they have in common, are to be distinguished as two stages in a progression towards adulthood, with the twenty-year-old *sphaireis* at the point of leaving youth and so also nearer to the city's centre.

Only the brevity of this book and the existence of excellent studies integrating sport into its community context dissuade me from pursuing this strategy here. Instead, I propose to discuss three issues of relevance to both ancient and modern sport. I will then make a short case for the value of my own emphasis on the place of sport in the Greek discourse on difference. First, then, sport and religion, sport and warfare, and the agonistic spirit of the Greeks.[7]

SPORT AND RELIGION

Twenty years ago, the American social commentator Michael Novak argued that 'sports flow outward from a deep natural impulse that is radically religious' and went on to describe football, baseball and basketball as a Holy Trinity and putting on shoulder pads as the equivalent of donning priestly vestments (Novak 1976:19). A strong position, strongly put. It is more common (as the title of Guttmann's *From Ritual to Record* reveals) to associate sport and religion with earlier times. Certainly there is a good case to be made for such a link in ancient Greece; another American right-wing ideologue opines that 'Greek philosophers considered sport a religious and civic – in a word, moral – undertaking' (Will 1990:2). Athletic and equestrian contests normally took place at regularly recurring religious festivals, where they joined many activities, including other competitions, to celebrate and worship one god or hero or more. The most important competitive festivals made up a circuit, the *periodos*. Originally there were four; if we may judge from Aristotle, their chronological and temporal relationships were well known (Arist. *Metaph.* 2.994a24, 5.1018b18):

(1) the Olympic games at Olympia in the region of Elis in the north-west Peloponnese, held in late July or August of every fourth year in honour of Zeus Olympios and supposedly founded in 776;[8]

(2) the Pythian games, sacred to Apollo, celebrated every four summers since 586 or 582 at his oracular shrine of Delphi in central Greece (Mosshammer 1982, Brodersen 1990);

(3) the Isthmian games at Poseidon's sanctuary on the Isthmus of Corinth, founded in 582 and held in the spring or early summer of alternate years (Gomme *et al.* 1981:23–4);

(4) the Nemean games, which took place in Zeus's honour above all in the north-eastern Peloponnese, first at Nemea and then, for much of antiquity, at nearby Argos; these were also held in alternate years, in September, starting in 573 (Perlman 1989).

---

[7] Excellent studies: Kyle 1987 on archaic and classical Athens, Hodkinson forthcoming on Sparta during the same periods.

[8] For the month, see S.G. Miller 1975a; for the date, Chapter 2 below.

Table 1. *The classical circuit* (periodos)

Olympiad and year	75.1	Olympia	July/August 480
	75.2	Nemea	August/September 479
		Isthmia	April/May or June/July 478
	75.3	Delphi	July/August 478
	75.4	Nemea	August/September 477
		Isthmia	April/May or June/July 476
Olympiad and year	76.1	Olympia	July/August 476

To win the same event in all four games marked an athlete as a *periodonikēs*, though the term itself is attested only from the second century of the current era, after other games – the Heraea at Argos, the Actia at Nicopolis, the Sebasta at Naples and the Roman Capitolia – had been elevated to the stature of the original *periodos*. A still more impressive feat was to sweep the original circuit within one Olympiad, like the Grand Slam in tennis or golf, or to win at all seven or eight of the games of the expanded *periodos* – a *periodos* or *periodonikēs teleios*; Nero, who ordered all the games of the circuit to be rescheduled to suit his Greek itinerary in 66–7 CE, styled himself a *periodonikēs pantonikēs*, 'all conquering circuit champion'. Nero is also said to have won 1808 crowns; though this is an exaggeration, the number at least hints at how many competitions there were, as countless local festivals augmented the panhellenic celebrations. (Harris offers a count, about 270, but there were certainly more.) The expectation that any festival would feature athletic competition at least was pervasive: when Julius Demosthenes offered to found a festival in honour of Apollo and the deified emperor Hadrian at his native Oenoanda in 124 CE, he apparently felt compelled to include athletic contests, though the fact that they were for citizens only, had no prizes, and were held on the twenty-second and last day of a rich and extended programme suggests that he himself had little interest in them (*SEG* 38 (1988) no. 1462). But there were festivals with no athletics at all as early as the mid-fifth-century celebration for Thasian Heracles; and competitions might take place on other occasions, notably at funerals for private (if well-born) citizens (Roller 1981). The nature and the strength of the association of sport and religion in ancient Greece warrant further reflection, best organized under three headings: cultic origins, sport and religion in the archaic and classical periods, secularization over time. Two

related topics, the heroization of athletes and funeral games, will be
treated later (below, Chapter 3). I will concentrate on Olympia, best
attested and most paradigmatic of competitive festivals.[9]

For the Greeks, the origins of the Olympic games were veiled in
myth. Many myths: Zeus wrestled Cronus or established games after
his triumph, with the younger gods as first competitors. Heracles of
Thebes marked his conquest of Elis and revenge over Augeas, its
king, by founding the games; another Heracles presided over an
inaugural race in which his brothers took part – they (with himself)
made up the five Idaean Dactyls of Crete. Other authors suggest
that Pelops was the founder, either honouring his chariot victory
over Oenomaus, king of Pisa, or Oenomaus himself, or the shadowy
eponym of Pisa, Pisus. Still others rationalized the competing views,
resorting to refoundations, or they mixed and matched, with the
Theban Heracles founding the games for Pelops. Bewildering today,
these variants were no less so in antiquity. Diodorus notes that the
Theban and Cretan Heracles were sometimes confused, and confuses them himself. We may see a trace of early debates on the two
Heracles in one of our first literary accounts of the origins of the
Olympics, Lysias's early-fourth-century Olympic oration (Lys.
33.1–2). Lysias praises Heracles for his efforts to bring Greeks
together, and goes on to say that he himself has not come to
Olympia to quibble over details or wrangle over terms (*onomatōn*) like
some useless Sophist but to discuss grave and urgent issues. The use
of *onomatōn*, normally 'names', suggests that one of the Sophists'
subjects for declamation at Olympia was precisely the identity of its
founder. Strabo has a commonsense response of his own to such
studies: 'One should disregard the ancient stories both of the
founding of the sanctuary and of the establishment of the games . . .
for such stories are told in many ways, and no faith at all is to be put
in them' (8.3.30 (355)).[10]

Sound advice, but modern scholars are loath to take it. Among

---

[9] *Periodonikēs*: E. Maróti 1985–8, Frisch 1991; but cf. Stefanis 1988 for a somewhat different
view. Nero: Dio Cass. 63.10.2; Kennell 1988. Festival numbers: Harris 1964: map 4, Pleket
1974:84 n. 133. Thasian Heracles: *IG* 12 Suppl. 414; Bergquist 1973:80–1 (despite Des
Courtils and Pariente 1991:71).

[10] Zeus: Paus. 5.7.10, 8.2.2. Heracles of Thebes: e.g., Pind. *Ol.* 2.1–4, 6.65–70, 10.23–85, Lys.
33.1–2. Another Heracles: Paus. 5.7.7–9. Pelops: Pind. *Ol.* 1.155, Bacch. 8.30–2, Phlegon,
FGrH 257 F 1.1, 6. Pisus: Phlegon, *FGrH* 257 F 1.1, 6. Theban Heracles and Pelops: Arist. fr.
637 Rose, Stat. *Theb.* 6.6–7, Hyg. *Fab.* 273.5, Clem. Al. *Strom.* 1.21.137, Solinus 1.27.
Confusion: Diod. Sic. 3.74.4, 5.64.6; 4.14.1, cf. Paus. 5.14.9.

recent writers who seek to isolate a core of historical truth amidst this welter of dissonant traditions, John Mouratidis argues that those singling out the Theban Heracles reflect an early period in which he was the hero the games honoured (Mouratidis 1984); the original connection to the cult of Heracles explains the exclusion of (almost all) women from the Olympic festival, as they were also prohibited from his shrines and sanctuaries elsewhere. The Cretan Heracles' brothers, the Idaean Dactyls, figure as both symbols of the regeneration of life – the foot-race revives the energy of nature by stirring up the earth – and as young initiates undergoing a ritual test (Lévêque 1982:8); Heracles himself may be identified with Iasius, and 'since it is highly probable that the celebration of the pre-Dorian sacred marriage between Demeter and Iasius-Hercules . . . was also observed in Olympia, the legend of the contest between the Dactyli may be regarded as a mythological account of an ancient, ritual suitors' race' (Drees 1968:27).[11]

Pelops's claims are the most insistent as he has had the most authoritative advocates. For Walter Burkert, the leading expert on Greek religion, the altar of Zeus, the stadium and the precinct of Pelops are the cultic centres of the sanctuary at Olympia, the polar relationship between Pelops and Zeus at the heart of its religious ritual (Burkert 1983:93–103). 'The Eleans honoured Pelops as much more than the other heroes at Olympia as they honoured Zeus among the other gods' (Paus. 5.13.1). The hero and the god went together like night and day – in fact, 'Pelops' may mean 'dark-face', the antithesis of the god of daylight, and his offering was a black ram. The god and the hero received the same number of sacrifices, lit by white poplar wood obtained from the 'woodman', *xuleus*, with Pelops's always preceding Zeus's (Schol. Vet. Pind. *Ol.* 1.149a); but while Pelops's offering was poured down into the sacrificial pit, Zeus's altar grew higher and higher with constant accretions of ash. Gregory Nagy concurs that 'the very festival of the Olympics was from the earliest times onward correlated with a myth that told how the hero Pelops was killed, dismembered, and served up by his father Tantalus as sacrificial meat boiled inside a tripod cauldron, to be eaten by the gods – only to be reassembled and brought back to life inside the same sacrificial cauldron by the agency of these same gods', though he parts company with Burkert in restricting the

[11] Advice: see the survey of theories of origins in Ulf and Weiler 1980, and cf. Weiler 1993.

implications of this story to the 'oldest aspect of the festival', the *stadion* race (Nagy 1986:79–81; see further below).

Despite its distinguished adherents, however, Pelops's place in the origins of Olympia is surprisingly insecure. Pausanias's comment on the pre-eminence of Pelops merely situates him among the heroes; it does not connect him, still less contrast him, with Zeus. The 'woodman's' duties may include other sacrifices as well as Zeus's and Pelops's, the priority of sacrifices to Pelops may concern only the annual sacrifice by the Elean magistrates rather than (as Burkert believes) all offerings, the opposition of pit to pile is in line with the distinction between heroic and divine cults in general. Nor is Pelops's black ram a polar opposite to Zeus's bull – it is just different. Finally, much of our evidence on the supposed complementarity of the two cults is very late, from Pausanias and after. Even if we accept that it justifies Burkert's reading for its own period, it may have nothing to do with the origins of the Olympics long before. The extant remains of the shrine to Pelops, the Pelopion, date only from the early fourth century. It was then an important place, close to the Altis and the altar of Zeus, and it has often been argued that it always was, even in Mycenaean times. But the current consensus is that the sanctuary's beginnings cannot be pushed back beyond the geometric period, that it was Zeus's from the start, that there is no early evidence for Pelops's cult. 'Thus, it becomes unnecessary to go into all the theories deriving the Olympic Games from the myth of Pelops' (Mallwitz 1988:89). We might say the same about any of the competing theories derived from ancient myth (cf. Ulf and Weiler 1980:29–31). Whatever their interest for the play of ideology – a subject to which we will return at the end of this chapter – they do not reveal the ancient history of the festival.

One positive result emerges from this sceptical survey, that later Greeks located the origin of the Olympic games squarely in the sphere of the divine; gods and heroes found and compete in them as well as simply receiving worship. Of course the Greeks may have extrapolated this connection from the competitive festivals they knew, but the consistency of this element in these aetiologies does testify to the continuity of the link between sport and religion, even if it does little to clarify its nature. For that we must turn to the organization and conduct of festivals in the archaic and classical periods.

Greek religion was essentially a matter of acts – rituals such as processions, sacrifices, feasts – not of creeds or dogmas. It might be argued that festivals, which brought together most of the acts characterizing Greek religion, were its most important public manifestation. By this token, athletic and equestrian competition, allied as it was with festival celebration, was intrinsically religious. Can we say more? Scholars in the English-speaking world are usually reluctant to speculate on the games' cultic origins; but they do not hesitate to pick out aspects with religious resonance. 'Though not necessarily inherent, the association of athletics with religion was harmonious and lasting. At Olympia athletics came under religious supervision and took on religious overtones with sacred oaths, truces, prayers and dedications' (Kyle 1987:13). Taken from a standard account, this is a careful and, I think, uncontroversial formulation. Let us look more closely at some of its elements.

The judges at Olympia, the *Hellanodikai*, had marks of distinction such as purple robes, elevated seats at the games, and, for ten months, separate living quarters, the *Hellanodikaion*, in the civic centre at Elis. Theirs were important duties (they supervised training, presented victory wreaths, presided over the festival's final feast), and they had powers of punishment over rule-breakers (Slowikowski 1989). But neither they nor their probable predecessors, the *diaitatores*, were priests or cult functionaries; and the cult functionaries we learn of in various sacred laws concerned with the sanctuary of Zeus, *iareis, iaromaoi, manteis, theokoloi*, have no role in the games (Siewert 1992a:116). As for oaths, adult competitors had to swear upon slices of boar's flesh that they had followed Olympia's training regulations for ten months; they also swore that they would do no harm to the games – an oath taken by trainers and by fathers or adult brothers for boy athletes; and those responsible for admitting boys and foals into their respective categories swore as well (Paus. 5.24.9–10; Lämmer 1993). These oaths were administered beside an image of Zeus with a thunderbolt in each hand, 'of all images of Zeus' (says Pausanias) 'the one most likely to strike terror into the hearts of malefactors'. However awesome the setting, such oaths were not unique to Olympia, but reflect the usual Greek practice in invoking a god or gods to guarantee a declaration; judges' oaths are particularly well known (Plescia 1970:33–57). Need we add that neither the religious overtones nor Zeus's thunderbolts ensured that these oaths were kept? Zanes, bronze statues of Zeus erected with fines from those who broke the rules, stood at the entrance of the stadium (Paus. 5.21). It is striking, however, that the fines were used for dedications to the god; so too that the gods supported each other in disputes which arose from judges' decisions. In 332, the Athenian Callippus bribed his opponents in the pentathlon and was caught (Paus. 5.21.5; Weiler 1991). The others paid, but the Athenians sent the orator Hyperides to Elis to have Callippus's fine remitted. When they were rebuffed, they boycotted the games until Apollo at Delphi, a dutiful son of Zeus, declared that he would not deliver any oracle to them while the debt was outstanding.

When we move on to the sacred truce we once again find both the attempt to mark off the festival as extraordinary and its occasional failure. The position of the Olympic festival within time is ambiguous. On the one hand, like other festivals, it represents a break in everyday life; thus it was irregular (though not illegal) for the assembly to meet on any of the upwards of 120 days of the festival calendar in classical Athens, and the games of the circuit coincided with lulls in agricultural activity (and with relatively good sailing seasons). This distinction was heightened at Olympia, which alone of the great panhellenic games imposed a thirty-day training period (at Elis) on athletes, perhaps to limit numbers by discouraging the poor or less proficient. But the Olympics also proved useful in designating secular time (see Table 1). As early as Thucydides, historians used Olympic victories to fix events (Thuc. 3.8, 5.49.1). The practice became prevalent after Hippias of Elis, a contemporary of Thucydides, drew up his list of Olympic victors with the *stadion* race leading off each festival (see below), though chronographers disagreed as to whether the Olympic year should be said to begin with the Athenian year (in summer) or the Macedonian (in fall) or some other. In this way, the Greeks staked a claim to time. They colonized the past by constructing and recording it through a festival which featured a distinctively Greek activity and was open to Greeks alone. Future time was appropriated rather differently, by means of the poems and monuments for individual victors (see below, Chapter 3). The Olympic truce, paralleled in the other circuit celebrations, was a period on either side of the festival during which competitors and other visitors were to be granted safe passage to and from Olympia (Lämmer 1982–3). Originally a month long, this was extended to two months as participants came from further afield (Luc. *Icar.* 22). It is important here to emphasize that the truce was quite restricted, an armistice (*ekecheiria*), not a period of peace (*eirenē*) throughout the Greek world; only open warfare by or against Elis was forbidden. Other wars could (and did) carry on – all that was intended was that they not disrupt the games. Notwithstanding the fact that a statue of Ekecheiria stood in the front hall of the temple of Zeus, even this limited goal was sometimes beyond reach. In 365, the Arcadians seized the sanctuary and proceeded to hold the Olympic festival of 364 along with the neighbouring Pisatans (who claimed to have been its original custodians). While the games were under way – wrestlers were still settling the pentathlon – the Eleans and their Arcadian allies invaded the sacred precinct, and a pitched battle ensued (Xen. *Hell.* 7.4.28–32). Again, as with the Zanes, the influence of religion was pervasive but not all-powerful.[12]

Other ties between religion and sport at Olympia are apparent. For example, the winner's prize, the olive wreath, came from a wild olive tree growing in the sanctuary of Zeus; a boy with both parents living, a *pais amphithalēs* – a good luck charm involved in many religious rites – cut the branch with a golden sickle. And the priestess of Demeter Chamune was the only (married) woman allowed to attend the games (Paus. 6.20.9). It seems best, however, to focus in conclusion on the central and defining act of Greek religion, sacrifice, now the subject of a stimulating discussion by David Sansone (1988, cf. 1991). For Sansone, all sport is the ritual sacrifice of physical energy – 'there is no essential difference between modern sport and the sports of other and earlier societies' (6) – with the competitor doubling as dedicator and dedication. Rituals of all kinds are patterns of behaviour that have acquired new meaning over time. In this case, the ritual is a remnant of man's many thousands of years as a hunter. Sacrifice, in which careful treatment of the victim's remains once represented the hunter's revival of the game he had killed, is transformed into the ritual slaughter of domesticated animals; the energy once expended in the hunt, left undepleted by the act of sacrifice, is spent in sport (61–3). Much of contemporary sport, then, is to be explained in the light of the hunt: teams bear names like Lions, Tigers, Sharks rather than Hamsters or Gerbils. Of Greek sport too: victory wreaths recall camouflage, olive oil and dust once masked the hunter's body odour. As for sacrifice, the music of the

---

[12] Thirty-day period: Philostr. *VA* 5.43, Joannes Chrysostomus, *In principium Actorum* = Migne, *PG* 51.76.5–10; Crowther 1991b.

aulos accompanies both competition and ritual slaughter, and the competitors themselves vie to determine which is the fittest offering to the god. The victor's head is bound with a wool fillet – so too the sacrificial victim's – and the *lebēs*, 'cauldron', common as a prize as early as the *Iliad*, was mainly used for boiling sacrificial meat.[13]

Much of this (as Sansone notes) has been said before. Sport is often regarded as ritual, however defined; the hunting inheritance, explored by specialists in ancient religion such as Meuli and Burkert, is a theme of Desmond Morris's *The Soccer Tribe*, where the ball is a weapon, the goal the prey, and the opposing team an embarrassment (Morris 1981). Roger Caillois describes athletes in terms like Sansone's: 'Dedicated to a divinity, they themselves constituted an offering of effort, skill or grace' (Caillois 1961:60). But Sansone's synthesis is unique. Is it credible (cf. Weiler 1989)? Less for some sports and some sportspersons than for others. The *aulos* was heard at a few events only (Raschke 1985). Combat athletes would rarely make unblemished victims of the kind preferred for animal sacrifice. (We may note that they make up a disproportionate number of the heroized athletes whose stories we will meet in Chapter 3.) Women's competitions can have little to do with the hunt if the division of labour among early hunter-gatherers was like that known today. Sansone himself pays special attention to the *stadion* race, 'at the ancient Olympics the most important event'. His account is worth quoting at length (82–3, cf. Nagy 1986:77–8):

The starting line was at the far end and the finish line nearest to the altar of Zeus. In fact, the stadium at Olympia was originally constructed in such a way that the finish line was directly in front of the altar. In other words, the one-stade race was a race . . . to the altar of the god. Now, in sacrificial ritual, it is of considerable importance that the victim be (or at least give the impression of being) willingly led to the altar. In the case of the one-stade race, there was an actual contest to see who could reach the altar first . . . In virtue of his willingness and of his expenditure of energy, the athlete is the sacrificial victim. But his rôle as sacrificer is also acknowledged symbolically. For, in the classical period the footrace took place on the central day of the five-day festival, the day on which the great sacrifice was made to Olympian Zeus. According to Philostratus, the victim, an ox, was slaughtered and . . . the consecrated parts of the victim were placed on the altar. Then the race was held, and the victor lit the fire in which the consecrated parts were burned up.

---

[13] Olive wreath: Paus. 5.15.3, Schol. Vet. Pind. *Ol.* 3.60.

We shall return to the original stadium at Olympia shortly. For the race and the sacrifice, our immediate concern, Sansone's evidence is Philostratus (*Gym.* 5). Let us overlook the fact that the timing of the *stadion* race in the programme, and its relation to the great sacrifice to Zeus, are quite unclear. (One plausible reconstruction, given in Table 2, puts the race and the sacrifice on separate days.) More disquieting (since Sansone does not notice it), Philostratus is not describing the classical period or the Olympia of his own day (perhaps the third century CE; see below, Chapter 2); he is recounting the supposed origins of the Olympic *stadion* race. If we believe that this passage accurately represents any actual Olympic competition, we should also accept the implications of other statements Philostratus makes in his series of aetiological remarks on various events (to say nothing of their mythological trappings): that second-places were enough to qualify for the wrestling in the pentathlon (3; see below Chapter 2), that the official delegates (*theoroi*) of the Greek states arrived during the *diaulos* (6), that Spartan soldiers fought without helmets (9). All are possible, none compelling. The *stadion* sacrifice least of all – spectacular, uncorroborated, uncopied; the contest established for the Eumeneia at Delphi in 160/59, in which a run towards the altar concludes with the winner lighting the sacrifice, is no parallel, since it is a torch race.[14]

I feel more comfortable with a tamer reading of sacrifice: it joins gods, humans and animals in one act which yet clarifies their divergent natures and roles – and so suits competitive festivals in which men and beasts honour the gods, sometimes together (another reason for the inclusion of equestrian events), sometimes not. Their relationship is ordered. But the same bodies which circumscribe the mortal condition may bring victors an immortality of their own, and challenge this hierarchy. Their *kudos*, their talismanic power, was a potent force on the battlefield and in the foundation of a city while they lived and might lead to their own worship as heroes after death. We will take up some of the tensions inherent in sporting success later in this book (below, Chapter 3).

For now, let us round off this section with a short essay on change over time in the relationship between sport and religion. Guttmann's model, of a trend towards secularization, is mirrored in many

---

[14] Sport as ritual: for accounts based on different understandings of ritual, see Birrell 1981, A. Krüger 1990. Eumeneia: *SIG*³ 671A.15–16 = Sokolowski 1962:89 no. 44.

Table 2. *The schedule of the Olympic Festival, about 350 BCE*

Day 1	Oaths of athletes and trainers
	Examinations of athletes and horses to ensure that they competed in the proper categories (men/boys, horses/foals)
	Contests for trumpeters and heralds
Day 2	Equestrian events
	Pentathlon
Day 3	Sacred procession and great sacrifice to Zeus
Day 4	Boys' contests
Day 5	Men's foot-races (*dolikhos, stadion* race, *diaulos*)
	Men's combat events
	Race in armour
	Crowning of victors in Temple of Zeus
	Banquet for victors in Prytaneum

Note: For evidence and discussion, see Lee 1992. Note that the programme changed over time; for example, the festival took up six days in Pausanias's time.

accounts of Greek sport as well. The context is often one of decline, itself linked to theories of the origins of Greek sport. Scholars who believe that the games sprang from cult are more likely to imagine that their degeneration involved abandonment of those roots. The idea goes back at least to Ernst Curtius in the 1850s and still thrives today. The view that Greek sport became progressively less embedded in religion can also be found among writers who eschew the rhetoric of decline and fall. But how to demonstrate this shift? The usual procedure has been to pick a date for the Golden Age of Greek sport, declare that decline began at the end of that era, and then assert that secularization was the cause, placing in evidence phenomena such as corruption, criticism, professionalization. How arbitrary and subjective this is can be deduced from the range of dates proposed for the Golden Age and its aftermath. Most, it is true, agree that the peak had passed by 400. This, unfortunately, has the consequence of labelling most of the history of Greek sport as days of decay; the *reductio ad absurdum* may be found in Drees, who sees secularization as a process lasting almost one thousand years, from the criticisms of Xenophanes to the prohibition of pagan festivals under the Christian empire (Drees 1968:154–60). The imagery of growth and decline is certainly appropriate to those scholars (like Drees) who believe the games stemmed from fertility cult; it loses lustre in view of the ongoing fecundity of the institution of the competitive festival: new local games were founded, and local upgraded to panhellenic, throughout the Hellenistic period and again, under philhellenic emperors and the *pax Romana*, in the second century CE. Nor are the symptoms of secularization reliable. Rule-breaking and corruption are envisaged in our earliest Olympic law, from the late sixth century (Siewert 1992b); professionalism is a term which confuses more than it clarifies (see below, Chapter 5).[15]

Still, there does seem to be one objective criterion by which a diagnosis of early secularization might be reached (though not, it must be stressed, any conclusions as to the patient's health). The classical stadium at Olympia (Stadium III), constructed about 450, was a considerable distance from the centre of the sanctuary, the Altis, and was cut off from it by a colonnade built perhaps one hundred years later. However, its late-sixth-century predecessor (Stadium II) was some seventy-five metres closer (Mallwitz 1988:79, 94–95; see Figure 1(a)). This is telling evidence for increasing separation of the areas of competition and cult, both through distance and a physical barrier, and excavators elsewhere have sought to identify parallel developments at their own sites. At Isthmia, for example, the placement of the early-sixth-century stadium close to the altar of Poseidon 'seems to have been modelled on the early stadium at Olympia' (Gebhard 1993:162). Here, however, the popularity of the festival and the easy access to it by sea and the main road to the Peloponnese soon caused the area for spectators to encroach onto the space in front of the altar; this mingling of cult and competition apparently lasted until the late fourth century, when the stadium was moved. So Isthmia provides little support for secularization. The early Hellenistic stadium at Nemea is a good quarter mile from the sanctuary of Zeus. Though no earlier stadium has been discovered, a late archaic votive deposit including apparatus for the pentathlon is taken to show that 'the situation is very like that at Olympia and Isthmia where the original stadia were relatively close to the religious and cult centre of the sanctuaries, but were moved away late in the classical or early in the Hellenistic periods to positions which allowed for more spectators' (S.G. Miller 1992:82). Not a word here about Delphi, where the topography required the stadium to be outside the sanctuary

---

[15] Decline: surveys in Weiler 1985–6, 1988b. Less embedded: e.g., Cartledge 1985:107, Tomlinson 1995:373.

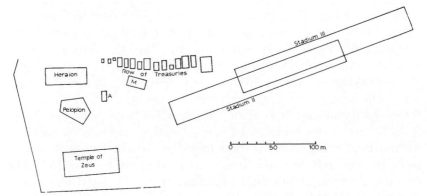

Figure 1(a). Olympia. The Altis. A = Altar of Zeus

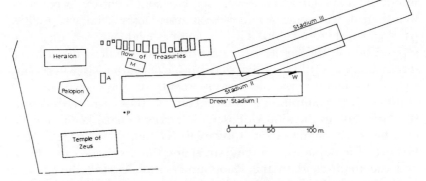

Figure 1(b). Olympia. The Altis with Drees's Stadium I. A = Altar of Zeus,
P = Pillar of Oinomaos, W = Archaic retaining wall

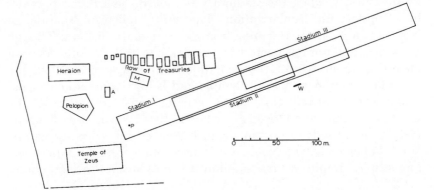

Figure 1(c). Olympia. The Altis with Brulotte's Stadium I. A = Altar of Zeus,
P = Pillar of Oinomaos, W = Archaic retaining wall

altogether and the hippodrome was far beneath in the plain of Cirrha.[16]

It would be more prudent to admit the possibility that each festival developed in its own way, conditioned by the terrain and by historical circumstances. An increase in spectators is only one of those circumstances; Nemea, after all, was destroyed by warfare towards the end of the fifth century, and the Argives who rebuilt it and took over its management from the neighbouring town of Cleonae may have chosen to make a new start. About Olympia itself (and its use as a model) there is a little more to say. Though Stadium II was closer to the Altis than its mid-fifth-century successor, it was still some seventy-five metres or so away from the altar of Zeus and at an angle to it. This is not quite the relationship implied by Sansone in the passage quoted above. However, Sansone's view does correspond to Drees's reconstruction of the earliest stadium at Olympia (Stadium I; see Figure 1(b), and cf. Siewert 1992b:8). Here the finish line for the *stadion* race does indeed come right in front of the altar; alas, the ground level of the surrounding area ensures that no stadium could have extended nearly so close. This conclusion is not affected by the latest attempt to place Stadium I in this vicinity (Brulotte 1994).[17] In fact Stadium I lay underneath Stadium II (Mallwitz 1988:94–5). Our conclusion here can serve for the whole of this section: There is surely something in the connection of sport and religion in ancient Greece, but it is a mistake to make too much of it. A lot depends on our perspective. Greek sport seems very religious in contrast with most of contemporary professional sport. Is it really exceptionally so in a society in which every part of life was pervaded by cult activity and invocations of the gods?

SPORT AND WARFARE

Richard Nixon christened his bombing of North Vietnam 'Operation Linebacker': war as a game. The metaphor moves the other way too today, when a pass in North American football can be

---

[16] Delphi: cf. Fontenrose 1988:145–6, with due caution for his assumptions about the siting of the early stadium.

[17] Brulotte relies in part on the supposed configuration at Nemea, a circular argument more in keeping with the shape of the modern stadium, and misstates the problem posed by the terrain. Since he suggests that the 'Pillar of Oinomaos' in Figure 1(c) was the turn post for Stadium I, and since all foot-races ended at the same place, his reconstruction also has the unintended result that the *stadion* race was run *away* from the Altar of Zeus.

called a 'long bomb', a good rightfielder has a 'howitzer' of an arm, and 'a cannonading blast from the point' became the trademark of Montreal hockey broadcaster Danny Gallavan. As Thorstein Veblen observed one hundred years ago, 'The slang of athletics . . . is in great part made up of extremely sanguinary locutions borrowed from the terminology of warfare' (Veblen 1924[1899]:256). Greek knows this overlap of terminology between sport and warfare as well (Scanlon 1988a). The seer Tisamenus of Elis, destined to win five great *agones*, at first took to athletic competition and came within one wrestling fall of being Olympic champion in the pentathlon (Hdt. 9.33–5). Realizing that his fate was linked to warfare instead, the Spartans made him a citizen and his presence helped them win five great battles – another sense of *agones*. Pindar's praise for successful athletes draws upon the elegiac vocabulary for war and assimilates the victor's homecoming to the soldier's (Perysinakis 1990). Parallels between sport and warfare extend beyond linguistic tropes (as is stressed by Lämmer 1985). The Dutch scholar Johan Huizinga's famous book on the play element in culture, *Homo Ludens*, noted (among other likenesses) that both are tests of the gods' will, owing much to chance (Huizinga 1970:89–104). Furthermore, Greek warfare, in the archaic and classical periods above all, was conventional, with inviolate heralds, truces for the recovery of the dead, and equipment and tactics standard enough to pass for rules of a game.[18]

Yet both athletics and warfare could be dangerous too. One of the several explanations for the fact that Eleans did not compete at Isthmia involves the sons of Prolaus. They were on their way to Isthmia to compete in *pankration* and wrestling when one was accidentally killed in practice. Combat sports could indeed lead to injury or death. The most famous example is of Arrachion (or Arrichion), who triumphed in the Olympic *pankration* of 564 even though he was strangled during the final match. (He expired as his adversary raised a finger to signal submission.) Other events might also be risky. A law-court speech (or rhetorical exercise) by Antiphon turns on a gymnasium accident in which a youth is transfixed by a javelin, and the discus is responsible for the mythological deaths of Acrisius and Hyacinthus among others. States needed laws to cover such accidental deaths in games. It is a cliché to call war the team

---

[18] Battles: cf. Xen. *Ag.* 3.1.21, where the gods are *agonothetai* of war.

game of the Greeks (e.g., Crowther 1995b:135). It is not quite true that they competed only as individuals; but what team sports there were – the ball games mentioned above, regattas, torch races – were generally the preserve of ephebes, young men moving from child-hood towards social maturity *via* a period of military training. Finally, Olympia's games may have come to prominence through the sanctuary's older and once greater claim to fame, as an oracle for war (and then colonization: Sinn 1991), and images of Ares and *Agōn* stood side by side on the table on which winners' wreaths were kept (Paus. 5.20.3).[19]

The foundation dates of the other games of the circuit, and of one of the defining institutions of Greek life (see especially Paus. 10.4.1), the gymnasium, seem to be associated with a momentous trans-formation in the dominant ethos of Greek warfare. The Pythian, Isthmian and Nemean games all arose (or were recast) in the first quarter of the sixth century. The first mentions of the gymnasium in literary sources can be placed in the same chronological context (Glass 1988:159–61); it retained its close links with warfare wherever free Greek cities relied on a citizen army (Gauthier and Hatzopoulos 1993:173–6). This is about the time that the so-called hoplite revolution was securely established: the leading role once played by individual, aristocratic champions – the aspect of battle highlighted by Homer – was now taken over by the hoplite phalanx. This was a formation of heavily armed infantry whose tactics depended on organization, discipline – each hoplite's right side was protected by the shield of his neighbour in the line – and esprit de corps. Hoplite warfare required enough courage to come to close quarters with an enemy's long stabbing spear and sword for hacking exposed body bits. It also needed fitness. Hoplite armour might weigh forty pounds or more; battles themselves were joined at speed, since one side hoped to break the other's line in the first shock; and the opening charge might lead to a more or less prolonged mêlée, with both sides pushing and shoving for their lives in the dust and hot sun. It is attractive, therefore, to imagine that both gymnasia and the

---

[19] Athletic dangers: R. Brophy 1978, R. Brophy and M. Brophy 1985, Poliakoff 1986. Eleans and Isthmia: Paus. 5.2.4, cf. 6.3.9, 16.2; Crowther 1988b:307. Arrachion: Paus. 8.40.1–2, Philostr. *Imag.* 2.6. Javelin: Antiph. *Tetr.* 2, cf. Plut. *Per.* 36.3. Discus: e.g., Soph. *Larisaioi* fr. 378, 380 Radt; Eur. *Hel.* 1471–5; Weiler 1974:227–9. Laws: Dem. 23.53, Arist. *AthPol* 57.3, cf. Pl. *Leg.* 8.831a. A spectator at a cheese toss in Poland was reportedly killed by a ten-pound block thrown by his son: *The Big Issue* no. 136 (26 June – 2 July 1995) 5.

new panhellenic games were responses to the demands of hoplite
battle (cf. Delorme 1960:24–30, Evjen 1986:54–5, 1992:103).

But whose responses? The hoplites themselves, prevailing on their
own communities to build gymnasia (public places) and on others to
give them the opportunity to test and display their athletic prowess?
Or the traditional elite, anxious to find another stage on which to
assert collective and individual superiority? (In neither case, we
should remember, are we dealing with a movement from below.
Hoplite equipment was expensive, out of reach of the majority,
perhaps two-thirds, of the fighting force in the cities where it had to
be provided by the soldier himself – all except Sparta. If the games
ever reflected the military métier of the mass of the citizenry, rowing
would presumably be more prominent.)

In favour of the first alternative, we may note that hoplite armies
engaged in athletic exercise and competition on campaign; Spartan
law even required it. Individuals might take athletic equipment
along – the Spartan commander Thibron was surprised and killed
throwing the discus with a friend on an expedition to Asia Minor
(Xen. *Hell.* 4.8.18). Training in the gymnasium is explicitly said to
have helped the (non-Greek) Sidonians to withstand Artaxerxes
Ochus in 351/0, the Thebans to hold off Alexander in 335/4.
Hermes Promachus, 'the champion', is supposed to have led the
ephebes of Tanagra in routing the Eretrians; he was armed with a
strigil (Paus. 9.22.2); the Spartan Isidas, 'turning from boy into man
at the age when the human flower blooms most beautifully', fought
the Thebans naked and anointed with oil like an athlete – and was
both crowned (as a victor) and fined by the ephors for his exploit
(Plut. *Ages.* 34.7–8). Protagoras remarks that parents send their sons
to the trainer (*paidotribēs*) so that physical shortcomings will not make
them cowards in war or other duties (Pl. *Prt.* 326bc). Inscriptions for
athletes regularly recount both athletic and military achievements
(Sani 1982).[20]

The race in armour, or hoplite race, *hoplitodromos*, is of special

---

[20] Armies and athletics: e.g., Thuc. 5.80.3, Xen. *An.* 1.2.10, 5.5.5; Plutarch criticizes the
Roman commander Crassus for failing to organize athletic contests on his disastrous
expedition to Parthia, *Crass.* 17.5. Spartan law: Xen. *Lac.* 12.5–6, cf. *Ages.* 1.25–27, *Hell.*
3.4.16–18, and the reflection of Spartan practice at *Cyr.* 1.6.17, 6.2.6. Thibron: I translate a
correction of the manuscripts' *diaskenōn*, 'retiring to his own quarters'. Sidonians and
Thebans: Diod. Sic. 16.44.6, 17.11.4; cf. Plut. *Mor.* 639f–640a. But only at Sparta would a
man be ashamed to work out at the palaestra with someone officially condemned as a
coward: Xen. *Lac.* 9.4.

importance here: Plutarch says that it comes after the other athletic events on the programme – where, he does not specify – because military fitness is the aim of exercise and competition (Plut. *Mor.* 639e, cf. Paus. 5.8.10). However, the open grounds of the gymnasium afforded space for horsemanship too: the Academy, one of the oldest gymnasia at Athens, was the site of cavalry processions and perhaps practice for the *anthippasia*, mass manoeuvres in which contingents competed by tribe – and the cavalry also competed on campaign. As for the hoplite race, its place on the programme may reflect the late date at which it was apparently added at Olympia (520) and Delphi (498). These dates seem to tell against a close early connection of either games with hoplite warfare. Nor do any of the games of the classical *periodos* include pyrrhic dancing, in which competitors wore body armour and carried a shield.[21]

All in all, the evidence supports the hypothesis that any link between the advent of the gymnasium, the expansion of athletic competition, and warfare must be made through the elite. Greek cities had a pyramidal social structure, with the top triangle relatively tiny; members of the elite within each city tended to share outlooks, activities and often family ties with their peers elsewhere rather than with their fellow citizens. Surely only they would have the interest or the capacity to found or refashion panhellenic games, or the leisure and means to travel the circuit they formed. In addition, the ideology of these games, made up of events in which individuals strove for a single prize, is more compatible with heroic excellence, to be the best and strive with the best, than with hoplite solidarity. Then too the new Pythian games included a horse race from the start and a chariot race from the second celebration – again an aristocratic pursuit (Paus. 10.7.5–7). Perhaps the most persuasive point, however, is one that often occurred to the ancients as well: the usual sports of the gymnasium and the competitive festivals were just not very well designed as preparation for hoplite warfare. A trenchant comment comes from a character in Euripides' satyr play *Autolycus* (fr. 282N.²):

---

[21] *Anthippasia*: Xen. *Eq. Mag.* 3.1, 11–14. Cavalry competitions: e.g., Xen. *Ages.* 1.25–7, *Hell.* 3.4.16–18, cf. *Cyr.* 8.3.25. Late date: Olympia, Paus. 5.8.10; Delphi, Paus. 10.7.7. It is unlikely that two fragments of an Etruscan vase, dated about 630–620, showing armed men running with lances in their hands as well as chariots and their drivers, have anything to do with the race in armour – a possibility raised by Camporeale 1993.

There are thousands of evils throughout Greece, but the worst is the race of athletes . . . What good wrestler, what swift-footed man has helped his city by winning a wreath hoisting the discus or smartly striking someone's jaw? Will they fight with the enemy discus in hand or drive out their ancestral foe by striking through the shields with their hands? No one who stands near steel is so stupid.

Plato criticizes the wrestling tricks of Antaeus and Cercyon and the boxing tactics of the equally legendary Epeius and Amycus as worthless in wartime; Homer's Epeius is a poor soldier, like a historical boxer, Boiscus of Sicily. Far better, according to Plato, to institute contests more closely linked to the demands of battle and to train soldiers through mock combat, despite inevitable casualties. The famous Theban general Epaminondas allowed his troops to wrestle, at least so long as they kept trim enough to fight, but advised his countrymen, 'If you want to be leaders of Greece, use the camp, not the palaestra' (Plut. *Mor.* 192cd, 788a; Nep. *Epam.* 5.4). His admirer Philopoemen went further. Himself a wrestler in his youth, he was persuaded that athletes did not make good soldiers and barred his men from competition (Plut. *Phil.* 3.2–4).[22]

Our conclusion must be akin to that on religion. No male activity could be far removed from warfare in a society in which hand-to-hand combat was a constant and periods of peace exceptional and short. But the relationship delineated here is for the most part indirect and oblique, a reaction against the dominant form of war rather than a preparation for it (cf. Poliakoff 1987a:112–15).

COMPETITION AND THE GREEKS

The Greeks were a competitive people. That Athenian comedies and tragedies were first staged in contests for a prize is well known. But we hear too of competitions for doctors (in surgery, the use of instruments, presentation of a thesis), for sculptors, for potters, for girls who carded wool, for dancers. There were beauty contests for boys at Elis and for girls in Arcadia, on Tenedus, on Lesbos. At the Dioclea in Megara, a crown of flowers was awarded to the boy with the sweetest kiss (Theoc. *Id.* 12.27–33). Among the peculiarities

---

[22] Not well designed: Kyle 1987:127–41, Poliakoff 1987a:94–103, 1990:93–6, Lavrencic 1991. Wrestling tricks: Pl. *Leg.* 7.796a, cf. 814d. Epeius and Boiscus: Hom. *Il.* 23.664–71; Xen. *An.* 5.8.23. Plato: *Leg.* 8.829c–831a, 832e–834a, cf. 7.813c and, on *hoplomachia*, *Lach.* 179a-180a, 181e-183d.

Aristotle ascribes to richer and more leisured cities are officials responsible for athletic, dramatic and other contests (Arist. *Pol.* 6.1322b38). What is more, to be capable of victory and yet fail to compete marked a man as a coward and a poltroon (Xen. *Mem.* 3.7.1, cf. *Cyr.* 1.5.10). No wonder, then, that some have adjudged the competitive spirit, the agonistic impulse, to characterize the Greeks above all other cultures, and have been led to suggest that such distinctive achievements as Greek philosophy sprang from the intensely competitive ambience in which people with ideas put forth their views (G.E.R. Lloyd 1987:85–91, 97–101). The idea is as old as Jakob Burckhardt's *Griechische Kulturgeschichte*, first published nearly one hundred years ago (Burckhardt 1902:87–122, 214–19), and thrives in standard works such as Gardiner's *Athletics of the Ancient World.* ('No people has ever been dominated to such an extent by this drive [to excel] as the Greeks were; no people has ever been so fond of competition' (Gardiner 1930:2, cf. 1910:3).) Since sport is a kind of competition, it follows that it too must be distinctively Greek, at least among contemporary cultures. So again Gardiner (1930:1):

The story of ancient athletics is the story of Greek athletics. The Greeks, as far as we know, were the only truly athletic nation of antiquity . . . The love of play is universal in all young things . . . But play is not athletics . . . The child plays till he is tired and then leaves off. The competitor in a race goes on after he is tired, goes on to the point of absolute exhaustion.[23]

In the last while, however, the ascription of a uniquely agonistic spirit to the Greeks has lost much of its appeal, appearing Helleno-centric at best, at times even racist. (According to Gardiner, 'The Egyptians, like all orientals, loved shows of every sort' – a statement he follows with references to acrobatic exhibitions in Xenophon, Petronius and his own day; Gardiner 1930:4–6.) Martin Bernal argues, unpersuasively as yet, that much of Greek culture was derived from Egypt; other scholars have explored the influence of the Near East, of the Phoenicians and Mesopotamians in particular, on Greek mythology, religion, art. It is in this changing climate, this re-evaluation of the Greeks' relationships with other peoples of the Mediterranean, that we find new suggestions: that the odd shape of

---

[23] Doctors: Ephesus, second century CE, Engelmann *et al.* 1980:108–12 nos. 1161–9. Sculptors: Aphrodisias, ?second century CE, *MAMA* 8 519. Potters: Athens, fourth century, *IG* 2² 6320. Wool carders: Tarentum, sixth century, Milne 1945:528–33. Dancers: Athens, later eighth century, *IG* 1² 919 = Jeffery 1990:431 no. 1. Beauty contests: Ath. 13.565f, 609f (boys), 610a (girls). Competitive spirit: a good account in Poliakoff 1987a:104–12.

the Greek discus stems originally from copper ingots like those found
in the Bronze Age Phoenician shipwreck off Cape Gelidonia; that
the stade, the six-hundred-foot unit of length that was the basis for
the Greek athletic venue (the stadium) and for all Greek foot-races,
was taken from the Babylonians – along with some athletic events. It
is appropriate, then, to revisit the question of the agonistic spirit of
the Greeks. More specifically: Did other ancient peoples of the
Mediterranean practise formal athletic competition – regular, recurring, regulated contests involving physical activity, in which out-
comes were determined by the strength, skill and good fortune of the
competitors themselves? And did any such competitions influence
the Greeks? We will briefly glance at evidence for the Phoenicians,
the Egyptians and the Minoans of Bronze Age Crete.[24]

The Phoenicians may enter first and exit most quickly. There is no
evidence that they practised athletic or equestrian competition early
enough to affect Greek sport; the claim that a stadium at Amrit was
in use in the mid-second millennium (Boutros 1981:57–78) flies in the
face of the excavators' date, the third century CE. Nor is it likely that
the Eleans were once the people of Êl (a Phoenician god) or that the
Olympics were founded in honour of the Phoenician deity Melkart
in the sixteenth century; in fact, there is no sure archaeological trace
of Phoenician influence in Elis at any time, and Melkart is a
relatively late arrival (ninth century?) even to Phoenicia (Evjen 1983).

About Egyptian athletics we know more, including indications of
wrestling, boxing, stick fighting, archery, equestrian activities, swimming, boating and ball play, and of the importance of the pharaoh's
physical fitness. Among the most significant pieces of evidence, wall
paintings from tombs at Beni Hasan (about 2000 BCE) show about
400 wrestling scenes (as well as acrobats, jumpers, ball players, stick
fighters); wrestlers, stick fighters and an audience to watch them
figure in carved reliefs in the tomb of Rameses III at Medinet Habu
(twelfth century); eighteenth-dynasty rulers demonstrated their
vigour and asserted their superiority through running and archery.
For Wolfgang Decker, the leading expert on Egyptian sport, this and
other evidence establishes that the Egyptians (and not the Greeks)
were the first athletic civilization we know: 'In Egypt, for the first
time in history, sport played a significant social and political role'

[24] Bernal: 1987, 1991: critiques in, e.g., Lefkowitz and Rogers 1996. Discus: Decker
1992a:44–5. Stade: Romano 1993:104. Phoenicians, Egyptians, Minoans: cf. Evjen
1986:52–3, 1992:95–9.

(Decker 1992a:ix). Unfortunately, this pushes the evidence (rich though it is) too far. The pharaoh's rejuvenating run was apparently a symbolic act (like Boris Yeltsin's disco dancing during the Russian election): no one ran against him. Nor did anyone compete with Amenophis II when he challenged allcomers to match his alleged feat in putting an arrow most of the way through a copper target several inches thick. To be sure, pharaohs did rival and surpass their predecessors and their own previous standards, in archery as in other ways. This, of course, is only an indirect form of competition, and one-sided; even if we can accept the historicity of the achievements they announce – no one has been able to duplicate Amenophis's feat today – pharaohs or their spin-doctors could pass in silence over occasions when they failed to measure up. The pharaoh's running and shooting have more in common with similar demonstrations (real or invented) of a ruler's vitality from the ancient Near East, such as Shulgi's run between two Sumerian cities in about 2000, a round trip of some 200 miles in one stormy day, than with Greek sport (Vermaak 1993, Lamont 1995:212–15).[25]

The combats from Medinet Habu are also problematic in this context. Here Egyptians fight foreigners. We cannot say (as we could with the run) whether we are dealing with a regular, recurrent event or with an unusual or unique display. It is clear, though, that it is Egyptian wrestlers who win in every case. This too must be a staged demonstration of superiority, of the Egyptians as a whole – and, again, of their pharaoh; one victorious Egyptian boasts to his Syrian adversary, 'Pharaoh, my lord, is with me against you.' Once more it is the other ancient peoples of the Mediterranean who provide a parallel, not Greek sport: a Hittite ritual involved a mock combat between Men of Hatti and Men of Masa (in western Asia Minor) in which the Men of Hatti, fighting with bronze against reed, inevitably won (Puhvel 1988:28–9). There may be indications of athletic contests – wrestling, fighting, weight lifting, shot putting – at Hittite religious festivals of the thirteenth century, but the identification of the activities is uncertain, their competitive nature speculative. As even an optimistic reader of the evidence admits, 'Athletic activities . . . are mentioned only rarely in the festival texts. Unlike the ancient Greek games, the Hittite contests did not develop to the

---

[25] Pharaohs: Decker argues that these rituals depend on the idea of a record, an achievement which betters all others, but he fails to note that today only records set in competition are recognized; Decker 1992a:55–9.

point where they dominated the religious activities of the festival'
(Carter 1988:185). Many years later, Herodotus found only one
athletic festival in Egypt, and the exception, in honour of Perseus–
Horus at Chemmis, may owe its Hellenized form at least to the
nearby Greek settlement at Neapolis (Hdt. 2.91; A.B. Lloyd
1976:369–70).

The case of the Minoans is the most intriguing, dwelling as they
did in what became part of the Greek world (on Crete and Thera)
and displaying in their art (our only avenue of access) one of the
most astonishing and attractive of arguably athletic activities, bull
leaping. This too seems to have been practised in the presence of
spectators, and the layout of Minoan palaces afforded space for both
participants and their audience. Regretfully, we must set bull leaping
aside here, since we know nothing about its context or even about
what actions can be represented in our depictions of jumpers
somersaulting over a bull's horns or using them to vault over its back
from the side (Younger 1976). (Can this be a competition? If so, how
was it scored? And how often did the bull win?) Still, there is other
evidence enough to have inspired the excavator of Cnossus, Sir
Arthur Evans, to give the figure he identified as the Mother Goddess
the sobriquet 'our Lady of the Sports' (Evans 1935:39, cf. Willetts
1977:120). Most prominent of possible competitive activities is
boxing, featured on the 'Boxer Rhyton' from Agia Triada (about
1500) and on a famous fresco from Akrotiri on Thera. The Agia
Triada boxers appear on the bottom two bands of their vase. Since
one group, on the higher band, wears helmets, hand coverings and
(in one case) sandals, and the lower boxers have no protection for
their bodies, these may represent two stages of a process of initiation
for Minoan males (Säflund 1987:230–2). Such initiations would
presumably be both regular and regulated, and might well count as
competition if victory (or putting up a good fight) were required to
move from one stage to the next. So important a role for combat
sport is of special interest in the light of our discussion of sport and
warfare: the Bronze Age Cretans are generally regarded as a
peaceable people. (The Romans too test the strength of that link,
since they were a great military power whose citizens did not
normally participate in sport.) In any case, sport is one of the many
aspects of Greek life often imagined to be an inheritance from the
Minoans *via* their complex interaction with the Greek-speaking
Bronze Age Mycenaeans (e.g., by Raubitschek 1980, cf. 1983).

We may prefer nevertheless to accentuate dissimilarities (cf. Mouratidis 1989). There is no evidence that the Minoans took part in chariot racing (a Mycenaean pastime; see below, Chapter 3). While both boxed, the protective helmets and footwear of Minoan fighters are unattested for Greece at any period. Gardiner's judgement on this point seems sound: Greek sport owes little to Minoan Crete (Gardiner 1910:11, 1930:14).[26] Furthermore, the great gaps in our knowledge of the nature and role of these activities on Crete and other Minoan centres ensure that the interest in and impact of sport among the Greeks remain unusual for their time and place.

GREEK SPORT AND THE DISCOURSE OF DIFFERENCE

I close this chapter with a quick demonstration of what I mean by the discourse of difference in Greek sport. I touch on two topics, distinctions among competitive festivals and the hierarchy of events.

In the first instance, Greek festivals were divided into those recognized as panhellenic and local games. The panhellenic competitions, held every two or four years, awarded only symbolic prizes, typically wreaths; they were therefore called *stephanitai*, 'crown games' and *hieroi*, 'sacred', later also *eiselastikoi*, 'games for driving in', since their victors won the honour (among many others) of returning home in a chariot. Local games, *agones thematikoi* or *themides*, might be of little account: Isocrates speaks of athletes entering where others don't think it worth their while (Isoc. 10.10). But they might also attract participants from all over the Greek world. Their defining characteristic was their value prizes – hence the designations *chrematitai* and *arguritai*, 'money games', 'cash games' (Poll. 3.153).[27]

There had once been only four *stephanitai*, the Olympic, Pythian, Isthmian and Nemean festivals. From the early third century, however, new crown games were founded – the first, the Ptolemaieia, by Ptolemy Philadelphus of Egypt, as part of a programme to enhance the status of his kingdom and its capital, Alexandria, among Greeks in the old cultural centres. At the same time, local

---

[26] Crete: nor is American baseball discussed on the Minoan Phaestos Disc, despite the entertaining argument of Bowman 1993.

[27] Panhellenic and local: Robert 1984; but cf. Pleket 1975:54–71 for some complexities. Chariot: Diod. Sic. 13.82.7, Vitr. *De Arch.* 9 *praef.* 1, *SEG* 41 (1991) no. 1003 II.46–50, Teos, third/second century. Some late sources add that a breach was made in the city wall for the chariot's entry, but this tradition may have been invented for or by Nero: Plut. *Mor.* 639e, Cass. Dio 62.20, Suet. *Nero* 25.1.

festivals were transformed into the more prestigious panhellenic celebrations, a process requiring the concurrence of other Greek cities (who agreed to send ambassadors to share in sacrificial rites) and, eventually, of the Roman emperor. By the first century BCE, the Peloponnese, already home to games at Olympia, Isthmia and Argos (then the venue of the Nemean games), boasted other stephanitic festivals at Sicyon, Epidaurus, Mantinea, Tegea, Lousoi, Cleitor, Mount Lycaeon, Hermione and Argos again (the Heraea). It was perhaps this proliferation of crown games which prompted the development of the designation *periodos*, to maintain the special status of the earliest panhellenic festivals. We have seen that even this place of honour came to be shared with the Argive Heraea and the new foundations of the emperors as time went by. But the reverence in which the original games of the circuit were held is indicated by the fact that many of the stephanitic games, newly founded or newly promoted, proudly styled themselves isolympian or isopythian or the like, to advertise that they patterned their programmes and prizes (at least in part) on the ancient models. There were no fewer than twenty Olympic games outside Olympia in the Roman imperial period.

This is not to say that games were regarded alike even at the most exalted level. They had different strengths and specialities. The Olympic games were 'the most athletic of contests'. The Pythian festival, said to have begun with a contest in singing a hymn to Apollo (Paus. 10.7.2), always emphasized musical and, later, other competitions in the arts. The site of Isthmia guaranteed large crowds – so Flamininus chose the festival to announce the freedom of the Greeks from Macedonian rule in 196 BCE – and may have encouraged a distinctive boat race. Nemea's race in armour was deemed exceptionally ancient (Philostr. *Gym.* 7).[28]

It is no accident, however, that I have mentioned Olympia first here: its preeminence was recognized throughout antiquity. Ancient writers may even use Olympia as a shorthand reference to all the great crown games (e.g., Arist. *Rh.* 1.1357a19, Plut. *Arist.* 27.2). Prose victory lists and agonistic epigrams generally present competitive successes in the order Olympia, Pythia, Isthmia, Nemea, with local games coming only afterwards, sometimes (when they are specified

---

[28] Olympia: *ton gumnikotaton tōn agonōn*, Luc. *Nero* 2. Isthmia: Livy 33.32; cf., for the festival's crowds, Strab. 8.6.20 (378), Dio Chrys. *Or.* 8.5–11.

at all) beginning with a festival of some special significance, say in the victor's home-town (E. Maróti 1990:135–7). The Actian games, Augustus's foundation, precede Isthmia or Nemea at times; the Heraea or Aspis of Argos is generally relegated to the rear of elite games, perhaps because (unique among them) it awarded a prize of value, a bronze shield (Moretti 1991:187). Mention of Olympia is occasionally delayed. Prose catalogues may be set out in chronological order; metre may affect verse. A decree of Byzantium lists the panhellenic festivals as Isthmia, Nemea, Olympia, Pythia – alphabetical order? But though the prose catalogue for the Chian runner M. Aurelius Heras sometimes lists his successes by event, sometimes chronologically or geographically, the verse epigram which accompanies it is careful to bring Olympia to the forefront, where it belongs. When the Athenians announced the birth of a boy with an olive wreath on the door, they wished to publicize both the family's present good fortune and its hopes for the future (Kauffmann-Samaras 1988:294); Plato's guardians are to have a life happier than the one men deem happiest, the Olympic winner's (Pl. *Resp.* 5.465d); a Spartan mother is supposed to have greeted the news of her son's death with the exclamation, 'How much better it is that he died in battle than if he lived prevailing at Olympia!' (Plut. *Mor.* 242ab); on one and the same day in 356, Philip of Macedon supposedly learned of a victory for his army, the birth of his son Alexander, and his racehorse's win at Olympia – three peak experiences of a great king (Hegesias *FGrH* 142 F 3 = Plut. *Alex.* 3); Critias prays for the wealth of the Scopadae, the magnanimity of Cimon and the victories of Arcesilas the Lacedaemonian, who won the Olympic four-horse chariot race (DK 88B8).[29]

Difficulties of transport, especially overland, ensured that geographical proximity was an important factor in competitors' decisions. The largest group of identifiable athletic victors at Olympia and Nemea, both inland, came from the Peloponnese; but Greeks from the west (Corcyra, Italy, Sicily) account for proportionately many more victories at Olympia, while Easterners (from the Aegean islands, Asia Minor and the Black Sea) were rather more prominent

---

[29] Prose catalogues: e.g., *SEG* 11 (1950) no. 831, Sparta, 221 CE or later, Spawforth 1984:273–4; *SEG* 37 (1987) no. 298, Epidamnus, late third century. Decree: Dem. 18.91 – but probably a forgery of a later date. Verse: Pythia precedes Olympia in *SEG* 11 (1950) no. 1223a = Moretti 1953: no. 32, Olympia, 464 or just after. Heras: *SEG* 37 (1987) no. 712, Chios, soon after 161 CE; Ebert 1988.

Table 3. *Geographical distribution of athletic victories in the games of the circuit, sixth century* BCE *— first century* BCE

	Olympia	Pythia (from 586) or 582)	Isthmia (from 586)	Nemea (from 573)	All Games
Peloponnese	175	31	67	102	375
Central and Northern Greece	115	37	68	61	281
Western Greeks	78	20	12	17	127
Eastern Greeks	76	28	113	59	276
Libya and Egypt	21	4	2	6	33
All Victories	465	120	262	245	1092

closer to home, at Nemea. The largest group of Pythian wins is contributed by competitors from nearby central and northern Greece. At Isthmia, so accessible by sea, islanders and coastal Greeks total going on half of all known victories, many more, both absolutely and in proportion, than in the other great games. (See Table 3. I derive the data from Klee 1918.) Rough as these calculations are — our evidence is too spotty for anything more precise — one conclusion is incontrovertible: Many more Olympic victories can be ascribed to an identifiable individual than anywhere else — about four times as many as at Delphi (where the Pythian games were also held every four years and, for most of this period if not all, with the same number of age classes) and double those at Isthmia or Nemea.[30] We may crudely calculate that we are four times more likely to know who won any given athletic event at Olympia than at the Pythian, Isthmian or Nemean games.

One reason is that a very important source of information, Pausanias, is interested in Olympic athletes almost to the exclusion of others (see below, Chapter 2). Of course, that preference is itself a reflection of Olympia's prestige. Similarly, when Philostratus begins *On Athletic Exercise* with a set of just-so stories on the origins of events, he says that he will always quote the authorities of Elis, as their

---

[30] The Isthmian and Nemean games were twice as frequent and there was an additional age class. The disproportion here is in fact even greater than these data suggest, since a large number of athletic winners at Isthmia and Nemea whose origin is known are not named but simply referred to in passing as family members or fellow citizens of the recipient of a victory ode, e.g., Pind. *Ol.* 13.96–100, Bacch. 2.6–10.

information is the most accurate (Philostr. *Gym.* 2). Later in his treatise, lamenting the corruption of contemporary sport, he excepts the Olympics: 'The wild olive of Elis is still unsullied because of its fame from early times – but those other games . . . !' (45). This is sentimental illusion; we have already found that the earliest extant Olympic law dealt with cheating. But the very stories which threaten to blemish Olympia's reputation also underscore the significance of victories there. According to Heracleides Ponticus, the Sybarites tried to bribe Olympic athletes to compete for their city (Ath. 12.521f). Cimon won return from exile by having the Athenian tyrant Peisistratus proclaimed as the owner of his victorious chariot team in 532 (Hdt. 6.103). Another tyrant, Hieron or Gelon of Syracuse, persuaded Astylus of Croton to win the Olympic *stadion* race of 484 or 480 as a Syracusan; in revenge, the Crotoniates turned Astylus's house into a prison and tore down the statue which commemorated an earlier win (Paus. 6.13.1, cf. 6.2.7, 3.11, 18.6). Accurate or not, such stories gain in impact from their setting at Olympia.

The hierarchy of competitive events is more controversial. I present (on p. 41) a list of the events at Olympia and the date at which they were said to have entered the programme (Table 4). Of course, this does not exhaust the events in which competitions were held. The Isthmian and Nemean games included the *hippios*, a middle distance foot-race of four stades (800 m, Paus. 6.16.4). At the Panathenaea, mounted ephebes threw the javelin at a target and tribes of Athenian citizens competed in the *euandria*, a test of physical fitness and fortitude that may have included a tug of war or shield manoeuvres and mock combat. The *taurotheria* at Larissa in the Thessalian plain was a kind of rodeo event in which the competitor leaped off his horse to grapple a bull into submission. Nor need events have been conducted in the same way everywhere: the *dolikhos*, the long race, varied between seven and twenty stades (1400 to 4000 m, Jüthner 1968:108 n. 232). Nevertheless, the Olympic programme provides evidence enough for our purposes.[31]

The Greeks divided athletic events into heavy (*bareia*) and light (*koupha*). Generally, it is the combat events which are called heavy. The word may bear a literal meaning, since the lack of weight classes in wrestling, boxing and *pankration* gave bigger athletes an

---

[31] *Euandria*: Crowther 1985a, Reed 1987, Boegehold 1996:97–103 (arguing that the event involved choral singing and dancing). *Taurotheria*: Heliod. *Aeth.* 10.28–30; Gallis 1988:221–5.

advantage. Philostratus, it is true, includes the discus as a heavy event alongside wrestling in the pentathlon (*Gym.* 3). Here the reference might be to the weight of the discus or to the effort required to throw it, a common metaphorical sense of *barus* and related words. Aristotle too seems to have effort in mind when he recommends that boys train only at lighter exercises (*Pol.* 8.1338b40). He is not talking about competition, however, so he may not be using the word as a technical term. Moreover, Philostratus's view, as often, seems to be shaped to suit his ideas about the athlete's physique: the pentathlete should be heavy rather than light and light rather than heavy, a balance mirrored in his account of the component events (*Gym.* 31). Galen (like other writers; see below, Chapter 5) disapproves of the training habits of heavy athletes and their consequences; but none of our sources offers judgements on the relative worth of the categories themselves except Euripides' Heracles, a fighter who distinguishes light from greater contests, boxing and wrestling (*ta meizona*, Eur. *Alc.* 1029–30). Aristotle observes that there is a sort of bodily exercise suitable for those naturally superior, but he does not say what it is (Arist. *Pol.* 4.1288b10–20).[32]

There are a number of signs of the significance ascribed to various events, though none is conclusive in itself and different indicators may point in opposing directions. Wrestling and the *stadion* race were both separate events and parts of the pentathlon. The importance of wrestling is otherwise confirmed by its association with Heracles and Theseus, legendary inventors and practitioners of its techniques; by the use of its Greek root, *palē*, in the name of a central institution in Greek sport and education, the *palaistra*; by the preponderance of inscriptions honouring wrestlers, and the rarity even of other heavy athletes, from Lycia and Pisidia in the Roman period (Jones 1990:487–8). We might object that Pausanias mentions more Olympic champions in boxing (56) than in any other sport (there are 48 runners of all kinds and 36 wrestlers). One response is that Pausanias is guided by aesthetic concerns, and above all by his interest in the sculptors of the works he describes. Moreover, it is never easy to be sure of the motivations for artists' or their patrons' choices of subjects.[33]

---

[32] Combat events: Aeschin. 3.179, Pl. *Leg.* 8.833d, Diod. Sic. 4.14.2, Plut. *Mor.* 724c, Gal. 6.487 Kühn. *Diskoi*: most competitive examples which have been found weigh between two and three kilograms; Gardiner 1930:156.

[33] *Palē* and *palaistra*: the etymology is recognized and debated in Plut. *Mor.* 638bd. Choices of

The *stadion* earns the biggest prize of all athletic events at the Panathenaea and leads off the athletic programme. Our source for this information, a prize list of the earlier fourth century BCE, is worth a longer look, since it involves several of the factors relevant here. The second largest prize did not go to wrestling at this famous festival but to *pankration* – the last athletic event. So much for the easy translation of priority into pre-eminence! Furthermore, in a festival at Aphrodisias in Asia Minor about 200 CE, the *pankration* offered a prize more generous not only than wrestling or boxing (3000 denarii for men as against 2000) but than the *stadion* race as well (1250). We might note here that the pattern of referring to an Olympiad by the name of the winner of the men's *stadion* does not predate the third century, and that the earliest uses of the Olympics to establish chronology in literature and inscriptions make use of pancratiasts. It appears that events were ranked differently from place to place and/or in diverse eras. Of course, prizes serve other purposes than simply representing an event's status. One (then as now) is to attract competitors; all prizes at the Panathenaea may have increased in the early fourth century in an attempt to raise the festival's competitive profile (Valavanis 1987:479–80). Whether this is so or not, they display some important distinctions. First, the athletic events at the Panathenaea were open to all comers. But there was another set of events for Athenians only, and these had noticeably smaller prizes. Whereas the winner of the boys' *stadion* race won fifty jars of olive oil, the best at throwing the javelin from horseback earned just five. Second, in both the open and the citizen categories, equestrian prizes far outstripped athletic rewards. The two-horse chariot race for grown horses had the top prize, 140 jars of olive oil, perhaps as much as double that for men who ran the *stadion* (the inscription is illegible here); victory in the same event for citizens brought thirty jars.[34]

This surely shows that it took some incentive for owners to enter

---

subjects: the race in armour, a late addition to the Olympic programme, is quite popular on vases – because it was a novelty? or picturesque? – but rare in sculpture. The discus is more evenly distributed across artistic media, the javelin rare in all.

[34] Panathenaea: *IG* 2² 2311 = S.G. Miller 1991: no. 84, dated about 380 in Valavanis 1987:476. Aphrodisias: *CIG* 2 2758 = *SEG* 39 (1989) no. 1103; cf. the praise of the *pankration* as 'the most perfect of *agones*' in another more or less contemporary inscription from Aphrodisias, *SEG* 34 (1984) no. 1045.20–2, third century CE. Pancratiasts: Thuc. 3.8, 5.49.1: *SIG*³ 557.15–16, Magnesia on Maeander, about 207/6. The first literary references to *stadion* winners for dating purposes: Xen. *Hell.* 1.2.1, 2.3.1.

their valuable teams and trappings at the Panathenaea. But it must
also indicate that the event was worth the cost. Such competition
was indeed given pride of place by some Greeks. Literally in the case
of Damonon, the wealthy Spartan whose stele boasts a carved relief
of a four-horse chariot in motion at the top and lists equestrian
victories before his numerous successes as a young runner. But not
by all – our cue to return to the Olympic programme and the stories
it tells. I will argue that the programme as we have it reflects
disagreement on just this issue, the relative worth of equestrian and
athletic competition, and that this disagreement influenced both the
reconstruction of the past and the fashioning of the present at
Olympia.[35]

The outline of the development of the Olympic programme is
straightforward. The earliest games comprised just one event, the
stadion race; other races, and then other athletic competitions,
followed over the next hundred years. The first equestrian event, the
four-horse chariot race, was contested in 680, the horse race in 648.
Boys' events began in 632; in 520, the hoplite race virtually
completed the athletic programme. Two new equestrian events were
introduced at the beginning of the fifth century only to be dropped
after fifty years; after this date, the programme grew to include a
number of new horse races and, finally, the boys' *pankration* in 200
(Paus. 5.8.6–9.2).

We will consider the earlier stages of this story shortly. Now, what
led to the adoption and then rejection of the *apenē* and the *kalpē*? The
question is as important to our understanding of the substance of
Greek festival competition as it is hard to answer. As Pierre Bourdieu
puts it, 'The *social definition of sport* is an object of struggles . . . in
which what is at stake, *inter alia*, is the monopolistic capacity to
impose the legitimate definition of sporting practices and of the
legitimate functioning of sporting activity' (Bourdieu 1978:826, cf.
Gruneau 1983:82). At Olympia, all such struggles must involve the
Hellanodikai, the prominent Eleans who had authority over the
competitions. Who else? Since three of the four winners we know for
the *apenē* were Greeks from the west (Anaxilas of Rhegium (480),
Hagesias of Syracuse (468), Psaumis of Camarina (456)), it is
tempting to see the impetus behind its appearance at Olympia

---

[35] Damonon: *IG* 5.1 123, 450–431 or (more likely) early fourth century; Hodkinson
forthcoming. Not by all: Crowther uses prize lists to argue that equestrian events were less
popular than athletic in the Roman imperial period (Crowther 1995a:121–2).

Table 4. *The Olympic programme and the traditional date when each event joined it*

stadion, 200 m race	776 BCE
diaulos, 400 m race	724 BCE
dolikhos, long race	720 BCE
pentathlon	708 BCE
palē, wrestling	708 BCE
pux, boxing	688 BCE
tethrippon, 4-horse chariot race	680 BCE
pankration	648 BCE
kelēs, horse race	648 BCE
stadion for boys	632 BCE
palē for boys	632 BCE
pentathlon for boys	628 BCE (dropped immediately)
pux for boys	616 BCE
hoplitēs, race in armour	520 BCE
apenē, mule-car race	500 BCE (dropped in 444 BCE)
kalpē, mares' race	496 BCE (dropped in 444 BCE)
sunoris, 2-horse chariot race	408 BCE
salpinktes, trumpeters	396 BCE
kerukes, heralds	396 BCE
tethrippon for foals	384 BCE
sunoris for foals	264 BCE
kelēs for foals	256 BCE
pankration for boys	200 BCE

coming from the wealthy and powerful tyrants of Sicily and South Italy and their associates, notorious for their eagerness to affirm their credentials among the long established aristocrats of the motherland by the speed of their horses (see Gardiner 1910:71, 460). Anaxilas marked his victory with an ode by Simonides and silver coins showing a pair of mules, their car and driver (Robinson 1946). By this reckoning, the mule car race will have been discontinued within a generation of the tyrants' expulsion and the democratization of Sicily and as a response to these events. But the first western win does not come until twenty years after the event's debut – and the *kalpē* has no known Sicilian connection (though it may appear on South Italian coins: Brauer 1974–5). The first and only identifiable winner was Pataecus of Dyme in the Peloponnese, and the event itself, a race for mares in which riders jump off at the end and run alongside their mounts, holding the bridle, is very like the *apobatēs*, a speciality of Athens and Boeotia (Harp. A 182 Keaney s.v. *apobatēs*).

Perhaps the *Hellanodikai* took over both *apenē*, attested in Attic art from the late sixth century, and *kalpē* from the Panathenaea (Kratz-müller 1993:89–90). Even if this is so, however, it is awkward to connect Athens with the events' removal from the programme, since Elis was friendly to Athens during the mid-fifth century and took part in the Athenian-inspired colony at Thurii in southern Italy in 444/3 (Hönle 1972:192–6).

An explanation based on the internal politics of Elis might work better. Dyme is virtually on the border of Elis – there may well have been local interest in introducing the *kalpē*. The 440s are more troublesome. There is no reason to believe that the Elean oligarchy became weaker at this time – if anything, the reverse (Arist. *Pol.* 5.1306a15). But it is just possible that there was a change in the composition of the board of the *Hellanodikai* during the time in which there were races for *apenē* and *kalpē*. Pausanias tells us that the office of *Hellanodikas*, originally hereditary and held by one man, was shared between two men appointed by lot from all Eleans beginning with the fiftieth festival, in 580, and that the number remained constant for a long time. Then the board expanded to nine – three for the equestrian events, three for the pentathlon, three for the remainder (Paus. 5.9.5). His text reads that this occurred at the twenty-fifth games – something must be wrong. The next clear chronological marker Pausanias provides is for the expansion of the board to twelve at the one hundred and third festival, in 384. We may therefore place the increase in the number of *Hellanodikai* at any time between 576 and 384; one attractive possibility is at the seventy-fifth Olympiad, in 480; another is after the unification of the villages of Elis into one *polis* in 471/0 (Diod. Sic. 11.54.1). We may further imagine that the confusion in Pausanias (or his text) extends to the allotment of the office, since that procedure seems to suit the fifth century more than the sixth. If so, the *Hellanodikai* who saw to the end of competition in *apenē* and *kalpē* will have been a larger and somewhat more representative group than those who had a hand in their introduction; though the commitments of time and money required for the post will have ensured that the candidates were generally well off. They might well be more sympathetic to a movement to rid the programme of two events of no great antiquity and accessible, in practical terms, to very few. At least they would have little reason to resist, on their own behalf (the *Hellanodikai* could field entries until 368, Paus. 6.1.4) or on that of the Elean elite in general. A curse forbad the breeding of mules in Elis – so much for local investment in *apenē* – and attestations of dismounting races outside Attica and Boeotia are late and do not include any in Elis.[36]

None of this inspires much confidence. Alternatives abound (cf. Bell 1989:173–4). There was disdain for the mules from the outset; Simonides is said to have refused Anaxilas's commission at first on the grounds that the fee and the event were beneath him (Arist. *Rh.* 3.1405b24, cf. Paus. 5.9.2). Did the elite (who probably competed in person, as in the *apobatēs*) find running alongside their horses to be beneath their dignity too? Did it simply require more effort than older horse owners (who made up the majority of equestrian victors; see below, Chapter 4) were prepared or able to expend? Also mysterious, but perhaps less purely so, is the introduction of the *sunoris*: Evagoras, the first winner, was Elean. It is in this context that the first list of Olympic victors, and so too the first account of the Olympic programme, was drawn up by Hippias of Elis around 400. We will consider the reliability of its dates below in Chapter 2. Here our focus will be on the programme's earliest development.

The pattern of Hippias's programme, of a small festival gradually growing over time, has seemed plausible to many (e.g., Lee 1988:111). Furthermore, the priority of the *stadion* race is a central element of treatments which stress the close connection of athletics and cult. But the late introduction of horse-racing is unsettling. Chariots appear to race in Mycenaean art, and the chariot race takes up by far the longest portion of the funeral games for Patroclus in *Iliad* 23 (see below, Chapter 3). Why would they not figure at early Olympia, an interstate sanctuary drawing visitors (as far as we can judge from dedications) from some distance away in the Peloponnese and attracting, along with other contests, 'increasing competition for status via the conspicuous consumption of wealth' (C. Morgan 1990:45)?[37]

We might also ask how Hippias knew that athletic contests were held for about one hundred years before the chariot race. We have few written records from archaic Elis, the oldest perhaps from a little before 580 (Jeffery 1990:216–21, 450–1). It is noteworthy that our earliest source, Pindar, offers a different (if overtly mythical) reconstruction: Heracles' first games included boxing, discus, javelin,

---

[36] Mules: Hdt. 4.30, Paus. 5.5.2, 5.9.2, Plut. *Mor.* 303b.
[37] Athletics and cult: e.g., Burkert 1983:95, Nagy 1986:81, cf. Sansone 1988:82. Late introduction: cf. Bell 1989:170–2, Peiser 1990:47–9.

wrestling and, yes, four-horse chariots as well as the *stadion* race
(Pind. *Ol.* 10.60–73). Even Pausanias, who follows Hippias in his
sketch of the growth of the Olympic programme, preserves traces of
other traditions elsewhere in his work. Zeus wrestled Cronus for the
throne of the gods at Olympia, or set up games to celebrate his
victory. In these, Apollo outraced Hermes and defeated Ares in
boxing (Paus. 5.7.10, cf. 8.2.2). At the funeral games for Azan,
contests were held at Olympia for the first time; these included horse
races – and Pausanias says he doesn't know what else (Paus. 8.4.5).
Pausanias's explanation for the programme's pattern may also give
us pause. There had been earlier celebrations, which fell into
abeyance. When these were revived by Iphitus, events were introduced as they were remembered (Paus. 5.8.5). This is not only
incredible in itself, it implies that even at Olympia there was a
tradition that there were competitions in many events at an early
date. It is true that we have no developed and explicit version of the
programme's history which contradicts Hippias's (unless we count
Plutarch's playful argument that contests in wrestling and boxing
were earlier than in running because of the contrasting ways they
are useful for war: Plut. *Mor.* 639d-640a). However, his absolute date
for the inception of boys' events, 632, did not command universal
assent.[38] We should recall that Hippias once came to Olympia
wearing only clothes he had made himself (Pl. *Hp. mi.* 368bc) – he
was a man who could make something up out of whole cloth.

More important, the Olympic festival's canonical charter myth is
based on a chariot race in which Pelops defeats King Oenomaus of
Pisa and wins the hand of his daughter Hippodameia, 'tamer', or
better, 'tamed by horses'. This story, the subject of the sculpture for
the west pediment of the Temple of Zeus built in the 470s, must
reflect early esteem for chariot racing. There is no answering role for
running in any early aetiology we know. Such stories – that the
Cretan Heracles matched his brothers in a race at the original
Olympiad, that Endymion's sons ran for his throne at Olympia – are
late. Instead, early sources offer alternative traditions, Pindar's
ascription of Pelops's triumph to the winged chariot he got from
Poseidon being countered by Sophocles' tale of the treachery of the
king's charioteer, Myrtilus, a figure on whom Pindar is silent. In this

---

[38] Hippias's knowledge: cf. Thomas 1989:287–8 and note Demosthenes' scornful scepticism
about the earliest history of Delphi, Dem. 18.149–50. Boys' events: Paus. 5.8.9 (632), cf.
Philostr. *Gym.* 13 (596).

second strain, favoured by Athenian authors, chariot racing is suspect from the start.[39]

We will take up the question of Athenian attitudes to equestrian competition in Chapter 5. For the moment, it is enough to identify in these stories evidence for both the antiquity of chariot racing at Olympia and hostility towards it. (There may be some hostility too in the tradition on Azan's games, in which Aetolus ran over a spectator and was exiled (Paus. 5.1.8).) The truth, I suspect, is that equestrian competition was part of the games from the beginning, as it seems to have been at Delphi (Paus. 10.7.5). Perhaps (as is sometimes said) the introduction of the four-horse race in 680 merely marks a shift from the two-horse chariot of epic (e.g., Gardiner 1910:56). But of course what matters is Hippias's silence on the subject, to be located within what I have called the discourse of difference in ancient Greek sport. Whether the entry of the *sunoris* into the Olympic programme in 408 represented a renewal of an old event or the insertion of a new one, it was a clear statement of the importance and legitimacy of equestrian competition in a festival which had known no athletic innovation in over one hundred years. It certainly struck Xenophon (*Hell.* 1.2.1). Hippias's list should be regarded as the expression of a rival viewpoint, one maintaining the ascendancy of athletics. The conflict between these two opposed elements of festival competition will recur in our discussions of contestants' age and sex as well as class. First, however, we must consider the nature of our evidence for Greek sport as a whole.[40]

---

[39] Running aetiologies: Paus. 5.7.6–9, cf. 8.2.2 (Heracles); Paus. 5.1.4, 5.8.1 (Endymion). Winged chariot: Pind. *Ol.* 1.69–87 – the gift is depicted already on the sixth-century Chest of Cypselus (Paus. 5.17.7). Treachery: Soph. *Oenomaus* in Apollod. *Epit.* 2.3–9, cf. Pherecydes *FGrH* 3 F 37a; Howie 1991.

[40] Hostility: note too the story of Salmoneus, known as early as Hesiod (fr. 30 M.-W.). He built a city in Elis and drove his chariot through it mimicking the thunder and lightning of Zeus until he and his city were blasted to oblivion by the real thing (Apollod. 1.9.7). A late commentator suggests that the provocation was all the greater because the region was one which worshipped Zeus with special fervour – a likely reference to Olympia (Servius on Verg. *Aen.* 6.588).

CHAPTER 2

The evidence and its limits

As I write, the Atlanta Olympics are about to begin. Media of every kind are full of stories – this athlete has passed the qualifying standard, that one a drug test, another counterfeit bills. One of America's great newspapers has devoted two pages of *Horizon* (its 'learning section') to a thorough and thoughtful account of the ancient Olympics (*The Washington Post*, 10 July 1996: H1, 4). Illustrated with a photo of Olympia, a map of Greece, and colour reproductions of vases, mosaics and coins, the story touches on the rule against women's attendance at the festival of Zeus and an exceptional case in which it was violated (see below, Chapter 4). 'Ancient chronicles tell of a widow from a wealthy family of Rhodesian exiles who wanted to watch her son box at the Olympics and arrived disguised as a trainer.' Confirmation of Martin Bernal's claims for the African roots of Greek culture? No, a simple slip (of 'Rhodesian' for 'Rhodian'). However, the story includes other information about the ancient games which is false or likely so: that a mule race was one of the original events, that wrestling and boxing were added about 600 BCE, that city states which accepted the Olympic truce were forbidden to bear arms, that the Olympic festival began on the third full moon after the summer solstice. I do not bring up these inaccuracies to embarrass a newspaper which has toppled presidents. In fact, *The Post* deserves credit for consulting in the story's preparation with three of the leading sport history specialists in the United States. My point is that our evidence for ancient sport is often so unsatisfactory that even the most august institutions may misrepresent its consequences and even the most eminent experts disagree. Why this is so should be clearer by the end of this chapter.

How do we know what we know about athletic and equestrian competition in ancient Greece? Why don't we know more? In this chapter, I outline an answer to these questions. I begin with a discussion of the available evidence in three categories, (1) literary texts; (2) texts engraved on stone (inscriptions), or scratched on potsherds (ostraca), or written on papyrus (papyri), or painted (dipinti) or incised (graffiti) on pots and other media; and (3) archaeology and art. As the treatment of texts under two different rubrics reveals, this scheme is essentially arbitrary. For example, one very important source of evidence, dedicatory epigrams, are literary texts often (and perhaps originally) engraved on stone bases or on other artefacts typically uncovered by archaeologists. Though commonly studied as isolated documents, they are best treated in the contexts of the objects they accompanied and the locations where these objects were displayed. The arrangement I propose here, then, is largely a matter of taste and convenience. The discussion is rounded off by a series of demonstrations of the difficulties raised by these categories of evidence and by the contradictions they so often display. I will offer brief object lessons on four controversial subjects: the jump, the date of the first Olympics, athletic nudity, determining the winner of the pentathlon.[1]

I stress at the outset two overriding drawbacks, more troubling even than the absolute silence of the sources on many subjects. First, nothing we read or look at or find was produced for our benefit. Whatever we may conclude from the evidence, we may be sure that the Greeks never intended that evidence to be used by us for our purposes. In that sense, to speak of *our* evidence is always wrong. Second, paradoxically, the evidence is sometimes too close to us. We still run, throw, jump and fight in programmes and ways which owe a great deal to Greek competition and our notions about it. But where the Greek *gumnasion* was an exercise complex, incorporating running tracks (both open and covered), ball courts, baths, dressing rooms, even auditoriums and libraries in an expanse of open space, itself located (at Athens at least) within a larger park-like precinct devoted to a god or a hero, the gym of our own experience is likely to be a small, stuffy room in a school basement. Our familiarity with some terms and techniques can hinder as well as help.

LITERARY TEXTS

Literary texts are evidence for the ideas and beliefs of their author; also, it may be, for the ideas and beliefs of others like the author (of

---

[1] Sources: Harris 1964:23–31 and, on the ancient world in general, Crawford 1983.

the same age, gender, social class, in the same time and place);
perhaps too for predominant attitudes, the way things were, what
really happened. I have presented these possibilities in the usual
order of reliability; it is generally more probable that any text
represents the beliefs of the author than of a group, beliefs of a
group rather than fact. But each text poses particular problems.
Take the prescriptions for female exercise and competition in Plato's
utopian works, *Republic* and *Laws*. In neither dialogue does Plato
appear by name as a participant; but there is little doubt that the
Socrates of *Republic* is the author's spokesman, still less about the
Athenian stranger in *Laws*. Other literary genres are less straightforward in this regard. The denunciation of the athletic activities of
Spartan girls, and the insinuations about their chastity, in Euripides,
Andromache 595–601, should be read in the context of the play first of
all, as part of the portrayal of the speaker, Peleus, as a harsh and
hostile old man – they need not be Euripides' own view. However,
the means used for Peleus's portrayal here may well be influenced by
the prejudices of many of Euripides' male contemporaries in the
Athenian audience, embroiled as they were in the early years of the
Peloponnesian war, and embittered as they may have been by
Sparta's annual incursions into Attica. In contrast, Plato's ideas are
idiosyncratic; he himself takes pains to let us know that women
exercising naked along with men may seem ridiculous. No doubt this
is true for Plato's own place and time; consequently, few believe that
his suggestions may be taken as good evidence for contemporary
Athenian reality. Plato, however, was a student and admirer of the
institutions of other Greek communities, notably Crete and Sparta,
and we may therefore accept his texts as evidence to confirm, in
essence, what Peleus presents so pejoratively.[2]

Each of the texts referred to so far is a short passage in a work
only incidentally concerned with sport. In fact, works which take
athletic or equestrian competition as their theme are very rare in
ancient Greece. Pride of place among them belongs to the praise
poetry for winners, the dedicatory epigrams and victory odes
discussed below in Chapter 3, and to our one extended text on the
subject, an odd treatise usually called *Gumnastikos* or *On Gymnastics*,

---

[2] Female exercise and competition: Pl. *Resp.* 5.452ab, *Leg.* 7.804de–805a, 813b–814c,
8.833c–834a. Ridiculous: Pl. *Resp.* 5.452ab, cf. *Leg.* 7.805a. Reality: but Perlman 1983 argues
that *Laws*' programme of races for girls reflects particular practices of the cult of Artemis at
Brauron (discussed below, Chapter 4).

but better titled *On Athletic Exercise* and ascribed to Philostratus (Billault 1993). Even this is incomplete. Furthermore, our usual assumption that this text represents the view of the author at least is vitiated by our uncertainty as to which of the several second- and third-century CE Lemnian intellectuals named Philostratus this was. The answer is of some significance in evaluating the work's contents. None of the candidates is known to have had any experience or expertise in competition. Yet *On Athletic Exercise* displays a keen interest in body aesthetics. A wrestler's neck, for instance, should be neither long nor set down into the shoulders; though this last is effective enough, it seems misshapen, like statues of Heracles, which are less pleasing and godlike because they have short necks (*Gym.* 35). Such confusions of form and fitness are not unknown today, when the suitability of curling as an event for the winter Olympics has been bedevilled by the inconvenient fact that successful curlers are often dumpy and middle-aged. Their prominence in On *Athletic Exercise* is all the more understandable if the author also wrote one of the series of *Imagines*, word pictures of artworks also transmitted under the name Philostratus. Of course, if they are the reflection of an exceptional interest in body shape, they may also be less indicative of the perceptions and priorities of others.

Indeed, it is otherwise evident that *On Athletic Exercise* does not speak for all. A rumination, among other things, on the decline in athletics and the part played in their denigration by contemporary doctrines, the work often criticizes prevailing theories on training and dietetics; unfortunately, its polemic sometimes takes the form of parody and misrepresentation (R. Brophy and M. Brophy 1989). So: *On Athletic Exercise* is evidence for the ideas of its author – but we can't identify him securely; its views are at times unusual, yet we cannot always employ them as a guide to what was normally thought or done. Does this text afford firmer footing in matters of fact? Of most importance here must be those places where Philostratus supplies information unavailable elsewhere: that a man who had previously won the race in armour at the Plataean Eleutheria was sacrificed if he ran again and lost (*Gym.* 8, 24), that only wrestlers could win a combat event *akoniti*, by default (11), that a large belly could be an asset in boxing, as it hindered blows to the head (34; Poliakoff 1982:143–8). Unhappily, the statement on wrestlers can be controverted by numerous examples from literary and epigraphic texts; that on boxers consolidates the author's reputation as a theoretician rather than an athlete or even a spectator. How about the hoplite race? The accuracy of Philostratus's text is accepted in the standard commentary by Jüthner and most recently by Sansone. But we may note that the first mention of the rule comes in an argument for the superiority of the Plataean race as the longest and the most arduous – the punishment for losing is just another extraordinary demand on competitors – and the second in a sequence of anecdotes on coaches' stratagems, where it offers a peg on which to hang an account of remarkable selflessness and inspiration on behalf of an unidentifiable Egyptian. Scepticism is in order.[3]

In the main, then, it is through casual comments, allusions, images that athletic and equestrian competition enters our literary texts. Their number and their distribution across all genres demonstrate sport's importance in the Greek world; these factors also go some way towards correcting the quirks and conventions of individual texts and their genres. Something of the flavour of these references may be explored through review of one work, Plutarch's *Lives*, the product of an educated Greek in the Roman Empire who had, as far as we know, as little in the way of special credentials in the area as Philostratus. Some of the evidence afforded by the *Lives* emerges from the narrative. We may adduce the vivid account of Mark Antony acting as gymnasiarch at Athens, carrying the rods, in Greek clothing and white sandals, taking young competitors by the neck and parting them (Plut. *Ant.* 33.4), of Leonnatus the Macedonian, on campaign with Alexander, bringing in camel loads of exercise dust from Egypt (*Alex.* 40.1). The narrative also offers important evidence for changes in the prizes at Isthmia (*Tim.* 36.1–3) and for Philopoemen's disdain for athletics as a preparation for war (*Philop.* 3.2–4). More frequent and more informative, however, are the similes and metaphors Plutarch (perhaps imitating Plato) uses or puts into the mouths of others. Many occur in military contexts – the field of war is a wrestling-ground (*Marc.* 27.2, *Pyrrh.* 23.6, cf. *Pelop.* 7.3). Antigonus III's resources let him wear Cleomenes III of Sparta down, just as well-trained athletes in time overcome those who excel merely in grace and skill (*Cleom.* 27.2). Similarly, Fabius fought

---

[3] Eleutheria: Jüthner (1909:201) stresses the original occasion of these games, as a celebration for victory over the Persians, and the bad omen that a winner's failure would entail in this context. Sansone (1988:117) regards the rule as 'a reflection of a time when the ritual sacrifice of energy was occasionally intensified to the point of actually involving human sacrifice'.

Hannibal like a good athlete – he easily baffled him when his holds had lost their vigour (*Fab.* 23.2, cf. 19.3). The same point is made through a different image in the life of Phocion (23.3). The Athenian general was asked about his city's prospects for revolt after Alexander's death. 'They are very good for the *stadion* race', he replied, 'but I fear the *dolikhos*, the long race of war, since the city has no reserves.' Vitellius's troops taunt Otho's as actors, pyrrhic dancers, spectators at the Pythian and Olympic games; the reversal of the usual conceit, that soldiers are athletes of war, so stings Otho's men that they beg their commander to throw them into the fray, and they beat back their tormentors' assault (*Otho* 6.1–2; cf. *Arat.* 27.2). Other troops, Verginius's and Vindex's, force their leaders into battle like charioteers who have lost control of the reins (*Galba* 6.3). A wrestler who does not move affords his adversary no advantage, thought Agesilaus; so too it is difficult to use stratagems against naive opponents who have no expectations to confound (*Ages.* 38.2).[4]

The other main context for references to athletics is another arena for competition among men, politics. The same image may appear in both contexts, as when invoking the *ephedros*, the athlete who has a bye and rests as others vie for the right to meet him. Some other references illustrate general truths: to call a man happy when he is still alive is like proclaiming and crowning a competitor in the midst of an event – a Greek idea put in a Greek idiom by Solon to a foreigner, Croesus (*Sol.* 27.7). We may sometimes wonder whether an image has not been distorted to suit Plutarch's purposes. It was Pelopidas's inspiration to make the Sacred Band one unit, but Plutarch is responsible for the more dubious proposition that explains the plan's success, that horses run faster yoked to a chariot than they do when men ride them singly (*Pelop.* 19.4). Nor does the epigraphic record bear out the allegation, a transition from Pompey's early achievements to his later triumphs, that adult winners take no account of their victories as boys and even leave them unrecorded (*Pomp.* 8.6). But in most cases, more or less incidental remarks of this kind must offer a glimpse of received wisdom among the literary elite of the Graeco-Roman world.[5]

---

[4] Athletics and war: see also Plut. *Caes.* 28.1–3, *Cim.* 13.3, *Pomp.* 17.2, *Sert.* 23.1, *Them.* 3.4, *Comp. Ages. Pomp.* 4.4, *Comp. Luc. Cim.* 2.1, 3.4.

[5] Athletics and politics: See also Plut. *Arist.* 2.3, *Caes.* 30.2, *Cato Min.* 45.4, *Demos.* 6.2, *Dion* 1.1–2, *Luc.* 38.4, *Per.* 4.1, 11.2, 28.4, *Comp. Arist. Cato* 2.3. *Ephedros*: Plut. *Caes.* 28.1, *Marc.* 3.2, *Pomp.* 53.6, *Sul.* 29.1.

These references in the *Lives* are pretty transparent. Not so others elsewhere. Fortunately, modern scholars have the benefit of ancient expertise, the encyclopedias and lexica and commentaries on Greek texts from the Hellenistic period until the end of antiquity and beyond. So Pindar mentions games at Epidaurus, but it is an ancient academic who tells us that these were the Asclepieia and that they were held nine days after the festival at Isthmia. But scholars are fallible, then as now. They made slips (as in giving the name of Theogenes' father as Timosthenes instead of Timoxenus: Masson 1994). They made guesses. (To what does Pindar intend to refer by the phrase *terma probais*? To a pentathlete throwing his javelin out of bounds? Or stepping over the line and fouling? Neither.) They make fools of themselves, as Hesychius does in explaining *mesoperdēn* and *mesopherdein*, lexicographers' coinages meant to elucidate the comic *mesoperdein*, 'to squeeze (out) a fart', as wrestling terms. But they also allow us to make sense of good, early evidence that we might miss without them. Two orations of Dio Chrysostom (28 and 29) make much of a certain Melancomas, a Carian boxer of the first century CE, whose fortitude and endurance were such that he could keep his guard up for two days without weakening and win without taking or delivering a blow. Much of our other evidence on Greek boxing stresses aggression, not to say brutality; Melancomas's tactics have been taken to typify a sport in decline, dominated by sluggish heavyweights with the energy and skill of a brontosaurus on valium. The scholars of late antiquity, however, know of a device, the *klimax* or 'ladder', to keep dilatory boxers within striking distance and so make Melancomas's methods impracticable. Though Melancomas is virtually unknown elsewhere, we might nevertheless prefer Dio's account to Hesychius and the rest; the plurality of sources could not be decisive, since such works (then as now, again) often borrowed from each other. But an entirely independent source of evidence, vase paintings of about 500, picture something that might be the 'ladder' the scholars describe; and a platform at Nemea – the contribution of archaeology – affords the confined space in which the 'ladder' might be placed. The result is to convict Dio of concocting fantasy for his own moralizing purposes, to vindicate ancient scholarship, and to improve our understanding of the development of Greek boxing (Poliakoff 1987b). More generally, it serves to underscore the importance of consulting as many different kinds of evidence as

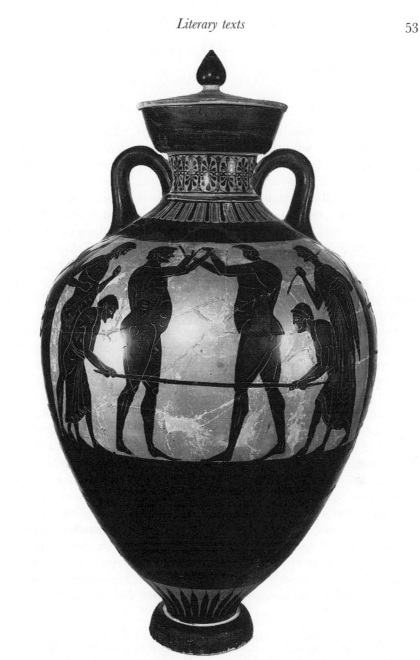

Plate 1. Two officials hold a rod (at knee level) to keep boxers at close quarters. Attic black-figure Panathenaic amphora, Cleophrades painter, early fifth century.

possible, and so leads the way to a consideration of inscriptions, papyri and related texts.[6]

INSCRIPTIONS, PAPYRI AND RELATED TEXTS

Such evidence has three main advantages. First, it is usually independent of other texts. Authors of ancient literary works, conscious as they were of writing within a living tradition, borrowed from one another no less than scholars did. Seneca, Plutarch and Philostratus all say that Spartans did not compete in boxing or *pankration*, because losers in these events might be forced to signal submission. Yet Philostratus also ascribes the invention of boxing to the Spartans (*Gym.* 9), the Spartan hero Pollux was a famous fighter, and a Spartan boxer is said to have won at Olympia. The matter is settled by evidence unlikely to feed off either literary tradition, inscriptions showing Spartan pancratiasts at panhellenic games and *pankration* competitions at Sparta itself.[7]

Second, new inscriptions, papyri and texts on other fabrics come to light continually. In 1995, Ulrich Sinn announced the discovery of a bronze tablet at Olympia, bearing the names of numerous Olympic victors, one of them the latest yet known, from 385 CE (Sinn 1995). If Sinn is correct to link the tablet with a shrine for Heracles, this is further evidence that the games retained their cult associations until the end. Third, most important perhaps, texts of this kind fill in many of the blanks left by the literary elite – details of festival programmes and schedules, the administration of gymnasia, money prizes, wages, other costs. No account of social status in ancient sport (like that below, Chapter 5) can be complete without some consideration of the workers, many of them slaves, who cleaned palaestras, tended baths, prepared and maintained stadia and other facilities. So an inscription from Delphi records payments of some 2000 drachmas to contractors for the Pythian games. The total sum must have been more: the inscription is only partially preserved. This can be true for literary texts as well (like Philostratus's), but it is

---

[6] Asclepieia: Schol. Pind. *Nem.* 3.147; Sève 1993. Out of bounds: Schol. Pind. *Nem.* 7.103b, c, d. Fouling: Hsch. s.v. *probais*; Lee 1976. 'Ladder': Hsch. s.v. *ek klimakos, Et. Gen. = Et. Mag.* s.v. *ek klimakos*, Eust. *Il.* 1824.48.

[7] Spartans don't compete: Sen. *Ben.* 5.3.1, Plut. *Lyc.* 19.4, *Mor.* 189e, 228d, Philostr. *Gym.* 9, 58. Spartan boxer: *Anth. Pal.* 7.88 = Diog. Laert. 1.73, cf. Pliny, *NH* 7.32.119, Tert. *De Anim.* 52. Inscriptions: *IG* 5.1 658, 669, 670; Crowther 1990c.

prevalent for texts on stone. A lacunose inscription from the island of Rhodes, published only some forty years ago, contains clues on the conduct of the pentathlon: entrants throw the discus five times, and the longest throw earns precedence in the jump. But more we cannot say. Nor can we be sure of the date, tentatively set in the first century BCE. And the assumption that the inscription refers to local games is just that. Even complete inscriptions with secure dates and unquestionable local reference can testify only to their own circumstances. The discus and jump may have been handled differently at other places and times, even on Rhodes. No less traditional a festival than the Olympics granted Cleitomachus's request in 216 BCE to hold the *pankration* before the boxing so that he might have a better chance in both (Paus. 6.15.5), and in the Roman period may have spread its events over six days rather than the original five (Lee 1992). Inscriptions' very vividness and minute focus limit their use; students of ancient sport must regard each one as a pointilliste painter's dot, contributing only a portion, however attractive, to the larger picture.[8]

All this, good and bad, holds for papyri too. They have the additional advantage that papyrus was a medium used for private communications, like Hierocles' letters on the training of Zenon's protégé. Yet by the same token they are more likely to have been written in haste; a slip of the pen combined with a modern expert's misreading to turn a commonplace reference to irrigation (*antletos*) into something rarer, more intriguing and chimerical, the payment of 200 drachmas to an athlete (*athletos*: Clarysse 1977). And of course papyri have survived only in extra dry parts of Egypt and the Near East. Texts on other media – a pentathlete's bronze jumping weight, a three-hundred-pound block of stone which Bybon threw over his head one-handed – are less numerous; the graffiti recently discovered in the tunnel which athletes used to enter the stadium at Nemea are unique (S.G. Miller 1992:85). The archon names on Panathenaic vases – vases of distinctive shape containing olive oil awarded to successful competitors at the Greater Panathenaea at Athens – serve to date the vessels and the events they depict: they

---

[8] Finds: a recently discovered mosaic, our most elaborate depiction of an athletic competition, from fourth-century CE Tunisia, provides further evidence of the unexpected vitality of Greek sport in late antiquity; Khanoussi 1991. Delphi: *Corpus des inscriptions de Delphes* 2.139 = S.G. Miller 1991: no. 60, 246 BCE. Rhodes: Moretti 1956 = S.G. Miller 1991: no. 46.

Plate 2. A fragment of a wrestling manual on papyrus. *P Oxy.* 3.466, first/second
century CE.

merit special mention (Hamilton 1993, Tiverios 1996). But here we
are on the border of our third category, archaeology and art.[9]

ARCHAEOLOGY AND ART

What is more familiar today than photographs of the sanctuary of
Zeus at Olympia, nestled in its shady valley between the Alpheus
and Peneius rivers, or of Delphian Apollo's, with Parnassus high
above? Yet the site of Olympia, buried beneath tons of mud, was
identified only in 1766, digging was delayed until 1829, and the
systematic excavations by the Germans began as recently as 1875. It
is hard to exaggerate how much we owe to archaeology since then.
We have already touched on the implications of Olympia's remains
for the history of the festival of Zeus. At Nemea, a layer of
destruction débris from the late fifth century attests to a pitched

---

[9] Hierocles' letters: *P. Cairo Zeno* 1.59060 = S.G. Miller 1991: no. 146, 257 BCE, *P. London* 1941.
Jumping weight: Knoepfler 1994. Bybon: *IVO* 717; Crowther 1977:112–13.

battle within the sanctuary itself – an extraordinary (though not unparalleled) event mentioned in no text; and the scarcity of artefacts from the period between about 410 and 340 confirms that the battle had far reaching consequences, including the abandonment of Nemea as a venue for games. Archaeological evidence for the starting lines at several stadia provides a control for textual evidence on the number of entrants in races (Crowther 1993:44–6). Measurements of stadia lend themselves to estimates of capacity – as many as 43,000 spectators at Hellenistic Olympia? – and show that the *stadion* race of 600 Greek feet differed in length from place to place; but the use of complex starting gates and curved starting lines at Corinth betokens exceptional care to give each runner an equal chance at victory at any given games (Romano 1993).[10]

There is of course – we have seen this too – room for disagreement on the inferences to be drawn from archaeological evidence, objective as it may appear. Even specialists sometimes need to be reminded that archaeological remains rarely come equipped with identifying marks as clear as the labels on site plans and museum cases. A cautionary tale: the great German archaeologist Wilhelm Dörpfeld thought he saw a tumulus of Mycenaean date under the remains of the classical shrine to Pelops at Olympia. But for Alfred Mallwitz, until his recent death the chief excavator at the site, this was less evident. 'What this row of stones actually was is hard to tell. It seems to me . . . to be merely a work of nature . . . ' (Mallwitz 1988:87).

The sanctuaries and other sites have yielded countless artefacts. Their evidence is as solid and, potentially, as opaque. What we recognize as jumping weights are sometimes exercise dumb-bells; perhaps future archaeologists will take them for cordless telephones. The most interesting among the finds for the sport historian (and the student of ancient art) are the most expensive and the cheapest, the life size (or larger) statues of victors in bronze or marble and the ubiquitous pots painted with athletic scenes.

Of the original statues, few remain; those of bronze were melted

---

[10] Battle: Stella G. Miller 1988. The fact that the provisions of the Peace of Nicias of 421 were to be engraved on pillars at Olympia, Delphi and Isthmia, but not at Nemea (Thuc. 5.18.10), may indicate that the sanctuary had already been destroyed at that time. Note, against this, the omission of Nemea at Hdt. 8.121. Care: The differences in the distances between 100–foot and 200–foot markers, and between those for 200 and 300 feet, at either side of the track at Nemea may be more characteristic; S.G. Miller 1990:177.

down in antiquity – the famous Delphi charioteer is a rare exception. Fortunately, Pausanias included Olympia in his tour of Greece in the 170s CE, and recorded the honoree, sculptor and occasionally the theme of something over 200 victory statues in the sanctuary of Zeus in his guidebook (Paus. 6.1–18). His account follows his somewhat eccentric journey through the site, and so supplements the evidence of the archaeological remains, especially for older statues and their contexts. Like his audience, he was nostalgic for the Golden Age of Greek independence which lay so far in the past; archaic and classical statues make up over 60 per cent of those which can be dated, with very few coming within 100 years of his own time (Herrmann 1988:123–5). Pausanias's reputation for trustworthiness received a recent boost from a leading authority: 'his faithfulness in reporting what he saw has, time and time again, been proven at a large number of sites and could easily be demonstrated at a good many others'. Still, his predilection for the archaic and classical means that his collection cannot be used as a representative sample even from Olympia. Indeed, he himself indicates that he will mention only the most notable, on artistic and athletic grounds (Paus. 6.1.2, 2.2). And it is only Olympia which engages him – he says very little about statues elsewhere, though he must have seen hundreds at Delphi alone (cf. Paus. 10.9.2).[11]

Individual biases are less troublesome for painted pottery, a relatively cheap art form found everywhere – it is almost indestructible – and in such numbers that we may well look for telltale patterns in what survives. (Among Athenian vases alone there are over 1500 stock athletic scenes, and many more referring to horse-racing or competitive victory: Webster 1972:214.) Like sculpture too – literary and artistic reverberations of Myron's Discobulus have fuelled most of the discussion on the ancient discus throw – the vases are of special interest for their depictions of equestrians and athletes in action. So it is Panathenaic amphoras which establish that mounted competitors threw their javelins at a target, not for distance as in the pentathlon (e.g., Gardiner 1930: no. 12; Luc. *Anach.* 27). Not that the vases are easy to interpret. Despite the prominence they now enjoy in histories of Greek art because of the virtual vanishing

---

[11] Bronzes: according to the fourth-century Cynic Diogenes, a bronze statue cost 3000 drachmas, tantamount to the price tag for an early cast of a Rodin bronze today (Diog. Laert. 6.35). Pausanias's reputation: Habicht 1985:63, cf. 77, Themelis 1994:1, Arafat 1996:1–2, 27.

Plate 3. Boxers bleed from the nose. Attic black-figure hydria, Leagrus Group, about 520.

of large scale painting, those who decorated vases were not artists of the first rank. (Note the five-legged horse on a Panathenaic amphora from Sparta.) The medium they worked on was anyway challenging, smallish, curved, awkwardly shaped. Nor did they specialize in photo-like representations of actual contests, but in genre scenes (in which several of the separate activities of the palaestra might be shown together as if part of one event or sections of a sequence) and in illustration of myth. (Could mortal wrestlers and pancratiasts perform the feats of Heracles or Theseus? How much can we generalize from pictures of Heracles subduing Antaeus in midair, since the Libyan giant had to be removed from contact with his mother, Earth, to be overcome?) Yet the very fact that vase painting was a minor art, produced in large numbers and affordable to many, may have encouraged painters to subvert the usual exaltation of the athlete in elite culture of the archaic and classical periods. Blood pouring from a boxer's nose on an Athenian vase may remind us of later depictions of the ravages of prize fighting, such as the bronze statue of a boxer from the Hellenistic period, his face scarred, his nose broken, his ears swollen. For the ancient observer, however, the nearest parallel may have been symposium cups and bowls on which men are shown urinating and vomiting under the influence of drink. But it is in respect to just such nuances of tone that our evidence, textual or not, is most elusive.[12]

THE JUMP

Present-day athletes triple jump because nineteenth-century academics thought the ancient Greeks did. The triple jump (or hop, step and jump) entered the programme of the 1896 Olympics and contemporary track and field because of two ancient athletes. Phayllus is said to have leaped fifty-five feet; a Spartan, Chionis, supposedly jumped fifty-two. Since the modern record for the long jump is just over twenty-nine feet, to accept these distances is to conclude that the Greek jump was something different. An investigation of the biomechanics of long jumping concludes that such a leap would be 'implausible, if not impossible on a horizontal surface', and credible only if the landing area were at least fifteen feet below the take-off point (Ward-Smith 1995:227). Ancient authors themselves thought that the jumping weights, *halteres*, made for distance (Arist. *IA* 3.705a17, *Pr.* 5.8.881b3), and jumpers had the additional assistance of flute accompaniment (Paus. 5.7.10, Philostr. *Gym.* 55; Raschke 1985). But neither ancient practice could help a modern athlete long jump anything like fifty feet. We should regretfully reject the theory that the feet in question are unusually small, perhaps those of Phayllus's little boy (Howland 1950–1). The Greek jump, then, must have been multiple; as well as the triple jump, candidates have included running double and quadruple jumps, three separate jumps (then totalled), a sequence of five standing jumps. This conclusion may be confirmed by a chance comment in an ancient (fourth century CE) commentator on Aristotle: 'For those jumping in the pentathlon do not make a continuous movement, because they interrupt part of the interval in which they

---

[12] Five-legged horse: Dickins 1906–7:151. The usual expedient, that a painter has chosen to present an unusual technique for the sake of variety, will not work here. For other problems in relating Panathenaics to practice, see Hamilton 1996. Athenian vase: Leagros Group, Vatican Museum 416, Beazley, *ABV* 365, Poliakoff 1987a:87 no. 91. Bronze statue: Terme Museum 1055, Poliakoff 1987a:74 no. 74.

are moving' (Them. *in Ph.* 5.3). (Artemidorus speaks of 'jumps' in the pentathlon, but his reference to 'javelins' makes this less helpful than we could wish (despite Harris 1972a:250; Artem. 1.57).) Still, the triple jump recommends itself in large part because its practitioners today regularly reach Phayllus's fifty-five feet.[13]

But did Phayllus? Obviously, his leap is more credible if Chionis could come so close to matching it. Unfortunately, that is far from certain. The evidence comes from the third-century CE victor list of Sextus Julius Africanus under the year 664: 'Chionis of Sparta won the *stadion* race; his jump was fifty-two feet.' However, the Armenian version of Eusebius gives the distance as twenty-two cubits. If the cubit is taken as about eighteen inches, this is over thirty feet, an extraordinary accomplishment in itself; but the divergence is unsettling. Besides, Africanus's account of Chionis's career is hard to reconcile with Pausanias's (3.14.3, 4.23.4, 10, 8.39.3). And his note is oddly elliptical. Are we to understand that Chionis won the Olympic pentathlon in 664? Other fast runners did – but no one says Chionis was among them. Did Chionis achieve his mark in another competition (either in the pentathlon or in a separate jumping event, occasionally attested for local games) or even in practice? If so, how does Africanus know of it? We need not believe that the idea of the record, like quantification, is a defining feature of modern sport. But, although Greek athletes' inscriptions make much of special circumstances surrounding their victories, and of the accumulation of distinctions throughout their careers, such Greek records of achievement in individual instances are rare, especially so early, and not to be explained solely by difficulties of measurement or variations in the length of the *stadion* (and other races) and in the weights of *diskoi* and javelins in different competitions (Ramba 1990). It's instructive that the stopwatch was invented primarily to time races – and not by the Greeks. What mattered to them was who won on a given day. 'Judge a man by the standard of the men of his own time,' Demosthenes tells Aeschines. 'Philammon did not leave Olympia without a crown [in 360] because he was weaker than Glaucus of Carystus and some other athletes of old; he fought best of those who

---

[13] Jump: sources in Doblhofer *et al.* 1992. A Delian inscription of the sixth century containing the word 'fifty' is too fragmentary to contribute, despite Ebert 1963:42–3. For modern opinions, see the survey in Crowther 1985b:80–1, adding Knoepfler 1994:340–1, E. Maróti 1994:18–20 (five standing jumps).

competed against him and was crowned and proclaimed victor as a result' (Dem. 18.318–19, cf. Aeschin. 3.189). This is the background against which Thucydides claims that his work is not an entry in a contest for the attention of his immediate contemporaries, but something with everlasting value (Thuc. 1.22.4).[14]

Having no ready answers, we should consider Phayllus's jump on its own merits. These too, however, are not beyond doubt. A man of that name, thrice victor at Delphi, was famous for coming with his own ship to help fight off the Persians in 480 (Hdt. 8.47, cf. Ar. *Ach.* 213, *Vesp.* 1206). But the early sources say nothing of a jump. It features in an epigram of uncertain date quoted by a series of scholiasts and lexicographers (*Anth. Pal. App.* 3.297), and from notices ultimately based on it, embellished with details which are at times contradictory (as on Phayllus's native city) or false (as in crediting him with an Olympic win):

Pent' epi pentekonta podas pedese Phayllos / diskeusen d' hekaton pent' apoleipomenōn

('Five and fifty feet flew Phayllus/But threw the discus one hundred failing five')

Epigrams often mimic a herald's proclamation – specifying an athlete's home, paternity and event. Mentioning none of these, this is probably not a contemporary verse to accompany a dedication; and though Pausanias singles out Phayllus's statue from all those on display at Delphi, he says nothing about this poem or the jump itself (Paus. 10.9.2). Instead, the epigram is marked by a preponderance of 'p' sounds, play with words for five and fifty, and an unimpressive discus throw. This all adds up to something of a joke, a gibe at an athlete who was (really or in the poet's imagination) an excellent jumper but fell short of the all-around excellence of the ideal pentathlete; the verse form, with its long line of six feet followed by a short line of five, parallels the pattern of the poem's contents. If this interpretation is correct – its main weakness, in my view, is our ignorance of just how the Greeks threw the discus (cf. Langdon 1990) – we may ignore the length of Phayllus's leap and feel free to posit any sort of jump we like, even a single jump from a firm surface into a dug-out pit – except for the weights, like the long jump today.

---

[14] Victor list: Euseb. *Chron.* 1.198 Schoene, whence John of Antioch, *FHG* 4 p. 540.27. The record and modern sport: Carter and Krüger 1990.

THE DATE OF THE FIRST OLYMPICS

For our second case study, we turn to the confrontation of literary and archaeological evidence. Whereas a new inscription extends the later history of the Olympic games, archaeology now calls their origins into question. The traditional date for the first Olympics, 776 BCE, derives from the victor list of Hippias of Elis, one of the chronographers who sought to date local myths and traditions from the mid-fifth century on. Hippias's list, compiled about 400, was the source of the Olympic dates supplied systematically (apparently for the first time) by the third-century Sicilian historian Timaeus and is followed by Pausanias. The list is now lost, though incorporated in the version of Africanus. But its first date has entered our own tradition. Almost at random I quote a standard textbook (Frost 1997:30): 'About the beginning of the eighth century, the Greek world once more began to have a history. There is one precise, if symbolic, date which may be recorded: 776 BC, the year of the first Olympic Games.' The most successful book on early Greece marks the year with an asterisk in its date chart as 'likely to derive from chronologically reliable lists, or certain for other reasons' (Murray 1993:309).

Yet Hippias's date did not go unchallenged even in antiquity. In the same breath that he credits him with the list, Plutarch says that Hippias had no starting point for it which would compel belief (Plut. *Num.* 1.4). Eratosthenes 'the pentathlete' – second best in this too – had the Olympics begin in 884, three hundred years after the fall of Troy; in this chronology, followed by Polybius, Aristodemus of Elis and Phlegon, 776 was merely the date from which winners were recorded. Callimachus too thought the Olympics had a history before Coroebus, Hippias's first victor, though a shorter one, thirteen Olympiads rather than twenty-seven (Euseb. *Chron.* 1.194 Schoene). Modern scepticism about the canonical date begins with no less a figure than Sir Isaac Newton (in a work published posthumously in 1728). Though it had little currency among nineteenth-century scholars – due perhaps to the desire to ensure Europeans a pedigree as long and lofty as the Orient – it was revived periodically and survives in some circles today. Certainly Hippias's motives merit scrutiny: disinterested inquiry or the accentuation of Olympia's antiquity and his home city's claim to it? The date itself may be as indebted to numerology as Eratosthenes', since 776 is three hundred

years, ten generations of thirty years each, before the first Olympiad
to follow victory over the Persians.[15]

Archaeology once seemed to support 776. The sanctuary yielded
eighth-century statuettes of charioteers and expensive metal tripods,
dedications or even prizes of early equestrians. But depictions of
chariots and charioteers are found at sites which never knew horse-
racing, the Olympia finds show two-horse chariots, not the *tethrippon*
introduced, according to Hippias's list, in 680 – the two-horse event
does not join the Olympic programme until 408 – and anyway the
eighth century is too early even for the four-horse race. Moreover (if
the earliest Olympics really were restricted to one event, the *stadion*)
the tripods are so numerous that 'we would have recovered a
complete set of victory dedications and more besides, an occurrence
unique in archaeology' (C. Morgan 1990:46). The latest results of
survey and excavation are still harder to reconcile with the pattern
of Hippias's list or its absolute chronology. Elis was essentially empty
in the early and mid-eighth century; even the largest of its sites, the
city of Elis, was tiny, just three or four families. How likely is it, then,
that the first, second and fifth victors came from this region, let alone
that the festival was under Elean control (C. Morgan 1990:63–4)?
More striking still is the appearance of wells in the eastern part of
the sanctuary, the place of competition, at the end of the eighth
century, growing ever more numerous as time went on – presumably
to provide water for contestants and their audiences (Mallwitz
1988:98–101). This would seem to encourage a downdating of the
first competitions to about 700 and renewed suspicion about Hippias's list.[16]

This evidence is not quite conclusive. Mallwitz himself imagines
that the wells may betoken an upsurge in interest as the games
(according to Hippias) added new contests. To telescope the interval
since the first Olympiads he suggests that the earliest festival was
annual; it became four-yearly only with the addition of the four-

---

[15] 884: Euseb. *Chron.* 1.194 Schoene, Phlegon, *FGrH* 257 F 1, cf. Paus. 5.4.5, 8.5. Scepticism:
Mouratidis 1985b thinks the games much older than 776, Peiser 1990 offers a survey of
opinions and a date in the early sixth century, more or less contemporary with the other
great panhellenic games.

[16] Tripods: we can hardly connect such expensive contests and lavish offerings to some small-
scale and insignificant games, at or near Olympia, unrelated to the festival for Zeus
Olympios, as in Lee 1988a. Eleans in Hippias's list: but the possibility that many early
dedications were made by Messenians does tally with their prominence among the list's
eighth-century victors; Crowther 1988b.

horse chariots in 680, the twenty-fourth Olympiad, a change arising from the reluctance of entrants to send their horses and chariots on the arduous trip to Olympia every year. This yields an original Olympics in 704, consistent with Mallwitz's dating of the wells, and retains too the outlines of Hippias's relative chronology. Yet the price, attributing a level of sloth and self-satisfaction to early seventh-century equestrians that would shame their descendants who ran horses year in, year out at the games of the *periodos*, may be too much to pay (Lee 1988a:114). Changes in dedicatory practice in the early eighth century have induced Catherine Morgan to toy inconclusively with reconstructions incorporating literary traditions on both the foundation and the revival of the games (C. Morgan 1990:41–2, 56, 92, 192, 212). She concludes, 'For the present at least, the question of the date of the institution of the Olympic games must remain open' (C. Morgan 1990:48). So Hippias still casts his spell; but for how long?

ATHLETIC NUDITY

The conventional costume of charioteers in Greek art is a long, close-fitting tunic, though some are shown nude. Jockeys, generally nude, may also wear a short-sleeved tunic. How about athletes? The name of the main Greek venue for training and competition, the *gumnasion*, derived from *gumnos*, 'naked'; it was a place for naked exercise. Sure enough, though some events required special body coverings – the shield and other armour of the hoplite runner, the thongs of the boxer and occasional pancratiast – and fighters might practise in leather caps and earguards, classical athletes usually worked out and invariably competed unclothed. This was not always so. Mycenaean and Geometric art sometimes seems to show nude athletes (and charioteers), but Homer's heroes don a loincloth (*zoma*, later *diazoma*, *perizoma*) passed through the legs and then knotted much as in Japanese sumo today (or Minoan athletics before). When did fashion change? Literary texts offer two answers. Pausanias identifies a pioneer, Orsippus of Megara, who let his loincloth fall because he thought he could run faster without it, and won the Olympic *stadion* race (Paus. 1.44.1). Other sources tell like tales. But they differ on the runner's name, native city, event, motivation and date (as early as 724, as late as 652). Moreover, all extant sources are late (though an epigram known from an inscription of the Roman

imperial period may be older, even Simonides'). The second answer
is given by a good early source, Thucydides, and echoed by Plato
(Thuc. 1.6.5, cf. Pl. *Resp.* 5.452c): 'In ancient times, even at the
Olympic games, athletes used to compete wearing loincloths over
their genitals, and it is not many years since they ceased.' 'Not many
years' is vague, but probably refers to the early fifth century – long
after any date for Orsippus or his doublets.[17]

Fortunately, vase painting offers plenty of evidence to compare
with these literary traditions. Unfortunately, it is as contradictory.
On the one hand, nude athletes appear in archaic art by at least 650,
with over 800 extant representations from the sixth century alone,
most presumably earlier than the shift envisioned by Thucydides
(Legakis 1977). On the other, a few pots, the so-called *perizoma* vases,
do depict athletes wearing loincloths; since these date from the last
decade of the sixth century, they have been taken to corroborate
Thucydides' chronology (Crowther 1982). It has even been argued
that they reflect the norm, and that the vastly more numerous nudes
are a conventional idealization (Thuillier 1988:34–7). This is the
kind of independent confirmation of a literary text which another
rarely guarantees; Plato's comment in *Republic* may stem from
familiarity with Thucydides, as the odd remark in Plutarch, that
pederasty crept into the *gumnasion* only yesterday or the day before,
after young men began to strip, clearly does with Plato (Plut. *Mor.*
751f; McDonnell 1991:191–3). Alas, it is illusory. The *perizoma* pots
are anomalous in many ways, including their shapes and their other
depictions – older, bearded and flabby athletes among them. Found
in Etruria, they were designed for Etruscan tastes, and have nothing
to do with Greek athletic reality (Bonfante 1989:564–5, McDonnell
1991:185–9, 1993). We are left to conclude that there is something in
the tradition about Orsippus after all, and that Thucydides, here as
elsewhere in this portion of his work, is fudging chronology to suit
his scheme of human progress (McDonnell 1991:189–90).

What of a related question, the meaning of athletic nudity? Those
who accept the testimony of Thucydides and Plato tend to find the

---

[17] Leather caps: Hyde 1921:165–7. Earguards: Aesch. fr. 102 Radt = Poll. 10.175, Plut. *Mor.*
38b, cf. 706c. Mycenaean and Geometric art: Mouratidis 1985a:218–21. Homer: *Il.* 23.683,
685, 710, *Od.* 18.67, 76. A stray line of Sophocles' *Peleus* may reflect this practice of the
heroic age, 'anointing through the folds of clothing' (Soph. fr. 494 Radt = Harp. 134.15).
Perhaps, however, the reference is to exercise, not competition (as in, e.g., [Arist.] *Probl.*
38.3.966b34, cf. 2.30.869a24). Orsippus: Sweet 1985:43–5, 1987:124–9.

Plate 4. Runners with loincloths. Attic black-figure stamnos, Michigan Painter, 510–500.

impetus for the adoption (or reintroduction) of athletic nudity in the late sixth or early fifth century in Greek conflict with the Persians, who (like other barbarians) were shocked by public nakedness (Crowther 1982). The superiority of their customs in this regard was a matter of course among Greek opinion makers. Wherein exactly did that superiority lie? 'Nakedness . . . ' (according to John Arieti) 'enabled the athletes to show the complete control they exerted over their bodies' in close quarters with other fit and attractive young men; *barbaroi*, in contrast, had to cover themselves to avoid arousing others and betraying their own lack of self-control – 'is that a javelin you're carrying, or are you just glad to see me?' (Arieti 1975:436; Barry 1995:15). For Thuillier, who denies that the crowd of naked athletes on vases represents reality, the late development of athletic nudity is a case of life imitating art, as the beauty of the male body modelled by sculpture and painting impelled athletes to conform (Thuillier 1988:41). Perverse – except for the fact that oil must have transformed an athlete into something dark and gleaming, a bronze that breathed. The earlier date implied by Orsippus and (for most) the vase paintings invites scholars to invest athletic nudity with more fundamental and far-reaching import. Sansone highlights hunting, though Greeks did not normally hunt naked (Sansone 1988:107–15; Lane Fox 1996:129–30). Mouratidis, who is most convinced that silhouetted figures with little anatomical detail on early vases are unclothed, regards athletic nudity as apotropaic, a protection against harm and a declaration of power and energy (Mouratidis 1985a). It is a nuisance for this view that the apotropaic penis is usually erect and athletes', in so far as they were special at all, were infibulated, the foreskin drawn back against the body by a thong.[18]

Consequently, the most sophisticated account of nudity as a costume in early Greek art distinguishes the apotropaic nudity of herms and comic phalli from athletic and heroic nudity, but links both with the initiation rituals of youth (Bonfante 1989:551–5). This accords well with the limited tolerance for display of the body in Greek culture, where Aeschines can accuse an enemy of throwing off his cloak in the Athenian assembly and disporting himself naked like a pancratiast though he was presumably underdressed rather than undressed. Most recently, Karen Bassi calls attention to the divergence in Greek conventions for showing or hiding male and female bodies. Women are clothed, to mark the discontinuity of their inner reality and outer appearance. But 'the public display of the nude Greek male may finally attest to the fact that . . . there is no discrepancy between what is seen (the full external view of the perfect human form) and what is not seen' (Bassi 1995:5). On the contrary, if this range of learned opinion leads to any definite conclusion, it is that nakedness is not so readily revealing. The temptation is to concur only with one of the interlocutors in Cicero's

---

[18] Superiority: Hdt. 1.10.3, Thuc. 1.6.5, Pl. *Resp.* 5.452c. Self-control: the verb *gumnazō*, 'visit the *gumnasion*' or 'exercise naked', is first found in a pederastic context of the late-seventh to mid-sixth centuries, Theogn. 1335–6. Infibulation: Sweet 1985:46–8, 1987:129–32, with the addition of the earliest literary evidence, Aesch. fr. 78a.28–31 Radt; cf. Lloyd-Jones 1971:544.

Tusculan Disputations: 'While I read, I agree; but when I set the book aside . . . all my agreement is swept away' (Cic. *Tusc.* 1.11.24). More productively, we may simply observe that good scholars can dispute which genres and which individual pieces of evidence should bear most weight. That assumptions about what is possible or plausible also count, will be evident in our last case study.[19]

DETERMINING THE WINNER OF THE PENTATHLON

One of the leading experts on ancient Greek sport, Don Kyle, recalls his student days, when an examiner asked about the pentathlon. 'I groaned internally and wanted to shout that I did not care how the Greeks scored the pentathlon, that I was interested in the social, cultural and political significance of sport, not in some antiquarian puzzle' (Kyle 1995:60). Instead, Kyle gave a low-key response – and later went on to write two articles on that antiquarian puzzle (Kyle 1990, 1995). Before Kyle, Joachim Ebert had also put forward a solution and later defended it (Ebert 1963:2–34, 1974), and Harold Harris too had a couple of goes, arguing for one way out only to revise it eight years after (Harris 1964:77–80, 1972a:34–5, 1972b). Hugh Lee is the latest recidivist (1993, 1995). There is still no consensus on 'perhaps the most puzzling problem in all Greek athletics' (Sweet 1987:56), despite a recent rash of research and response. What explains this perennial fascination? No doubt the challenge. Then too there is the nature of the evidence. Many sources combine to establish that there were five events – *stadion* (E. Maróti 1994:1–3), discus, jump, javelin, wrestling – that the wrestling was scheduled as the finale, and that three wins guaranteed victory. But how to reconcile these facts with the one literary text which may allude to the procedure when no clear winner emerged after the opening triad (Philostr. *Gym.* 3)?

Before Jason and Peleus, the jump used to be crowned individually and the discus and the javelin were enough for victory in themselves in the time the Argo sailed. Telamon was the champion with the discus, Lynceus with the javelin, the sons of Boreas ran and jumped the best. Peleus was

---

[19] Aeschines: *gumnos epagkratiazēn*, Aeschin. 1.26, cf. 1.33. For other rebukes for revealing too much of the body in inappropriate contexts, see Theophr. *Char.* 4.7, 11.2, 18.4, 22.13, Philetaerus fr. 18 KA, Herod. 5.44–6.

second best at all these, but would triumph over all in wrestling.
Accordingly, when they were competing on Lemnos, they say that Jason
joined together the five events as a favour to Peleus, and in this way Peleus
gained the victory.

It is beguiling to accept that this is based on the way a real athlete
could win the pentathlon, at least in Philostratus's day: that, like
Peleus, a pentathlete could come out on top even though victorious
in no event except the last. But Philostratus (as we know) often errs;
and here his tale may have as much to do with the reputations of
Jason and Peleus (inferior to his son Achilles and, often, to his female
wrestling adversary Atalanta; see below, Chapter 4) as second-raters.
So some scholars ignore Peleus altogether and devise schemes based
on their ideas of what was likely or appropriate for the Greeks. But
there is a lot of room for disagreement in such an exercise: it is one
thing to argue that no human being could long jump fifty-five feet,
another to be sure about what one group of people, the Greeks,
considered fair or fitting. Yet (as Kyle notes) the investigation of the
principles scholars invoke or reject may lead to important gains in
our understanding of the aims and expectations of Greek competitors and their audiences.

For example, it is alleged that Peleus's limited success as a runner-
up could not qualify him for victory overall: 'it runs counter to the
whole Greek outlook on victory'. Yes, Pindar exalts victory and
draws a sorry sketch of the losers; theirs 'the most hateful return, the
dishonouring tongue, the secret by-path' (Pind. *Ol.* 8.68–9, cf. *Pyth.*
8.81–7). This ideology suits his purpose, to praise victors, and victors
in the great crown games at that, which indeed awarded first prizes
only. These games in addition were made up entirely of individual
events, perhaps because sharing even victory was felt to diminish its
glory. Yet at other games, including the fourth-century Panathenaea
at Athens and the Asclepieia on second-century Cos, second prizes
were available to both athletic and equestrian competitors; much
smaller prizes, to be sure – at the Panathenaea, only one-fifth the
amount of first prizes for athletes – but presumably still worth
having for the panhellenic cast among entrants in events open to all-
comers at both important festivals. Socrates supposedly tried to
dissuade Charmides from competing in the *stadion* at Nemea.
'Perhaps I will not win', replied Charmides, 'but I will benefit by the
effort of exercise' (Pl. *Thg.* 128e, cf. Porph. *VP* 15.16–18). In fact, later
athletes do claim credit merely for taking part in competition

(Robert 1960:355–8). Nor were team sports unknown, though (as we have seen) these were local and directly connected to training for war (Crowther 1995b).[20]

This issue should not be confused with another, no less overarching, the standing of pentathletes among others. While today's track and field aficionados may regard the all-rounder, the winner of the Olympic decathlon, as the world's premier athlete, many casual fans focus on the more spectacular sprints. So Dan O'Brien, for all his versatility, is less well known than another Olympic champion, Michael Johnson. Greek opinions varied as well, though not necessarily on similar grounds. Agesipolis sought to outdo his rival king of Sparta, Agesilaus, in every way, like a pentathlete – a measure of the currency of the ideal of all round excellence (Xen. *Hell.* 4.7.5). Aristotle thought competitors in the pentathlon the most beautiful, as naturally gifted with both strength and speed (Arist. *Rh.* 1.1361b10, cf. 26), and sculptors often chose a pentathlete as their subject because of his balanced proportions (cf. Pl. *Leg.* 5.728e); Polyclitus's *Doryphorus* may carry a pentathlete's javelin and exemplify the sculptor's ideal of physical harmony. The young Hysmon of Elis, afflicted with a muscular disease, took up the pentathlon as therapy and so strengthened himself that he won at Olympia and Nemea (Paus. 6.3.10). And the name Pentathlus, surely positive despite counter examples such as Aeschrus, 'shameful', was borne by a Cnidian of some distinction, leader of a colony to Lipara (Diod. Sic. 5.9.2–3, Paus. 10.11.3). On the other side, pentathletes were known to be less adept than specialists in running and wrestling – as a winner in the Nordic combined at the Winter Olympics will lose to those who concentrate on ski jumping or cross country (Ebert 1974:258 n. 6) – and the Hellenistic scholar Eratosthenes was called 'beta' and 'the pentathlete' because he was only second best in every field of study (*Suda* ε 2898). At Olympia, the boys' pentathlon was held only once, in 628, and then abandoned (cf. Lämmer 1992:110). Most instructive here are the prizes awarded for pentathletes at the Panathenaea in the earlier fourth century – less than in the *stadion* and *pankration*, though equal to those for boxing and wrestling – and at Aphrodisias some five hundred years later, where pancratiasts,

---

[20] Victory: Harris 1964:78, cf. Merkelbach 1973:261, Langdon 1989:117, Kyle 1990:302, E. Maróti and G. Maróti 1993:55. Second and other prizes: Crowther 1992b, with the additional examples of S. Follet, *BE* (1993) 499 no. 249.

wrestlers and *stadion* runners won six, four and two and a half times as much as pentathletes.[21]

The interest and importance of individual events may be more relevant. Some believe that the run was the first event in the competition, followed by discus, jump, javelin and wrestling. More prevalent, however, is the view that the distinctive contests, discus, jump and javelin, led off and the race and wrestling came after. Exceptional athletes swept the first triad or had three victories after four events, and so won *akoniti*, without needing to raise up a dust cloud in struggle or (perhaps) without needing to dust up as in wrestling. But often there was no clear winner. The most awkward result would be three contenders, two with one win and one with a pair (likely the run and the jump or the two throws). Harris's hypothesis, of a preliminary contest as a prelude to the wrestling finale, now holds sway among those who discount Philostratus and the elaborate schemes involving second places, relative victories and points that he has inspired. But what kind of contest? Harris himself thought of a wrestling contest between the two pentathletes with individual victories, the winner to wrestle again for the prize. It's true that this accords a great deal of importance to wrestling (Lee 1995:44). On the other hand, wrestling was a staple of Greek physical education, something any all-round athlete should be able to do and do well. Kyle objects that a wrestling *repêchage* would consume too much time – stand-alone wrestling matches required three falls for victory, whereas a *stadion* run-off would be over within half a minute – and lead to an anticlimactic finale, in which a fresh fighter would have an unfair advantage. A qualifying race may be supported by the fact that we know more successful runners, *stadion* runners especially, who won pentathlons than heavy athletes (E. Maróti 1994:12–23).[22]

Yet how can we tell what bored a Greek spectator? Americans reputedly find cricket too slow and ice hockey, on television anyway, too fast (they can't follow the puck). So for everyone who feels that a reprise of the *stadion*, in which one runner had already demonstrated

[21] *Doryphorus* as pentathlete: Waddell 1991:99, rebutted by Lorenz 1991. Less adept: Pl. *Amat.* 135e-136a, 138e, cf. [Long.] *Subl.* 34.1, Diog. Laert. 9.37. Panathenaea: *IG* 2² 2311 = S.G. Miller 1991: no. 84. Aphrodisias: *CIG* 2 2758 = *SEG* 39 (1989) no. 1103; Ebert 1966:383–5.

[22] Run: Langenfeld 1991:8–9, Waddell 1991:101–3, E. Maróti 1994. Distinctive contests: e.g., Kyle 1990:293, Jackson 1991:179, Matthews 1994:133, Lee 1995:41. *Akoniti*: earliest reference is *SEG* 11 (1950) no. 1227 = Moretti 1953: no. 8, Laconia, 525–500 BCE; Wachter 1995.

superiority, would be as unfair and as uninteresting (Lee 1993), another is intrigued by the prospect of javelin- and discus-heaving heavyweights struggling in a race for which neither has a knack (Sweet 1983:290). Nor is efficiency a cross-cultural universal; if it were, fifth-century Athenian democracy would have run very differently. As a matter of fact, at least one pentathlon did cause a delay in the programme of the Olympics, in 472; the response was to reconfigure the festival schedule, not to alter anything in the conduct of the pentathlon (Paus. 5.9.3). Furthermore, the Greek notion of fairness in combat sports – like wrestling – encompassed matches between adversaries of different sizes as a matter of course (since there were no weight classes within age categories) and a critical advantage to the *ephedros*, the competitor who drew a bye (as in Harris's solution; cf. Langdon 1989:118). Finally, it shouldn't go unnoticed that the pentathlon must often have ended with precisely the event least likely to be conclusive: wrestling matches (unlike runs, jumps, throws) were apt to be drawn, yielding two winners or none, with the crown dedicated to a god (as in a pentathlon at the Thespian Erotidea). So the evidence does not allow a final solution to this puzzle, as opposed to the profit to be gleaned from pondering some of its implications. We may close as we began, with the words of Don Kyle: 'Let's not turn the debate . . . into a marathon, which we all know was not a Greek athletic competition' (Kyle 1995:65).[23]

This short survey of sources should underline the importance of choosing an approach to Greek sport: their nature, scarce and skewed, demands a context, a framework to impose shape and elicit significance. At the same time, they are just numerous and varied enough – and Greek sport is integrated into Greek society so fully – that they support many different modes of address. In the next chapter, I return to the path I have pointed out in this introduction to the subject by discussing the simplest sort of distinction made in Greek sport, that between winners and others. Literary representations will take up the foreground. We will be sensitive as well to the resonance of literature with another sort of source, art, and especially to the rivalry of praise poetry and victory monuments.

[23] Bye: it was a mark of distinction to be crowned as a victor without the benefit of a bye: *IVO* 225 = Moretti 1953: no. 64, 49 CE; Crowther 1992a. Erotidea: *SEG* 3 (1929) no. 335, second century CE.

CHAPTER 3

Reflections of victory in literature and art

Plato's *Symposium* celebrates a literary event, the victory of Agathon at the Lenaea in 416. Xenophon wrote one too. The symposium in his work honours an athlete, Autolycus, winner in the *pankration* for boys at the Greater Panathenaea in 421. Callias, its host and Autolycus's lover, avoids any suspicion of impropriety by including the boy's father in the festivities. These are presented as anything but risqué. Autolycus's beauty, joined as it is with modesty and moderation, causes some to grow silent and others to strike attitudes; his chaste love gives Callias a more tender look and a gentler voice (Xen. *Symp.* 1.9–10). At the end of the party, a rather dull affair – the interruption by Philip the buffoon does not carry the charge of Alcibiades' in Plato, and the desultory philosophical chitchat cannot replace Aristophanes' creation myth of the sexes – Autolycus leaves with his father. Only then does a Syracusan impresario offer some adult entertainment. Two slaves impersonating Dionysus and Ariadne kiss and caress – a scene all the more affecting in that the young man and woman play their parts with real passion. Unmarried guests swear to take wives, those already wed ride off to enjoy their company. And so the symposium ends (9.2–7).

We turn now to a less edifying event, the party thrown by Chabrias to celebrate his victory in the four-horse chariot race at the Pythian games of 374. Those in attendance include Phrynion and his companion, the famous courtesan Neaera. At some point Phrynion fell asleep and 'many had sex with Neaera while she was drunk, even Chabrias's servants'. This has a more authentic ring. Symposium scenes illustrated on Attic vases often display revellers, satyrs as well as humans, in a variety of homosexual and heterosexual pursuits (and captures). Pindar, more discreetly, depicts enhanced attractiveness as one of the benefits of victory: girls watched Telesicrates win at Athens, and wished he were their husband (Pind. *Pyth.* 9.97–9),

Pythian crowns (or an Olympic wreath to come) make Hippocleas desirable to his age-mates and elders, and keep him in the young girls' thoughts (*Pyth.* 10.55–60; Hubbard 1995:41–5). Many centuries later, a discussion of trainers' tactics includes the tale of Promachus of Pellene, whose trainer assured him (falsely) that the girl he fancied would welcome his love if he won the *pankration* at Olympia (Philostr. *Gym.* 22). He did, in 404.[1]

The place of sex among the pleasures of a carousing victor must have been especially prominent if the abstinence reportedly observed by some athletes during their preparations for competition was widespread. Iccus of Tarentum (so they say) never touched a woman in training, or even a boy (less tiring); nor did other famous athletes of old, though they had more sexual vigour than the rest of us. A story about the renowned *hetaira* Lais has her fall in love with Eubotas of Cyrene, an Olympic *stadion* champion, and propose marriage. Fearing what she might do if he refused, Eubotas agrees to marry her after the games, but does not have sex with her. He wins, and then brings her picture back to Cyrene with him, saying that this fulfills his promise. The Theban athlete Cleitomachus left a symposium if anyone so much as mentioned sex. Many names and stories recur in our sources, however, and most belong to the past, often the distant past: such continence seems exceptional, rather than the enforced observance of a taboo.[2]

In any case, what matters here is not that orgies such as Chabrias's took place, let alone what may have motivated them. The point is that both symposia serve an author's purpose: Xenophon's, for the most part, to exalt the reputation of Socrates, Apollodorus's to destroy Neaera's. And mine: highly coloured, indeed overdrawn, as they are, they demonstrate the resonance of an athletic or equestrian victory, not just a significant achievement and occasion for display but a potent symbol. The literary and

---

[1] Chabrias's party: [Dem.] 59.33–4. Licence prompted limits: it was illegal at Athens to give a slave or a freedwoman, flute girl or prostitute the name of any of the great crown games (Harp. N 10 Keaney s.v. *Nemeas*, Ath. 13.587c).

[2] Iccus: Pl. *Leg.* 8.839e–840a; Fiedler 1985. Eubotas: Ael. *VH* 10.2, cf. Istrus *FGrH* 334 F 55 in Clem. Al. *Strom.* 3.50.4, where a similar story involves one Aristoteles of Cyrene. Cleitomachus: Plut. *Mor.* 710d, cf. Ael. *NA* 6.1, *VH* 3.30. Taboo: so Lloyd-Jones 1983:99; *contra*, Fiedler 1985:169 n. 44. Note that venues for athletic exercise were prime pederastic pick-up points: see (for Athens) Ar. *Vesp.* 1023–8, Aeschin. 1.135, Pl. *Charm.* 153a, 154c, cf. Theophr. *Char.* 27.14.

artistic exploitation of that symbol in other contexts will be the theme of this chapter.

Athletic and equestrian victors earned rich rewards; in Plato's Myth of Er, the soul of Atalanta sees the honours of (male) athletes and chooses their lot for its next sojourn on earth (Pl. *Resp.* 10.620b). To be sure, the great games of the circuit, the so-called crown games, merely bestowed wreaths as symbols of supremacy – wild olive at Olympia, laurel at Delphi, at Nemea fresh celery and at Isthmia, pine until the early fifth century, dry celery to the second century, both pine and dry celery thereafter (Broneer 1962). But this was only a beginning (Buhmann 1972:104–36). Athenian victors in all these games won life-long invitations to meals in the public dining-room in the Prytaneum, and those at Olympia and Isthmia at least also received cash bonuses of 500 and 100 drachmas respectively, amounts said (probably anachronistically) to go back to Solon and to have been reductions of earlier rewards at that. They were not alone. An early sixth-century athlete from Sybaris dedicated a tithe of his Olympic prize, presumably a gift from the community, to Athena, and the monument to Thespians killed at the battle of Delium in 424 identified one as Olympic and another as Pythian champion, surely a reflection of other honours during their lifetime (*IG* 7 1888b). Such recognition might include statues and coins, seats of honour in the theatre and games (*prohedria*), and exemption from duties and taxes (*ateleia*); a third-century inscription from Tralles in Asia Minor simply speaks of 'the same honours as Olympic victors' (Poljakov 1989:36 no. 25.5). Spartan victors had a unique right, to fight at the king's side in battle (Plut. *Lyc.* 22.4, *Mor.* 639e). Other, less prestigious games did not require victors to defer material gratification. Known prizes range from the paltry – ten obols for heavy athletes in a local festival in fifth-century Attica (*IG* 1³ 1386), a top prize of ten drachmas at the Apollonia on Delos in the earlier third century (*IG* 11.2 203a.65–70), just enough to defray daily expenses or the costs of travel – to the substantial, such as the woollen cloaks awarded at Pellene, the bronze objects at Tegea, the Theban Iolaeia, the Heraea at Argos, to the munificent. Silver goblets were at stake at Marathon, Megara and Sicyon, amphorae of olive oil at the Greater Panathenaea, as many as 140, each holding thirty-five or forty litres, for the owner of the winning two-horse chariot team (see further below, Chapter 5). But of all the fruits of success, none has been more long-lasting than the victory song.[3]

It is an index of the importance of competition in ancient Greece that it gave rise to a distinctive art form, the victory song or epinician: a poem in praise of a victor and his victory, commissioned by him (or a family member or friend), sung at the festival at which the victory was won or (these, more elaborate, make up the majority of extant examples) as part of a homecoming celebration in the victor's own community. It is just as illuminating that the form had a relatively limited life span of about 120 years, from just before the mid-sixth century to just after the mid-fifth. The victory cheer at Olympia – *tenella kallinike*, 'hurray for the champion' – was said to be taken from the seventh-century poet Archilochus (324.1 West, *IE*[2]). But it was long supposed that the first writer of victory songs was Simonides of Ceos, a small island off the Attic coast, who lived from about 556 to 467. However, recent papyrus finds include fragments of three or perhaps four poems for victors written by Ibycus, a native of Rhegium in southern Italy who was active about the time of Simonides' birth (Barron 1984:20–2, Jenner 1986). One of these (282B (ii) Campbell = S221 *SLG*) was composed for a Callias. If this is the Athenian who won the Olympic chariot race in 564 and also won at Delphi, Ibycus's poem, and the origin of victory songs as a genre, fit the context of the remarkable upsurge of organized athletic and equestrian competition which marked the first half of the sixth century. The other fragments, for a Spartan victor in games at Sicyon, for a runner from Leontini, perhaps for a wrestler, already reveal some of the characteristics of later epinicians: references to the event and place of victory, praise of the victor's city, narratives of myth linked to either locale, the description of competition and praise poetry alike as *ponos*, 'toil' (cf. Angeli Bernardini 1992:970–1).

Simonides' own work is rather better attested, but still fragmentary. Known as the first poet to write for pay, he is nevertheless – or consequently – portrayed as the peer of the most powerful figures of

---

[3] Rewards: Buhmann 1972: 104–36, Kyle 1996 (distinguishing prizes given at the site of games, symbolic honours [like the herald's victory announcement], and rewards offered by home cities on the victor's return). Cash bonuses: Plut. *Sol.* 23.3, Diog. Laert. 1.55. For the reliability of the tradition, see Weiler 1983, Kyle 1984b; the relative chronology of Solon's term of office, Athens' first coins and the foundation of competitions at Isthmia is especially problematic. Sybaris: *SEG* 35 (1985) no. 1053 = S.G. Miller 1991: no. 160, Ebert 1972:251–5.

his day, a guest of Hipparchus, son of the tyrant Peisistratus at Athens, an associate of Hieron, tyrant of Syracuse, able to advise and admonish even Pausanias, the arrogant victor of Plataea and regent of Sparta. He was also regarded, at least in later antiquity, as something of a sage – there may have been a collection of 'Sayings of Simonides'. In one extant apophthegm, he is asked, 'Who are the noble?', and replies, 'Those with old money' (Arist. fr. 92 Rose). The sentiment would not disturb those who commissioned his poems, prominent among them the horse-loving elite of Thessaly. But there might be an edge to his work too, as in his poem for Crius, an Aeginetan wrestler (507 Page, *PMG*). Simonides notes that he did as he deserved when he came to 'the splendid and well-wooded precinct of Zeus' (at Olympia or Nemea): he was shorn, a pun on his name, which means 'ram', and a reference to the wrestler's custom of cropping the hair.

More still remains of Simonides' nephew Bacchylides, most of it from a papyrus, purchased in Egypt in 1896, containing fourteen epinicians and six other poems; the epinicians date from the middle or late 480s to 452. Like Ibycus and Simonides, Bacchylides wrote poems of many different kinds. The victory songs are not the works of specialists, but of versatile and accomplished men; their abilities prompted wealthy winners to seek their services, their skill in other genres confirmed the value of their epinicians. Like Simonides, Bacchylides wrote for victors near and far, from Ceos and Aegina to Sparta, Macedon and Syracuse; three poems are for Hieron, his uncle's friend. He liked puns too, playing in the opening lines of poem 6 on the name of Lachon, Olympic champion in the boys' *stadion* race in 452, and the verb *lakhe*, 'allotted'. Another kind of word-play honours Pherenicus, the great racehorse which brought Hieron victory at Delphi in 478 and at Olympia in 476. In the poem for this last occasion, Bacchylides claims that 'no dust (*konis*) from horses in front of him ever yet dirtied Pherenicus as he rushed towards the finish of a contest' (5.42–5). The effect is to make the horse win *akoniti*, 'dustless', the term applied to a champion whose reputation or performance so impresses others that he faces no competition. Pherenicus ran like the wind, *aellodroman* (5.39). The image recurs in a different form in poem 10: a runner panted out a hot storm of breath (*aellan*) at the finish line of the *stadion* race at Isthmia, and then wet with his oil the cloaks of the spectators as he fell into the packed crowd in winning the four-length race (10.21–6).

This vivid picture of what actually went on during competition is unusual in epinician. There are certainly items of information to be gleaned from the victory songs of Bacchylides and his Theban contemporary Pindar. In respect to the four-horse chariot race, for example, we learn that it was twelve laps in length; that teams were usually made up of mares; that as many as forty-one teams once competed at Delphi. In athletics, Pindar gives reason to believe that the javelin came right before the wrestling in the pentathlon (Pind. *Nem.* 7.70–4; Segal 1968:39–40). The poets may sometimes describe personal characteristics to individualize victors: the boxer Diagoras is 'enormous', and goes straight at his opponents, while the pancratiast Melissus is, like Heracles, a small man, not much to look at, but adamant in spirit (Pind. *Ol.* 7.15–17, *Isthm.* 4.49–52). It may be that Pindar himself saw some of the feats he celebrates, or took special pains to master the details of a competitor's career (Angeli Bernardini 1985:123–41), though we may be reminded at times of a clergyman's quick caucus with family members before eulogizing a communicant he never met. Furthermore, the poems' imagery and mythic narratives occasionally reflect the victor's event. Pindar is a javelin thrower in two poems for pentathletes, a runner standing at the starting line set to praise the winner of the *diaulos*, like a man struggling against opponents as he decides which theme to develop in a poem for a wrestler. 'Pindar adapts language denoting accuracy, speed, and distance . . . in new, explicit ways to the sports he celebrates, adding in the process a sense of the challenge and the danger involved in sport' (Lefkowitz 1991:168); he presents himself as an athlete to express his fellowship with the victor and his appreciation of his different area of excellence.[4]

But in the main the victory song is less preoccupied with what sets any one win or winner apart than with the transcendent nature and

---

[4] Twelve laps: Pind. *Ol.* 2.50, 3.33–4, *Pyth.* 5.33, cf. *Ol.* 6.75; Lee 1986:170–3. Mares: Bacch. 3.3–4, fr. 20c.4, Pind. *Pyth.* 2.8, *Nem.* 9.52, *Isthm.* 5.5; McDevitt 1994a. Forty-one teams: Pind. *Pyth.* 5.49–53. This has been doubted, on the grounds that fields at Olympia were restricted to no more than ten because of the size of the hippodrome (Ebert 1989, 1991a, 1991b, cf. Decker 1992b:138); but Pindar's text seems secure, and whatever the case at Olympia, it need have no relevance to arrangements in the plain of Cirrha at Delphi (cf. Crowther 1993:46–8). Twenty-one two-horse chariots race in the frieze around the antechamber of the third ('Prince's') of the late fourth-century Macedonian royal tombs at Vergina; Andronicos 1991:202 and plates 167–8. Victor's event: Poliakoff 1982:137–41, Steiner 1986:99–100, Lefkowitz 1991:161–8. Javelin thrower: Pind. *Ol.* 13.91–5, *Nem.* 7.71–3. Runner: Pind. *Nem.* 8.19–21. Struggling: Pind. *Nem.* 4.33–43; cf. the wrestling imagery at 57–8 and 91–6 and the chariot imagery in a poem for the four-horse race, *Isthm.* 2.1–2.

impact of victory itself. Victory is the product of four factors in combination: natural ability (*phua* – mostly inherited), hard work (*ponos*), wealth and the willingness to spend it, the divine favour which was the Greek equivalent of good luck (Willcock 1995:15). It places a man on a continuum with the legendary heroes of the epinician's myths (who may themselves be associated with athletic or equestrian competition), and with his city's and family's champions in the far and recent past – these are often named or enumerated. 'The victor has sweet fair weather for the rest of his life on account of the contests' (Pind. *Ol.* 1.97–8). And, provided that a poet be found to sing his praises, victory may guarantee him memory everlasting for the future. This is so above all for a victory at Olympia. The best thing is water, and gold shining like fire, begins the poem which stands first in our collections of Pindar's epinicians, but we will hear of no contest greater than Olympia (Pind. *Ol.* 1.1–8); it is the peak of contests (Pind. *Ol.* 2.14, cf. *Nem.* 10.31). If a man has won at Nemea, the poets wish him success at Delphi and Olympia; an Isthmian champion may look to Olympia or Delphi or both; victory at the Pythian games may presage Olympic success. But what can an *Olumpionikos* still expect? Only triumph in a more prestigious event, or more of the same for himself or other members of his family. Failure to achieve Olympic glory sometimes requires an excuse. Alexidamus should have won the boys' wrestling – but either a god was responsible or the unreliable judgements of mortals cheated his hands of the top prize; Aristagoras might have matched his record in local games at Olympia and Delphi had not his parents' hesitation held him back.[5]

We have already seen that this pre-eminence of Olympia was not unusual. Indeed, it influences the shape of Pindar's work as we now have it. Whereas Simonides' epinicians were arranged by event, and Bacchylides' at least partly by the victor's community, Hellenistic scholars divided Pindar's into four books according to the festival at which victories were won in the order Olympians, Pythians, Isthmians, Nemeans. Within each book, poems commemorating the most important events (as the scholars saw them) were placed first. The collection's initial poem, however, is an anomaly, celebrating a

[5] Expectations: Pind. *Ol.* 1.106–11, 13.101–3; Cairns 1991, A. Miller 1991:170–1. Alexidamus: Bacch. 11.24–36, cf. 4.11–13; McDevitt 1994b. Aristagoras: Pind. *Nem.* 11.19–29, cf. *Isthm.* 4.28–35.

horse race rather than the four-horse chariot race, and owing its precedence to Aristophanes of Byzantium's admiration for its majestic opening or to its theme. And Pindar himself can change his tune to suit circumstances; Pythian victory is the best of joys in a Pythian ode (*Pyth.* 8.64–5), even the games for Adrastus at Sicyon merit a description to match Olympia, 'the peak of contests for horses' (*Nem.* 9.9). This hierarchy, and its manipulation, remind us that this is the realm of rhetoric and representation. As Peter Rose comments, 'To insist . . . that a peculiar physical activity, which the structure of economic life in Greece . . . substantially confined to the small class of males who could afford the leisure to train and the luxury of professional trainers, represents the summit of human happiness is supremely ideological' (Rose 1992:169).

There was also tension inherent in this ideology. The victor who left home to compete as an equal returned as an exceptional, almost heroic, figure. Our appreciation of the role of the victory song in resolving this tension has been greatly enriched by the work of Leslie Kurke, to which I am indebted for much of what follows (Kurke 1991). This social and political element of the victory song coheres best, perhaps, with the traditional understanding of its performance by a choir which sang and danced in a public presentation. Some scholars now believe that epinicians were sung solo before an audience of invited guests. Even on this assumption, however, the song was one portion of a celebration of which part was public, and neither poet nor victor would have any motive for preventing its circulation; Pindar's seventh *Olympian* was indeed written in letters of gold and kept preserved in the temple of Athena at Lindus on Rhodes because of its panegyric of that island. There is something perverse about the idea of private praise poetry. An additional corroboration for the usual view is the lack of late archaic and classical victory songs for Spartans, perhaps a result of that community's strict control over the kinds of public occasions on which they were presented elsewhere at that time.[6]

Of whom did the poet sing? Of the victor, naturally, of his past achievements and future hopes as much as of the occasion for the poem. Parts of some poems read like a curriculum vitae in verse; even Aristagoras, an incoming magistrate on Tenedus and not a

---

[6] Kurke: for an opposing view, see Lefkowitz 1995:143–4. Choir: Carey 1991, K. Morgan 1993. Solo: Heath and Lefkowitz 1991, Lefkowitz 1991:191–206. Lindos: Gorgon, *FGrH* 515 F 18.

festival victor at all, is furnished with a suitable résumé, first sixteen times in games nearby (Pind. *Nem.* 11.19–21). Family members figure too. *Trisolumpionikan* trumpets the initial word of the poem for Xenophon of Corinth – 'three times Olympic champion' (Pind. *Ol.* 13.1). Xenophon is also the first to win both the *stadion* race and pentathlon at Olympia (30–1). Even he finds an equal in his father, who won the Pythian *stadion* and *diaulos* on the same day and three times at Athens within a month (37–9), and rivals among a family with seventy victories at Isthmia and Nemea and many more elsewhere in a list that stretches from Sicily to Euboea (97–112). Nor is the winner's city forgotten. Not only does the current triumph crown it or proclaim it or make it famous (Saïd and Trédé-Boulmer 1984). Glorious as it is, it is joined by many others – seventy crowns for Ceans at Isthmia, for example (Bacch. 2.9–10). The trio of victor, family and community echoes the formula of the herald's proclamation at the festival itself – name, patronymic, city. But the poet's care to include others in his praise also serves to alleviate envy and dispel suspicion that the victor's extraordinary good fortune will inspire him to *hubris*, arrogant disrespect for the rights and status of others. In this way, he is reintegrated into his family and his community. Moreover, it is victory which reveals that he is a true member of each: whatever his heritage, 'performance proves the man' (Pind. *Ol.* 4.18, cf. *Nem.* 3.70–1).

It is instructive in this regard to consider those on whom the poet does not normally bestow a share of the winner's fame. The race-horse Pherenicus comes in for praise; but of jockeys we hear nothing. These must have been boys, whose weight would be of special importance given the small size of Greek horses. Perhaps some boys rode their own horses. Aegyptus's victory monument portrayed a young boy, *paidion*, on horseback (Paus. 6.2.8). But we should be wary of interpreting the image too literally: his father Timon was a victor too, in the *tethrippon*, and his monument boasted an image of a young woman – Pausanias takes her as Nike, victory – as charioteer (Paus. 6.12.6). I suspect that jockeys were often boy slaves, beneath the notice of the victory song as not strictly necessary for victory: Pheidolas's mare threw her rider but he was declared winner of an Olympic horse race all the same (Paus. 6.13.9). As for charioteers, some owners drove for themselves, others may have owned or hired drivers (Lefkowitz 1984:41–2). Two attain prominence in Pindar. One is a brother-in-law of the victor. The time and

detail allotted to the description of Carrhotus's race, guiding Arcesilas's team safely through where forty others crashed, and to his
dedication of the chariot to Apollo, are remarkable, and might risk
overshadowing the praise of the victor himself (Pind. *Pyth.* 5.26–62).
Pindar therefore makes a point of Arcesilas's own expertise at the
reins (115–17). Carrhotus thus is a kind of surrogate for Arcesilas; in
heading home from Delphi to Cyrene he associates its king with
Battus, its legendary founder, whose journey also began at the
sanctuary of Apollo (Dougherty 1993:103–19). The other, Nicomachus, is also a man of some standing, perhaps a *proxenos*, or honorary
representative, of the Eleans; he drove Xenocrates' team to victory
at Athens and his brother Theron's at Olympia (Pind. *Isthm.*
2.18–29). The connection lets Pindar link Xenocrates, who died
before the poem was composed, with the Olympic victory he can
now never win.[7]

Trainers appear more often, always (or nearly so) in poems for
heavy athletes competing as boys or youths (Hamilton 1974:106–8,
Barrett 1978:19 n.27). In one instance, the trainer is mentioned
merely to add suspense. Pindar's *Olympian* 10 opens with the news
that a son of Archestratus has won an Olympic crown (1), establishes
his community (13), supplies the event, boxing for boys (16), advises
gratitude to the trainer (17), and only then yields up the victor's
name (18). There are more elaborate references, however. After all,
association with a famous and successful trainer may enhance a
beginner's reputation: Alcimedon is Melesias's thirtieth winner
(Pind. *Ol.* 8.65–6); the pancratiast Pytheas is guided to a win at
Nemea by Menander, whose Olympic victories amount to a subtle
hint of the poet's ambitions for the boy (Bacch. 13.190–8). Trainers
(many of them Athenian) may guide a young athlete like a helmsman
(Pind. *Isthm.* 4.65–7) or a charioteer (Pind. *Nem.* 6.64–6). This seems
an odd way to speak of someone approaching heroic proportions. Is
it part of a programme of cutting the victor down to size? Hardly.
Boys and youths were not yet full members of the community,
neither lifted above it like adult victors nor able to gain access to the

---

[7] Pherenicus: Bacch. 5.37–49, 182–6, fr. 20c.8–10, Pind. *Ol.* 1.18–23, *Pyth.* 3.72–6. Jockeys:
Pausanias saw Hiero's dedication for his three victories at Olympia – a man in a chariot
flanked by two boys riding horses (Paus. 6.12.1). Vases begin to show boy jockeys around the
traditional time of the introduction of the horse race into the Olympic programme in 648, a
convention followed by Panathenaic prize amphorae; Maul-Mandelartz 1990:105–16,
210–11.

resources and personal influence needed to be thought a threat. The grammar of praise is modified accordingly. So too Pindar's poems for rulers make no effort to defuse the envy they attract; this is taken for granted, accepted, desired (Kurke 1991:195–224).

SONGS OR STATUES? THE END OF EPINICIAN

Pindar's earliest datable poem belongs to 498, his latest to 446. We have most of the epinicians he wrote during those years, or at least most of those which were known to Callimachus and other Alexandrian scholars. One of the forty-five was written for the Tenedan official Aristagoras, one for a musician, a champion *aulos*-player. A few commemorate victories in local games. In the great majority which remain, those for athletic and equestrian victors in the panhellenic festivals of the *periodos*, Pindar praises owners of chariots and racehorses (the largest group), heavy athletes and runners, men of immense wealth and power such as Hieron and Theron in far off Sicily, and young boys in Aegina close to home. He wrote two songs for some victories; some victors commissioned (or had arranged for them) songs by two poets, Pindar and Simonides, Pindar and Bacchylides. And then after Pindar's death there is nothing. Thirty years later, Euripides (or someone else) wrote an epinician for Alcibiades, a poem by then as out of step with the norm as the extraordinary Olympic performance it praised (and probably exaggerated) or as the victor himself (755, 756 Page, *PMG*; Bowra 1970:134–48).

Such a change in fashion needs more explanation than the death of one man. One can be suggested, however tentatively. Victories continued to be won and valued; the expansion of the equestrian programme at Olympia and (especially) Delphi and Athens in the fifth century must reflect ongoing and even increased interest among the panhellenic elite (whatever the vagaries of local conditions). They were merely commemorated differently. Pindar had proudly contrasted his work with another form of advertisement and display, the victory dedication. I am no sculptor, he begins *Nemean* 5, fashioning my statues to stand unmoving. No, on every ship I bid my song go forth (1–8). The theme is reprised obliquely later in the poem: when it's a matter of praising wealth or might of hand (the victor is a pancratiast), I need a wide jumping space: there's a light spring in my knees (19–20). This is not a boast a statue could make and, as Simonides said, 'stone is broken even by mortal hands' (Simon. 581 Page, *PMG*). The two strategies of commemoration were not mutually exclusive, for the very rich or showy at any rate; Hieron and Alcibiades commissioned sculptures too, Alcibiades paintings as well. But from the mid-fifth century victory statues and their accompanying dedicatory epigrams prevail, and praise songs die out. The reason, I suspect, lies in the very communal context of praise poetry which is now the subject of debate.

I have already stressed the coincidence of the development of the epinician genre and the efflorescence of athletic and equestrian competition in the earlier sixth century. Epinician had other contexts too, among them the more or less contemporary sumptuary legislation, attributed to Solon, which restricted display at funerals at Athens. Wealthy Greeks had always to balance their impulse towards conspicuous consumption with their concern for the envy it might bring from the many less blessed. This might entail replacement of one form of display by another – elaborate obsequies by the commissioning of victory songs – and influence the ideology of any: the praise poets present victory as a public good, a benefaction from the victor upon the city, achieved only with much expense and toil. I suggest that this was an image of which the competitive elite had by and large grown weary by 450 or so. They lost interest in providing their fellow citizens with rationales for their competitive pastimes through the words of poets, and preferred instead to erect monuments, in their own home-towns and in the great panhellenic sanctuaries. Here too there seems to have been some unease that such monuments elevated the victor dangerously close to gods. We hear of traditions that only those who had won three times were permitted to have their own likeness represented in portrait statues at Olympia and that statues were to be life-size and no larger. Nevertheless, the distinction between a votive to honour a god and a monument to immortalize a victor must have been easily elided. 'Even the earliest victor statues were regarded as honorific representations of the athletes . . . this signal honor soon contributed to the aura which surrounded both men and statues' (Lattimore 1988:255). This was all the likelier given that statues of the archaic *kouros* type were used for representations of gods and successful athletes (such as Arrachion, Paus. 8.40.1) alike and that athletic images often served as models for the sculptural decoration of temples, including, most appropriately, the mid-fifth-century Temple of Zeus at Olympia (Raschke 1988b:42–5).[8]

The late sixth and early fifth centuries seem also to have been a fertile period for a series of picturesque tales of heroized athletes, regularly (though not invariably) involving victory statues. Theogenes' statue at Thasos fell on an enemy, was cast into the sea, recovered by fishermen and restored to alleviate a famine; Theogenes himself was then worshipped as a hero. Two statues of one of Theogenes' early-fifth-century rivals, Euthymus of Locri, were struck by lightning on the same day, many miles apart; he too was the object of cult. Oebotas, the first Achaean to win at Olympia (in 756) did not receive the recognition he thought fitting. None of his countrymen could match his feat – so goes the story, inaccurately – until the Achaeans set up his statue at Olympia. Sostratus of Pellene then won the boys' *stadion* race of 460. Even in Pausanias's time, Achaeans competing at Olympia made offerings to Oebotas and crowned his statue when they won (Paus. 7.17.13–14). We may suppose that victory statues came to seem less numinous in the mid-fifth century. Or did appearing to be arrogant matter less? After all, whatever else the statues were, they were gifts to the gods, whose envy might be appeased by the same magnificence which antagonized ordinary men. They were also messages to the victors' own kind, those Greeks who had the leisure and means to visit with some regularity the precincts where they stood. From this perspective, the abandonment of epinician, the shift from song to statue, reflects the closure of one channel of communication between mass and elite in Greek society. No doubt it occurred earliest in communities where elite competition had itself lost some of its lustre, such as at Athens (see below, Chapter 5); it may be significant here that the last datable epinician for an Athenian, Pindar's *Pythian* 7 for Megacles, is as old as 486, that Alcibiades' may have been sung at Olympia and not at Athens (Angeli Bernardini 1992:973–4), that it had some success, if it contributed to his election as *strategos* (general), but no successors.[9]

Or almost none. We have fragments, some substantial, of three poems by the great Hellenistic scholar and poet Callimachus in honour of athletic and equestrian victors. One is for Sosibius, an important political figure in the courts of Ptolemy III and IV of

---

[8] Three times: Pliny, *NH* 34.9.16. Life-size: Luc. *Pr. Im.* 11. For the reliability of these traditions, see Hyde 1921:45–6, 54–7.

[9] Heroized athletes: Fontenrose 1968, Bohringer 1979, Kurke 1993:141–55.

Egypt (fr. 384, 384a Pfeiffer). The second commemorates one Polycles' victory in the *hydrophoria, amphorites* or *amphiphorites* at Aegina, in which competitors raced to pick up a vessel of water and run back with it to the finishing line. Composed sometime in the late 240s, like the poem for Sosibius, the third treats the victory of Queen Berenice II in a chariot race at the Nemean games (254–68c *Suppl. Hell.*). Ancient commentators termed Sosibius's poem an elegy, Polycles' an *epinikos*, Berenice's proudly proclaims itself an *epinikion* in its third line (254.3 *Suppl. Hell.*): the discrepant labels reflect the poems' mixture of genres (Fuhrer 1993). They are written in elegiac metre, like dedicatory epigrams, but (in the cases of the poems for Sosibius and Berenice anyway) are longer than agonistic epigrams and incorporate characteristic features of epinicians: a mythic aetiology for the festival at which the victory was won (in the poems for Polycles and Berenice), abrupt transitions, verbal echoes. For Sosibius, Callimachus constructs a victory catalogue of a familiar kind, though of unusual range; Sosibius won the boys' *diaulos* at games for a Ptolemy, the Panathenaic wrestling for youths, and chariot races at both Isthmia and Nemea. The hierarchical (rather than chronological) order of festivals the poet follows can be exampled elsewhere, as too the use of an athletic metaphor – at Corinth's competitions, 'fair judgement outruns gold' (14). We are surprised, however, to recognize Sosibius himself as a speaker in one section of the poem, that devoted to his youthful exploits, and to learn that he now knows what keeps the people friendly and does not forget 'little people', a quality called rare in a rich man who has no sense (53–6). Where Pindar played the athlete, Callimachus flatters Sosibius by arrogating to him the poet's prerogative – he himself takes the role of audience or recipient of the news of victory (Fuhrer 1992:218–19) – and by stressing his condescension, an adherence to the credo *noblesse oblige.*[10]

This poem aims less at reintegrating the victor into his community than at reinforcing his status at its top; nothing in Pindar or Bacchylides separates rich victor from poor townsfolk so explicitly. One explanation is that Sosibius must be situated within two communities, Alexandria and the wider Greek world. Another speaker in the poem is the river Nile, only now able, thanks to

---

[10] *Hydrophoria*: Callim. fr. 198 (with *Dieg.* 8.21), 220, 222, 223 Pfeiffer. Echoes: in *The Victory of Berenice*, as it is usually called, 'Callimachus combines a handful of Pindaric gestures in his first line' (Parsons 1977:45) and echoes Bacch. 5.43–5 in lines 6–10.

Sosibius's victories, to claim its rightful place among the paltry streams of others' homelands (27–34). The Ptolemies too used athletic and equestrian competition for the purpose of establishing their panhellenic credentials; they were doubly outsiders, inheritors of the name of a Macedonian general from the fringes of the Greek world and rulers of a barbarian people (cf. Tancke 1991:112–27). So Berenice competed often; the priestess of her posthumous cult bore the designation 'prizebearer of Berenice the benefactress'; a series of small bronzes shows her husband, Ptolemy III, as a naked wrestler besting a barbarian (Kyrieleis 1973). Berenice was further removed from the victor's norm: hers is our only epinician for a woman. The unusual mention of women of Colchis and the Nile weaving tapestries, teasingly incomplete as it is, seems meant as a foil for Berenice's achievements in an arena less likely to be regarded as women's work (255.11–16 *Suppl. Hell.*); as elsewhere in Hellenistic poetry, the private world of textile production is juxtaposed with the public display of palace society (cf. Theocr. 15; Whitehorne 1995). Callimachus's learned play with convention thus modifies and supplements the epinician tradition, but remains rooted like earlier examples in contemporary reality.

HOMER'S HEROES

Accounts of athletic and equestrian competition are as old as Greek literature (Laser 1987:1–88, 185–9). Funeral games take up much of the third day of the obsequies for Patroclus, killed in a confrontation with the Trojan hero Hector, and of *Iliad* 23 (257–897). Achilles presides, Patroclus's great friend; the most prominent of the Greek fighters compete for prizes, some taken from among the dead man's possessions, some Achilles' own. Valuable in themselves, their associations make these rewards doubly precious: both moral and material incentives are original in Greek sport. First in order and importance among events – it takes up over half the space devoted to the games (257–652) – is the chariot race. The five contestants draw lots for post positions and drive themselves in the two-horse chariots they use in war, rounding a turn marker set far off on the plain; Achilles deputes his old squire Phoenix to make sure they keep to the course. Skill is as important as speed, the veteran horseman Nestor tells his son Antilochus, advising him to keep as close as he can to the turn-post; in the event, it is Antilochus's sharp practice, driving dangerously close to Menelaus at a narrow spot in the course, which brings him home ahead – after an appeal to his stallions not to let a mare beat them proves ineffective (407–9). The gods too make a difference, playing favourites as they do in battle: Apollo dashes the whip from Diomedes' hand, Athena brings it back, and then for good measure breaks the yoke of Eumelus's chariot and hurls him headlong to tear his body on the ground (382–97). All this occurs out on the course. The spectators can only keep a lookout as the horses head for home. Themselves prominent warriors, they squabble and offer bets over what they see until Achilles makes peace (448–98). Diomedes proves to be the winner, and carries off first prize, a woman and an eared tripod 'of 22 measures'. In fact, no entrant leaves empty-handed. Achilles allots a prize for Nestor too, since his days of competition are past; the old man repays him with a lengthy memoir of his exploits at the funeral games of Amarynceus, when he won in boxing, wrestling, running, spear-throwing – every event but the chariot race and even then he lost only to Siamese twins (615–50).

Both competitors in the next event, 'painful boxing', are also guaranteed awards, a hard-working mule for the endurance of the winner (652–99). This is Epeius, unique among his fellow competitors in admitting shortcomings in war (667–71) and elsewhere identified as a craftsman, the carpenter who made the Trojan Horse (*Od.* 8.492–3, 11.523). Other events follow: wrestling (also 'painful'), in which Odysseus seems set to defeat Telamonian Ajax despite his size and strength (and the crowd's expectations?) until Achilles declares a draw (700–39); a foot-race around a turn-post and back – Odysseus wins this from behind, passing the other Ajax, the son of Oileus, when he slips in cow dung after a push from Athena (740–97); an unsettling and indecisive armed combat between Telamonian Ajax and Tydeus (798–825); a weight throw, in which Polypoites wins the event and the *solos*, the lump of iron used in it, and Epeius's feeble effort reveals yet another unheroic dimension (826–49); an archery contest (850–83). The last contest to be announced is spear throwing, but this does not take place: acknowledging Agamemnon's pre-eminence, Achilles awards him first prize and Meriones second, the spear itself (884–97), and then declares the games at an end.

Athletics figure in the *Odyssey* too, though in different contexts and briefer compass. The Phaeacians of Scheria entertain Odysseus with feasting, songs of the Trojan War, and a series of contests – running, wrestling, jumping, discus and boxing. The Greek visitor, in disguise, is invited to show his own athletic prowess by Laodamas, the winning boxer and one of the sons of the king; Odysseus has the look of an athlete in his lower legs and thighs, his arms and neck. 'There is no greater fame for a man than what he wins with his footwork or the skill of his hands', Laodamas sums up. When Odysseus declines, he is taunted by one Euryalus, who has just won the wrestling. 'You don't resemble a man who knows about contests', he jibes. 'No, you remind me of a merchant who sails from port to port with no care for anything except cargoes and profits. You are no athlete.' Piqued, Odysseus answers taunt with taunt and then, still fully clothed, hurls an extra-large discus beyond any earlier throw – an achievement reported by his ever-present patron Athena, also in disguise, who marks it. He then challenges his hosts to test his mettle further in boxing or wrestling or throwing the spear – even in running, sore-kneed though he is. The Phaeacians hush. Finally, king Alcinous breaks the silence to commend Odysseus's spirit and to back off from his challenge: his people are not fighters after all but runners and sailors, eaters and musicians, dancers who love luxury (*Od.* 8.97–255).

Athletic competition returns in a different key later in the poem, when Odysseus, disguised again, has reached his home on Ithaca (*Od.* 18.1–107). A beggar and gofer nicknamed Irus (after Iris, the female messenger of the gods), despises his apparent age and shabbiness and challenges him to a fist-fight. Irus's claims that he will hit with both hands and knock out all Odysseus's teeth echo Epeius's boasts in *Iliad* 23; and the suitors, amused at the prospect of a fight between two paupers, offer appropriate prizes, the haunch of a goat and a standing invitation to join them at dinner. Odysseus's physique, enhanced by Athena, impresses them and causes Irus to shiver in fear. Fortunately for him, Odysseus decides to go easy lest he arouse suspicions of his true identity; even so, Irus's bone is shattered by a blow beneath the ear and he drops, bleating, into the dust to the laughter of the suitors. Odysseus drags him by the foot to the courtyard wall as if to indicate that the prize fight is at a lower level than the *Iliad*'s literally as well as socially: Epeius caught his opponent as he fell and kept him upright until his friends could help him leave, still on his feet (*Il.* 23.690–8).

Much in these Homeric scenes recurs in later competitions: the mix of equestrian and athletic contests, the role of judge (Phoenix and Athena) and of trainer (Diomedes acts as the loser's second in the boxing, *Il.* 23.681–4), the engagement of the onlookers, the premium placed on success, the ignominy of failure. (If you crash, Nestor tells Antilochus, you will be a joy to the others and a shame to yourself, *Il.* 23.342–3.) Though the heroes drive for themselves in Patroclus's games, Neleus, like later owners, sent a charioteer along with a four-horse team to a competition in Elis (*Il.* 11.698–702). Other elements are more unusual. The boxers wear loincloths (like the wrestlers) as well as thongs (*Il.* 23.684–6, 710). *Pankration* is absent – it is said to have been the last of the combat sports to be introduced at Olympia – its place taken by events ignored at the great crown games: armed combat, archery, perhaps the weight throw. (Epeius, whirling, seems to be throwing a discus, *Il.* 23.840; but then his result may be laughable precisely because his technique is wrong: Howland 1954–5:16.) The jump, discus and spear throw are not brought together as part of the pentathlon. The passages (and other incidental references, especially in similes) raise questions important for the historian of sport.

The funeral games for Patroclus and Amarynceus are only two of many attested in Greek myth; Homer himself refers to those for Oedipus (*Il.* 23.677–80) and Achilles (*Od.* 24.85–92), and we hear elsewhere of such honours for legendary heroes like Paris and Peleus (Malten 1923–4:307–9). Such games were thought to have been the beginning of many competitive festivals, including the great crown games – for Oenomaus or Pelops at Olympia, for the serpent Python at Delphi, for the babies Melicertes/Palaemon and Opheltes/Arche-morus at Isthmia and Nemea. Later Greeks established regularly scheduled competitions as part of the cult of civic benefactors who were made heroes; famous men, in some cases (Miltiades, Brasidas, Timoleon, Philopoemen), but not only those (Roller 1981). One Critolaus of Amorgos founded an annual festival at Aegiale for his dead son Aleximachus in the late second century (*IG* 12.7 515). Athletic victors, men and boys, were to receive portions of the meat of animals sacrificed in Aleximachus's honour. Groups too received such recognition, as the Eleutheria for those killed at Plataea and Athens's annual Epitaphia for its war dead. We also learn of once-only competitions for the dead, unnamed or unknown in many instances, from many regions of the Greek world. The prizes which have been found, bronze vessels and marble *diskoi* dedicated to deities or buried in their owners' graves, were valuable enough to attract competitors from a distance – from Athens to Boeotia, from Notion to Lampsacus. Such games may be very old, Mycenaean. Men fight with swords in a funerary context on a thirteenth-century larnax from Tanagra, a pot from Tiryns shows chariot racing on one side and a goddess of the underworld on the other (Decker 1982–3).

The Swiss scholar Karl Meuli thought that beneath the Greek *agōn* lay a kind of trial by combat to determine and punish the man responsible for the death it marked (Meuli 1968[1926]:30–4, 56–7; 1941). Competitions, by this reckoning, grew from armed duels through combat events to the rest of the programme. Gregory Nagy sees in early Greek athletic activity rituals of compensation, in which death or mock death appeases the anger of the deceased and the guilt or pollution of those surviving (Nagy 1986:76). The narrator of Margaret Atwood's *Cat's Eye* might concur:

Andrea writes for a newspaper. 'This is for the Living Section', she says. I know what that means, it used to be the Women's Pages. It's funny that they now call it Living, as if only women are alive and the other things, such as the Sports, are for the dead. (Margaret Atwood, *Cat's Eye* (Toronto 1988) 88)

The connections between death and competition do run deep, from the myths in which a discus throw ends in death to the folk-tale reshaped in Euripides' *Alcestis*, in which Heracles wrestles Death and wins, to the use of tombs as turning posts and of the racecourse as a place of burial (McGowan 1995). But as early as epic there is more to equestrian and athletic contests than that. The Phaeacian games are far from funereal; nor is there any indication that those in Elis, where Neleus sent his chariot, or the Theban games in which Tydeus excelled are linked to death ritual. Achilles' Myrmidons enjoy their discuses, throw javelins, shoot arrows, much like the suitors waiting for Penelope. This may be recreation, not competition. Even so, the casual references to the lengths of a discus throw or a javelin cast which a man might make 'in a contest or in war' as measures of distance imply that Homeric competition was the stuff of everyday life as well as an important adjunct to funerary ritual. It might be best to ignore origins and to stress the fact that the figures, real or imaginary, who were honoured by equestrian and athletic competition were not just dead, but heroes. The contests affirmed their special status at the same time that (as we have seen) they revealed that of living victors. The link is made explicit by a condition of Critolaus's foundation at Aegiale: at each festival, his dead son was to be declared winner in the *pankration*.[11]

All this invites a further question: whose competitions do the epics describe? Schliemann's discoveries seemed to establish that Homer was history, the history of the Bronze Age. This was denied in the influential work of Moses Finley, who thought that the world of Odysseus was set neither in the Mycenaean era nor in the time of the composition of the poems, but sometime in the intervening Dark Age, the tenth or ninth century; a sharp break after the fall of the palaces became archaeological orthodoxy too. Recently, however, scholars, including specialists in sport history, have preferred to pick out elements of continuity between Mycenaean and later Greece. Funeral games are one, chariot racing and boxing and perhaps spear-throwing and foot-races others (Rystedt 1986, cf. Evjen 1992:99–100). But there are phenomena in epic for which Mycenaean parallels are rare or lacking – three- and four-horse chariots, contests in archery, prize tripod vessels (cf. Renfrew 1988:17); and some features, such as armed combat and the provision of prizes for all participants, may be Mycenaean and Homeric but counter to later Greek custom (Mouratidis 1990). The Homeric epics are thus likely to be something of a patchwork in their presentation of equestrian and athletic competition. Furthermore, any reading of them by the sport historian must be literary as well as literal. When Achilles halts the wrestling, he bids Odysseus and Ajax carry away equal prizes; an awkward task – they are a tripod valued at twelve oxen and a four-oxen woman (*Il.* 23.700–5, 736–7). We are not enlightened as to how this is done, nor does it matter; the poet has other priorities, to which we now briefly turn.[12]

Patroclus's games serve a variety of purposes within the poem. They allow a last glimpse of the Greek heroes, few of whom will be involved in the final scenes in Book 24. What is more, they are glimpsed in characteristic guise: crafty Odysseus, Ajax, strong but not blessed with success. He is in danger of losing to both Odysseus and Diomedes, and one of those bested by Polypoites in the weight throw, an intimation of the disastrous loss in the contest for Achilles'

---

[11] Death: see above, Chapter 1 (on sport and warfare). Elis and Thebes: Hom. *Il.* 11.698–702, 4.387–90. Myrmidons and suitors: Hom. *Il.* 2.774–5, *Od.* 4.625–6, 17.167–8.
[12] Homer and history: Morris 1997 provides a sketch of scholarship in this area.

armour which (in other poems) later leads to his madness and death. His swifter namesake, quarrelsome and 'best in abuse' (Idomeneus's words) as a spectator of the chariot race, is rendered foul-mouthed in earnest after his fall in the dung during the footrace (*Il.* 23.483–4, 777). Most important is the transition the sequence affords between the bloody turmoil of the poem's earlier books and its peaceful close with the ransoming of the corpse of Hector. This transition is effected by the games, not by the funeral rites in general; these include one of the poem's most savage acts, Achilles' slaughter of twelve Trojan youths over his friend's grave. In the games, however, we see conflict resolved time and again. Menelaus, his heart 'full of bitterness and anger against Antilochus', upbraids him for cheating; conciliatory in tone, Antilochus apologizes for his youthful misjudgement and offers to give up the mare he has won – a generous gesture Menelaus, mollified, refuses (*Il.* 23.566–611). Epeius's braggadocio is transformed into solicitude for his battered opponent. Both the wrestling and the armed duel are called off before anyone loses or is seriously hurt. Achilles, *agonothetēs* and arbitrator, is at the centre of this movement from conflict towards calm. It is he who quiets Ajax and Idomeneus and calls a halt to the wrestling. We are thus prepared for his gracious reception of Priam at the end of the poem, and his willingness to give up his anger along with Hector's body. What a distance we have travelled from the opening book of the poem, in which Achilles' fury at the seizure of his prize by Agamemnon almost provoked him to draw his sword against the king. In Patroclus's games, Achilles provides an extra prize to Eumelus from his own stores, at Antilochus's urging. Fittingly, the book ends with Achilles acknowledging Agamemnon's superiority in throwing the spear, and declaring him winner of the first prize without a contest. In a way, Priam will recover his son's body as another prize.[13]

The Phaeacian games occur earlier in a poem with another denouement, Odysseus's revenge on the suitors. Accordingly, while the contests of the Achaean warriors in *Iliad* 23 play down conflict in favour of harmony – the provision of prizes for all, perhaps a reflection of the distribution of battle booty, mitigates the sting of defeat – in the games on Scheria we may sense overtones of war

---

[13] Agamemnon's superiority: for a contrary opinion, see Postlethwaite 1995.

(Louden 1993:22–6, Visa 1994a). King Alcinous's banquet closes with songs of Troy, the scene of Odysseus's warrior past, and the disguised hero reduced to tears; his vigorous and impressive response to the taunts of Euryalus prepare us for the successful battles that lie in the future. More particularly, the ease with which Odysseus overawes the soft-living Phaeacians presages his achievement in killing the suitors against extraordinary odds; his emphasis on his prowess as an archer and his claim to be first in shooting a man in the midst of a host of enemies points to the weapon he will use (*Od.* 8.214–22).

ORESTES: CHAMPION AND CHUMP

From these beginnings (and partly due to their example), athletic and equestrian competition continued to inform Greek literature of all kinds. Sometimes surprisingly. 'Of all writers in Greek, he is perhaps the most fruitful source' (Harris 1976:54, cf. 13): not everyone would immediately identify the informant on athletics referred to in this sentence as Philo of Alexandria, the Jewish theologian and polemicist who wrote in the first decades of the current era. Yet Philo is rare or unique among our literary texts in alluding to tripping fouls in foot-races and body blows in boxing, in describing the tying of victory ribbons (*tainiai*) and a coach matching his runner stride for stride in training. The subject is too vast to survey in a book like this. Diverse strategies for selection are on offer in recent research: to investigate the presentation of a single event, such as boxing (Fiedler 1992), or of a single image – life as a foot-race, perhaps. We might concentrate on a single genre: Richard Seaford notes 'the surprising association of dramatic satyrs with athletics' (Seaford 1984:40). His own explanation invokes the participation of men or boys dressed as satyrs in athletic contests at the Anthesteria – contests, however, for which no good evidence exists. Or we might focus still more narrowly, on just one passage, ideally illuminating some aspect of competition as well as the text itself. So Valerie Visa's elucidation of Euripides' *Hippolytus* 1268–71 builds on the distinction between racecourses with and without turns, *akamptoi*, to reveal Aphrodite as a victor who drives her charioteering opponent, Hippolytus, off the track (Visa 1994b). I propose here another tack, in keeping with the theme of difference and its implications, to study the depiction in tragedy of Orestes as a victor.[14]

The core of Orestes' story is clear enough. He is the son of king Agamemnon and Clytaemnestra, who joins with her lover Aegisthus to kill the king on his triumphant return from Troy. At Apollo's prompting, Orestes comes back disguised from exile in Phocis and avenges his father's murder with the deaths of Clytaemnestra and Aegisthus, his sister Electra and friend Pylades his main allies. His mother's Furies hound him to Delphi. There, the oracle of Apollo sends him on to Athens; he is tried for murder at the court of the Areopagus and acquitted by the vote of Athena, who presides. Even for this core, however, variant versions thrive – the setting is sometimes Argos, sometimes Mycenae or Sparta; Aegisthus's death precedes and follows Clytaemnestra's – and Orestes' later career is still more fluid. He figures as an exemplar of heroic behaviour as early as the *Odyssey*, and later poets too (as usual) employed and transformed the tale according to their ends. Still, his connection to athletic and equestrian competition comes close to being a constant. I begin not with literature but with art, and not at the tradition's start but with our newest evidence: an oversize red-figure calyx crater attributed to the Aegisthus Painter, dated to about 470 yet discovered only in the early 1980s.[15]

This great vase bears a continuous band of decoration depicting the death of Aegisthus. Its memorable images are many: Clytaemnestra, axe in hand, tries vainly to save her lover; an excited young woman – Electra? – rushes in from the right; a nurse holds a baby amidst the carnage, the child of Clytaemnestra and Aegisthus in all probability, and so a reminder that the queen is a mother too. Not that we need to be reminded: Orestes is at the centre of the scene, his sword plunged into Aegisthus's chest, his head turned to Clytaemnestra's attack. He is 'spectacularly nude' (Shapiro 1994:139).

Why nude? Well, Orestes is often nude in early Greek art. Among

---

[14] Tripping fouls: *Quod Deus sit immutabilis* 75. Body blows: *De agricultura* 114. Victory ribbons: *De agricultura* 112. Coach: *De migratione Abrahami* 166; Harris 1976:51–95. Life as a foot-race: Bruyère-Dumoulin 1976, M. Davies 1985:101–10, Nollé 1985:133–5. No good evidence: Kyle 1987:45–6, Hamilton 1992:58, 67–8, 173. Orestes in tragedy: cf. Visa 1992a:276–89, 434–65.

[15] Aegisthus Painter: Malibu, J. Paul Getty Museum 88.AE.66, Prag 1985:106–7 and plate 46.

Plate 5. Orestes kills Aegisthus: the avenger as athletic victor. Attic red-figure calyx krater, Aegisthus Painter, about 470.

examples of the theme illustrated on this crater, the death of Aegisthus, we may note a series of bronze Argive-Corinthian shield bands from the first quarter of the sixth century (Prag 1985: nos. C1–6). Four of these were found at Olympia, one at Isthmia, both, of course, sites of major panhellenic competitions, Isthmia's dating from about the time the shield bands were made. Orestes is very much the victorious warrior in these pictures, triumphing over his enemies by stealth and strength. Is he to be thought of as an athlete too? Festival competitions rivalled war as occasions for young men of the elite to gain glory; their home-comings might be as packed with meaning as those from battle. Is this the reason that a red-figure stamnos by the Copenhagen Painter, which shows a fully-armed Orestes killing Aegisthus, also bears a palaestra scene on its reverse? Does the young man, partially naked, who appears on a Mycenaean crater from Enkomi carry a pick-axe in his left hand and, in his right, the marking-stake or strigil of an athlete (M. Davies 1969:215–23)? Is he Orestes about to take his revenge? In fact, Orestes is clothed more often than not in scenes of Aegisthus's death; the shield bands are found outside athletic contexts too, at Olbia, and often show others naked – Aegisthus, Agamemnon; 'the palaestra scene has no obvious connection with the killing' (Prag 1985:20); the young man of Enkomi does not carry a marking-stake or strigil after all (Prag 1985:9), and likely has nothing to do with Orestes (cf. M. Davies 1969:218–23).[16]

So this evidence from art does not permit us to assume that Orestes was generally thought of as an athlete returning in victory or to triumph in the archaic and early classical periods (let alone the Bronze Age). We should consider nevertheless the possibility that this image stands in the background of a poem by Pindar and makes it easier to understand. *Pythian* 11 honours Thrasydaeus of Thebes, probably the victor in the boys' *stadion* race at Delphi in 474 (though he may have been the men's *diaulos* champion in 454 instead). A digression links Thrasydaeus with Orestes through Pylades – Delphi is said to lie 'in Pylades' rich plough-fields' (15). The young men (I assume that Thrasydaeus is the *stadion* runner) are to be contrasted: whereas Thrasydaeus returns home to his father Pythonicus (43), placing a third victory wreath on his native hearth (13–14), Orestes' father was dead (17) and his home-coming the occasion of a third murder to join those of Iphigeneia and Agamemnon (Young 1968:1–26). But they may be alike too, if to the hospitality Orestes received as *xenos*, 'guest', from Strophius and his son (16, 35) we may compare the Delphians' *xenia* for Thrasydaeus, feasted with other victors in the Prytaneum (Slater 1979:63–8). The threads in the text seem thin and winding in such a summary, yet they would be obvious enough if the assimilation of Orestes to an athlete were already established; the competitive credentials of other mythological figures mentioned in the poem, Iolaus and the Dioscuri, are unquestionable (cf. Angeli Bernardini 1993:423–5).

To refer to competitive imagery in Aeschylus's *Oresteia*, produced fifteen years after Pindar's poem, causes less controversy. Wrestling is especially prominent, from the 'much heavy-limbed wrestling' sent by Zeus in the chorus's entry-song in *Agamemnon* (63–4) to the house of Atreus, too long stretched out on the ground in *Choephori* (963–4), to the final image, through which Orestes wishes the people of Athens 'a wrestling trick enemies can't escape and the victory-

---

[16] Orestes nude: Sarian in Sarian and Machaira 1994:76. Copenhagen Painter: once Berlin F 2148, Prag 1985: no. C18. Revenge: an interpretation broached but rejected by Vermeule 1958:104.

bearing salvation of the spear' (*Eum.* 776–7; Poliakoff 1980). As this last instance indicates, Orestes is implicated in this recurrent imagery. He asks his dead father to send him justice to help him grip his enemies as Agamemnon was held (*Cho.* 498); the chorus says he has a bye in a wrestling competition and wishes him victory (*Cho.* 866–8); the Furies rejoice at his admission of matricide – it is the first of the three falls they need – but Orestes, not yet on the ground, warns them not to exult too soon (*Eum.* 589–90). Equestrian competition figures too; against Aeschylus's usual practice, it may be announced visually, in the entrance of Agamemnon on a wagon, *apenē* – still an Olympic event at this time – before it appears in the imagery of the text. This also involves Orestes. In *Choephori*, he is both a young colt yoked to a chariot of troubles – the chorus prays Zeus to provide him a winning gait (794–9) – and a charioteer, driving off the course, overcome by ungovernable wits which lead him away (1021–5). He is urged not to yoke himself to ill-omened words (1044–5); but his madness has turned victory to disaster.

The most elaborate development of the motif comes in Sophocles' *Electra*. The play cannot be dated; sometime soon after 415 is attractive, since we might then see the Athenian who wins the Pythian chariot race reported in the great messenger speech (680–763) as a reference to Alcibiades. This speech, the longest single account of Orestes as an athlete, is well prepared. Early on in the play, Orestes compares his slave to an old thoroughbred horse who hasn't lost his spirit in the midst of danger; it is a warhorse he has uppermost in his mind, but the image recalls a passage of Ibycus where the horse is competing for a prize (Ibycus 287.5–7 Page, *PMG*, cf. Pl. *Parm.* 137a). He then hatches a plot: the old man must tell those within the palace that he is dead, victim of a chariot accident at Delphi (47–50). A later chorus invokes the chariot race of Pelops, full of troubles, and the curse of his driver Myrtilus, which still hangs heavy over Atreus's house (504–15). The speech itself gives a vivid, circumstantial and fictitious report on Orestes' performance at the Pythian games, victorious in running and all the other athletic events he entered, then killed battling for the lead in his chariot. This was a festival many in Sophocles' audience would know well by autopsy or reputation; nothing is more plausible than the conclusion that what they heard in the theatre of Dionysus matched what they could see every four years at Delphi. This is truest, of course, of items which are corroborated by other evidence for Delphi or other festivals: the form of the victory proclamation (693–5), the scheduling of athletics before horse-racing, held early in the morning of a different day (698–700), the prominence of Thessalians and other northern Greeks among the chariot entries – even Orestes has Thessalian mares (701–8) – the drawing of lots for post positions (709–11). Unique details need not be dismissed either, such as the placing of foot-races first among athletic events (684). The description of Orestes' crash also carries credibility (720–48). I give it here in the Loeb translation of Hugh Lloyd-Jones (1994):

And Orestes, keeping his horses near the pillar at the end, each time grazed the post, and giving his right-hand trace-horse room he tried to block off his pursuer. At first all had stood upright in their chariots, but then the hard-mouthed colts of the Aenian, carrying him on in his despite, on the turn as they finished the sixth and began the seventh round dashed their foreheads against the chariot from Barce. One driver crashed into and smashed another in a single disaster, and then the whole plain of Crisa was filled with the wreckage of chariots. Seeing this, the cunning charioteer from Athens pulled his horses away and paused, avoiding the surge of chariots all confused in the middle of the course. Orestes was driving last, keeping his horses in the rear, confident in the result; and when he saw the Athenian alone was left, he sent a sharp command through the ears of his swift horses and went after him. They brought their chariots level and drove on, with the head of now one, now of the other projecting from the chariots. Throughout all the other rounds the man and his chariot remained upright; then as the horse turned he relaxed his left-hand rein, and unawares he struck the end of the pillar. He broke the axle box, slid over the rail, and was caught in the reins, and as he fell upon the ground the horses plunged wildly into the middle of the course.

No doubt any other Greek crowd would also cry out with pity if such a splendid youth were mangled beyond recognition before their eyes (749–56). No wonder scholars have relied on this speech. Still, caution is not amiss. Much of this messenger speech is reminiscent of other genres. The earlier part puts us in mind of epinician; we see the same praise of the site of competition (681–2), the quick résumé of earlier successes (688–9). We even find the word *epinikia* (692), though its translation here – 'prizes'? 'victory songs'? – is uncertain. The finale recalls the chariot race of *Iliad* 23, from verbal echoes to Orestes' tactics and the fate failure in them brings (cf. Machin 1988). Sophocles is not writing a textbook for courses in Greek sport – a pity, for the copyright would have expired long ago. He is producing a play for an audience that may have enjoyed some safe titillation and make-believe carnage on the track, and cared as little for absolute accuracy as fans of *Die Hard 3* (and counting). At the same time, he works within a literary tradition in which epic accounts were reference points as relevant as contemporary competitions, and must consider that his audience – the same audience – was as conversant with the one as the other. Here, Sophocles has taken two seemingly contrasting elements of the tradition, the motif of Orestes as an athlete and victor and the baneful horsemanship of Pelops, and combined them in a manner both intellectually and emotionally satisfying. The messenger speech offers a continuation of the Pelops theme, another chariot race which brings ruin to the House of Atreus, and a modification of the depiction of Orestes as a competitor, since he now loses as well as wins. As it turns out, of course, the catastrophe is a prelude to and means of achieving victory; and that victory is the more welcome when it comes because of the detour through defeat.[17]

Youngest of Athens's great tragedians, Euripides returns often to the Orestes myth, in *Andromache* (?425), *Electra* (before 415), *Iphigeneia among the Taurians* (before 412) and *Orestes* (408). Some of his stories will be unfamiliar to those modern readers who know only the extant versions of Aeschylus and Sophocles (and at times surprised their first audiences too). Clytaemnestra's brothers, Castor and Pollux, send Orestes to Athens for judgement (*El.*); he and Pylades flee to the Crimea and meet Iphigeneia – not sacrificed after all (*IT*); he stays in Argos, condemned to death for his murders, and makes an attempt on Helen's life (*Or.*); he kills Neoptolemus (*Andr.*). Orestes is still an athlete – this was apparently too integral or at least attractive a part of his legend to ignore. The image of competition may merely colour the action: in *IT*, Orestes' madness keeps him on the move, like a chariot wheel (82, cf. 36–7, 971, *El.* 1252–3). But the Euripides who renders problematic the use of traditional tales as exemplars and of heroes as models is at work here too. In *Electra*, Orestes has the hair of a well-born man raised in the palaestra (527–9, cf. 686–7), and his task, the killing of Aegisthus and Clytaemnestra, is referred to as a contest (751, 987), its accomplishment as a victory (590–1, 675). Orestes has come to win a crown (614) and does (854–5, 872), to be hailed as *kallinike* by his sister and

[17] Scholars: e.g., Lacombrade (1959), arguing that the race course at Delphi replicated Olympia's. Verbal echoes: *homoklesantes*, 'shouting in unison', in 712 imitates *Il.* 23.363 and is found nowhere else in tragedy.

co-conspirator (880, cf. 761, 865); the word is taken from the victory song at Olympia, the occasion said (in an uncertain text) to be greater than those there (862–4, cf. 883–5). But what exactly is this glorious victory? Orestes, invited to a sacrifice, kills his host from behind as he leans over to inspect the entrails. The subterfuge to which Orestes resorts to gain access to his victim – he claims to be a Thessalian on his way to Olympia to sacrifice to Zeus – undermines the appropriation of athletic analogies to valorize his deed, just as the perverted sacrifice of the murder calls into question its moral legitimacy. We might go on to ask, what kind of athlete is Orestes supposed to be? A wrestler, yes, but a runner as well: he skins the sacrificial calf faster than a runner completes a double *diaulos*, the race called the *hippios* (824–5). So it is that when Electra reflects on the punishment of the wicked, who think they've outrun justice before they've reached life's finish line, she directs her words at Aegisthus's corpse (953–6). We, however, may think of Orestes, and Castor tells him at the play's end that his race is not yet run (1264; Myrick 1994:138–41).

Much of *Orestes* too is taken up with conflict; *agōn* and other words formed from the same root occur thirteen times, more than in any other extant play. At issue is Orestes' fate. A sick man, jumping up from his bed like a colt running wild from under the yoke (45), he is also a wrestler fearing to lose the third fall and the match (434) and a runner in a race for his life (878–9). His peril takes the form of a trial for matricide in the assembly of Argos. One citizen recommends he be crowned for avenging his father; he uses the patronymic, 'Orestes son of Agamemnon', as a festival herald might do (923–4). But it is another man, who advocates that Orestes and Electra be killed, who wins (*nika*, 944–5). Only with difficulty does Orestes manage to exact a concession, to kill himself and his sister by his own hand; he is no victor here. The news prompts Electra to lament Pelops's chariot, Myrtilus's death, the curse on Atreus, breeder of horses; these led to an awful prodigy, as the sun's chariot reversed its course and the Pleiades were forced to run another route (988–1006). These allusions to chariots are followed by the appearance of Pylades, guiding Orestes like a trace-horse (1013–17). Will these chariots lead to triumph, as in Sophocles' play? No. Desperate plots, to kill Helen, to kidnap Hermione, to torch the palace, end in stalemate; only by Apollo's intervention is the situation saved. *Orestes* is a play in which the ethos and appurtenances of athletic and equestrian competition avail very little. If (as we read in the ancient introduction to the play ascribed to Aristophanes of Byzantium) it has bad ethics and, Pylades aside, base characters, it also has a loser for a hero.

This chapter has treated the most elementary form of difference, distinctions winners demonstrate and earn. Their implications are less simple than they may seem. By revealing their difference from other mortals, victors also approach the gods, a movement facilitated by the fact that these were envisaged anthropomorphically, much like mortals in form and action. The irony is that the body, doomed to decay and death, allows the competitor to claim immortality. But how to secure this claim? We have touched on two strategies. The victory statue represents the body and does so in a genre associated with divinity; however solid and well-made, it is liable (like the body itself) to destruction, by accident or (as in the stories of angry heroes) by design. Song is insubstantial, fleeting and (perhaps) therefore safe. The individual's choice (as I have suggested) was made in the context of communication between groups within and outside Greek communities. It is to sport's role in framing and fashioning group divisions – between young and old, male and female, rich and poor – that I turn in the next two chapters.

CHAPTER 4

Divisions of age and sex

'The test reveals who is the exceptional boy among young boys, the man among men, and also among those older' (Pind. *Nem.* 3.70–3). Competitions for boys, *paides*, were said to have been an afterthought at Olympia, added only (in Hippias's view) in 632 (Paus. 5.8.9), but age classes were a regular feature of this and all other festivals we know of from that time on. They were made up of boys (sometimes in more than one grouping), youths, and men. Males only: women were not normally competitors, against men least of all. Yet they were not totally excluded from equestrian and even athletic activities. In this chapter, I discuss distinctions of age and gender and their implications.

AGE CLASSES

At Olympia, athletes competed as boys (*paides*) and men (*andres*). So too at the Pythian games from their first celebration (Paus. 10.7.5). The involvement of 'beardless youths', *ageneioi*, at the other games of the classical *periodos*, at Nemea and Isthmia, is attested from the early fifth century and probably goes back to their first celebrations one hundred years before. *Ageneioi* also appear in the early fourth-century prize list for the Panathenaea (*IG* 2² 2311). Since they competed in a local games in the mid-fifth century BCE (*IG* 1³ 1386, found at Salamis), it seems safe to assume that they were part of the Panathenaea too as early and likely at its reorganization in 566. Later festivals featured four age classes – at the Asclepieia of Cos about 200 BCE, our earliest example, *paides Puthikoi*, 'Pythian boys' and *paides Isthmikoi*, 'Isthmian boys' as well as *ageneioi* and *andres*. At the Athenian Theseia, reorganized soon after 167 to mark the recovery of Lemnus, Scyrus and Imbrus, boys competed in three groups, in the first, second and third age class; there were *ageneioi* and *andres* as well – five classes in all – and the torch race had divisions for *paides*, ephebes, ex-ephebes, *neaniskoi* and men (Bugh 1990). Hellenistic inscriptions from Boeotia, apparently referring to the Erotidea at Thespiae, mention *pampaides* and *paides presbuteroi* (*IG* 7 1764, 1765); other games elsewhere reveal a bewildering array of *paides katharoi*, *paides kriseōs tēs Agesilaou*, *paides Olumpikoi*, *paides Aktiakoi*, *paides Ptolemaikoi*, *paides Klaudianoi*, *paides Sebastoi*, *paides Artemisiakoi*, sometimes two at the same festival, occasionally the coinages of an individual *agonothetēs* (Robert 1939:239–44).[1]

The boundaries of these age classes are generally quite uncertain. At Olympia, for which we have the clearest evidence, there was apparently a minimum age for competitors, at least in some events, since Pherias of Aegina was prevented from wrestling with the boys in 468 because he was too young and unready; he was still a *pais* when he won four years later (Paus. 6.14.1). Two statues of boy boxers noted by Pausanias bore inscriptions which made a point of their youth – perhaps because it was older boys who usually had the strength and endurance for victory (Paus. 6.3.1, 6.7.9). The youngest victor for whom we have a precise age is not a combat athlete: Damiscus of Messene was twelve when he won the boys' *stadion* in 368. The upper limit of the *paides* at Olympia was probably seventeen; any boy who turned eighteen in the year of the games was excluded (Crowther 1988a). Nicasylus of Rhodes, eighteen, had to wrestle with the men (Paus. 6.14.2); the Phoenician pancratiast Aurelius Helix won in 213 CE as *anēr ek paidōn*, 'a man when he had just left the age class of *paides*' (Philostr. *Her.* p. 147.22 Kayser).

As for other festivals, Pytheas of Aegina may have been victor in the boys' *pankration* at Nemea as young as twelve in the early fifth century (Robbins 1987:26–7); Onasiteles of Cedreae won the *stadion* at the Isthmian games three times as a boy some three hundred years later (*SIG³* 1067 = Moretti 1953: no. 50); 'Pythian boys', presumably named for the boys' age class at Delphi, are younger than 'Isthmian boys' at the Coan Asclepieia, boys at the Panathenaea older (according to late and emended texts, Phot., *Suda* s.v. *Panathenaia*). Klee offered the following scheme for the Asclepieia, based on the appearance of the same athletes among the victors in different age classes in subsequent festivals: *paides Puthikoi*, 12–14;

---

[1] Four age classes: these may be referred to in the iconography of a theatre in Roman Phrygia: Chuvin 1987.

paides Isthmikoi, 14–17; *ageneioi*, 17–20 (Klee 1918:46–8). But it is not easy to generalize his conclusions; variation seems assured. Boys at the Panathenaea may well have entered and/or left the class of *paides* later than at Isthmia. But Onasiteles cannot have won three times in just four years. And what of the Pythian boys? At the lower end, we have excluded competitors younger than twelve; at the upper, it seems odd that the age class of *paides* should end earlier at the Pythia, where there were no *ageneioi*, than at Isthmia. Under these circumstances, some scholars have looked for radical solutions, hypothesizing that there was after all an age class of *ageneioi* at the Pythian games from about the third century (Ebert 1965), or concluding that precision in setting ages to these classes is as misleading as it is unattainable.

The early Greeks had no birth certificates, many states probably considered all children born within the same year to be of the same age for civic purposes (as Sparta and Athens did), these years did not all begin and end at the same time: all this would bedevil the allocation of athletes to the proper age class, left to the judgement of officials, *egkritai*. It has been argued that these relied mainly on the athletes' size while also making use of specific signs of physical development, so that boys competed as *paides* from the time that their milk teeth had fallen out and the second molars grown until the appearance of genital hair (Frisch 1988). Certainly physical phenomena must have led to the disqualification of one of Lycinus's team from the four-horse chariot race for foals in 384 (the year the event was introduced at Olympia) or sometime after – and to the entry of the team in the race for fully-grown horses, which they won (Paus. 6.2.1–2). The same motif occurs in accounts of athletes (Pind. *Ol.* 9.89). But in their cases, physique and other externals are unlikely to have been decisive in themselves. Chronological age was probably the main determinant of competitive classes after all: when the *Hellanodikai* at Olympia matched wrestlers for training, their criteria were age and ability, not size (Paus. 6.23.2). Nevertheless, there was room for argument and influence. Due to the intervention of King Agesilaus of Sparta, the son of Eualces competed as a *pais* at Olympia though he was 'largest of the boys' (Xen. *Hell.* 4.1.40, Plut. *Ages.* 13.3). Perhaps Agesilaus, like his friend Xenophon, observed that 'in the case of those who have reached their full growth when still young, there is to be seen a certain freshness which betrays their youth' (Xen. *Cyr.* 1.4.3). Or did he rely on precedent, since Eualces' son may have been admitted among the *paides* at his native Athens or elsewhere during the year of the Olympic festival? An anecdote about an analogous situation may be relevant. The son of Iphicrates, the Athenian commander of the fourth century, was pressed to pay for public services when he was still too young. 'If you consider tall boys men', Iphicrates objected on his behalf, 'you must vote that short men are boys' (Arist. *Rh.* 2.1339a35).

Whatever the criteria for these age classes, it is plain that they became more numerous over time. Explanations include the increased popularity of boys' competitions as professionalism decreased the numbers of men involved in athletics, the improved status of children in Greek society and fair play. We might also ape the methods of successful researchers in another field and consider motive and opportunity. Who won the new competitions for boys and young men? Eleans excelled at Olympia, providing 87 (10.5 per cent) of the 832 victors with identifiable cities of origin among men, as compared to 75 Spartans, 41 Alexandrians, 40 Athenians (Crowther 1989). Strong though this showing is, it falls far short of their dominance in boys' events: Elis produced 28 (22.5 per cent) of those 124 winners whose home-towns are known, nearby Lepreon 3 more; its closest rivals, Sparta and Miletus, had just 5 each. It is easy enough to see how the superiority of Eleans may be exaggerated. The names of many victors derive from Pausanias's report on the statues dedicated to victors; the right to set these up was controlled by the Eleans, and Pausanias was dependent on local guides for some of his information. However, Elis's standing is consistent with the domination of the Peloponnese as a whole, home to over one half (57.5 per cent) of all locatable boy victors, and (more significantly) it is paralleled by home-town heroes in boys' competitions at other festivals. Thebes boasted three boy winners at the Pythian games, the largest contingent known among victors down to the first century BCE, and Phocis another (Klee 1918:76–88); that athletes from Ceos and Aegina are most numerous among boy victors in the Isthmian and Nemean games mostly mirrors the disproportionate share of our evidence drawn from the poems of Pindar and Bacchylides. Arcadians won 9 of 25 events for men in fourth-century competitions at the Lycaea, but almost all – 8 of 9 – for boys (*IG* 5.2 549, 550). Coans at the Asclepieia were successful in 7 of 49 events for men (less than Carians and Ionians) and in just 3 of 29 for *ageneioi*, but made up by far the largest group of winners among both *paides*

Isthmikoi (15 of 41) and *paides Puthikoi* (12 of 36). Athenian *paides* won 5 of 8 events at the Amphiaraeia at Oropus in the fourth century (*IG* 7 414), Boeotians 7 of 19 in the first (*IG* 7 416–20).[2]

More is at work here than just geography; Oropus did not move between the fourth and first centuries, its control passed from Athens to Boeotia. But clearly distance and familiarity of surroundings (which should be understood to include the security supplied by political control) influenced competitors' plans, and their parents'. The career of Socrates of Epidaurus may be paradigmatic. He won many foot-races as a boy, almost all nearby in the Peloponnese. The trip to Olympia was particularly daunting. Not only was Elis distant, hot and uncomfortable, poorly provided during the first 500 years of the festival with facilities for visitors and competitors alike, but athletes had to spend thirty days at the site before the games began. Boys would need, even want, the company of an adult member of their family for the journey, the training period, and the festival – perhaps six weeks in all. Pindar censures the parents of Aristagoras of Tenedus, a small island in the north Aegean, for failing to let him prove the prowess he had demonstrated in local competitions in wrestling and *pankration* at Delphi and Olympia (Pind. *Nem.* 11.19–29), but many others surely saw things their way. Eleans among them: in contrast to their success at home, only 1 of 15 boy Pythian victors whose citizenship is known came from Elis, and only 4 of 32 boys and *ageneioi* at the Nemean games.[3]

Yet fathers and (surprisingly?) mothers remained deeply interested in their sons' athletic endeavours and success. Example was important. Victory ran in families – rather, in the most successful family, that of Diagoras of Rhodes, it punched and kicked. Diagoras, a *periodonikēs* in boxing, was joined in time at Olympia by his three sons, boxers and pancratiasts, and his grandsons, two more boxers. Victory statues might therefore be erected in family groups (Hintzen-Bohlen 1990). For good reasons, then, Philostratus advises the trainer to look into the ages, breeding and health of both an athlete's parents (Philostr. *Gym.* 28–30). Nor should we underestimate the effect of exposing boys to competition at an early age, as the Ionians once did on Delos and continued to do at the Ephesia in Thucydides' day (the late fifth century; Thuc. 3.104.5–6). Of course,

[2] Popularity: Klee 1918:44–5. Status: Papalas 1991:167, on the inclusion of *paides* at Olympia. Fair play: Frisch 1988:181.
[3] Socrates: *IG* 4² 1 629 = Moretti 1953: no. 53, about 100 BCE.

encouragement counted too. The mother of Deinolochus of Elis set him to athletics as she had dreamed, when pregnant, that he would be born wearing an Olympic crown; he won the boys' *stadion* in 380 (Paus. 6.1.5); Peisodorus of Thurii was accompanied to Olympia by his mother Pherenice or Callipateira, Diagoras's daughter. The lot of Aristomenes of Aegina, boy victor (perhaps in wrestling) in 446, contrasts with the losers'; they will have no sweet return from Delphi, hear no light laughter from a mother's lips (Pind. *Pyth.* 8.83–7). Mothers boast of their sons' skills as charioteers before the fatal race with Oenomaus (Soph. fr. 471 Radt). A luckier competitor, M. Antonius Callippus Peisanus of Elis, had a victory statue set up by his mother (*IVO* 223, 89 CE). Among fathers, Lampon's contribution to his sons' wins at Isthmia and Nemea is also praised by Pindar; he is a Naxian whetstone among other stones in urging his boys on, a sharpener of bronze (Pind. *Isthm.* 6.72–3). Himself the son of the successful heavy athlete Melesias and a wrestler of note, Pericles' rival Thucydides made sure his sons got the best training available, and indeed they were the best wrestlers in the Athens of their time (Pl. *Meno* 94ac, *Virt.* 378d). Other fathers were less careful – the absent-minded man, says Theophrastus, makes his children (*paidia*) wrestle and forgets to have them stop until they're worn out (Theophr. *Char.* 14.10) – or less scrupulous. So anxious was Damonicus of Elis for his son Polyctor to win the boys' wrestling at Olympia that he bribed his opponent's father (Paus. 5.21.16–17, 12 BCE).[4]

The desire for victory supplies the motive for the introduction of new age classes. It is coupled with opportunity, the oversight and management of local and (to a great extent) panhellenic festivals by the same neighbourhood elites whose sons tended to predominate among their younger competitors. An explanation of this kind has the advantage of accounting for a related phenomenon, the expansion of the programme for young athletes. Olympia put on only one race for boys, the *stadion*, introduced the pentathlon for them only in 628, and never held it again, and did not allow them to contend in

---

[4] Diagoras: Moretti 1957: nos. 212, 287, 299, 322, 354, 356. For other examples of Olympic victors within the same family, see nos. 61+82, 132+189+313, 149+195, 154+249, 167+170, 194+257, 276+331+338, 298+335, 305+339, 340+363, 364+365, 536+562, 691+783, 853+880, 865+884 (fathers and sons), 428+508, 475+557 (grandfathers and grandsons), 190+192, 489+506 (brothers). Peisodorus: see below for Pausanias's account and, for others, Moretti 1957: no. 356.

the *pankration* until 200, 'after an unconscionable delay' (Philostr. *Gym.* 13). But boys contested the *diaulos, dolikhos* and pentathlon at the Pythian games from the start, and the *pankration* from 346; the athletic programmes for *paides* and *ageneioi* at Isthmia and Nemea were the same as for men, a pattern that became the norm (with some exceptions: for example, the youngest two age groups at the Theseia did not run the *dolikhos*, the *pankration* was often closed to *paides* and the race in armour always). The expectation was that local boys would win more than their share of these events.

These efforts testify to a high regard for the athletic victories of the young; they had the prestige and symbolic resonance of men's and, like them, prompted commissions for the best and best paid praise poets and sculptors. 'No one among the Greeks' (writes Bacchylides of his fellow Cean Liparion), 'won more victories in equal time – boy or man' (Bacch. 8.22–25); there is no intimation here that a boy's victories are to be discounted. The Clazomenians dedicated a statue for the boy runner Herodotus because he was their first Olympic champion, in 292 (Paus. 6.19.2); perhaps the boy wrestler Polyxenus, for whom the Zacynthians put up a statue, was their first too – we know of no other (*IVO* 224, first century CE or later). An inscription discovered only in 1987 accompanied a statue erected by the people of Cos for the previously unknown Heliodorus, who defeated four other boys in the wrestling at Olympia in the late first century BCE or shortly thereafter (Höghammar 1993:131 no. 21). The people of Stratoniceia in Caria buried Athenion, winner of the Pythian *diaulos* and *dolikhos* for boys (*SEG* 38 (1988) no. 1104, undated). When Antipater of Miletus won the Olympic boys' boxing in the early fourth century, the Syracusans paid his father to have him proclaimed as a citizen of theirs. Antipater, however, refused to go along, and his statue adds to his identification as a Milesian that it is the first dedicated by an Ionian at Olympia (Paus. 6.2.6). Oebotas's curse supposedly prevented Achaeans from winning at Olympia until he was appeased; the sign that the curse was broken was a victory by a boy, the runner Sostratus (Paus. 7.17.13–14). Epichares is one of the few Athenian *paides* or *ageneioi* to win at the great panhellenic games during the archaic and classical periods, first finisher in the Olympic *stadion* for boys in the early fourth century, garnering a 'wreath for the city' and respect as long as he lived (Dem. 58.66). Our source is his grandson, who makes the achievement a claim on the sympathy of a jury. Polynicus won the Olympic wrestling for boys in 448. When he was killed at the battle of Delium twenty-four years later, the community of Thespiae erected a monument for him and his fellows – and distinguished him as an *Olumpionikas* (*IG* 7 1888b). For boys too victory brought immortality of a kind, a kind the Greeks treasured; so Hellenistic sarcophagi show dead children as athletic victors or (we might better say 'including') Heracles – 'les héros de l'athlétisme, eux aussi, participaient à l'immortalité' (Lambrechts 1957:333, cf. Bonanno Aravantinou 1982:82).

Nevertheless, while Olympic glory exalted all those boys who attained it, we know less about them than about men: we can attach names and/or home cities to about a quarter (23.5 per cent) of the victors in men's events, to a little more than half as many (13.5 per cent) of boy champions (Crowther 1989:206). It is instructive in this context that Pausanias can find no record of boys' contests in his ancient Olympics, those held before Iphitus's renewal of the games, and says that the Eleans simply established them because they wanted to – that is, without legendary precedent or aetiological myth for legitimation (Paus. 5.8.9); so too that Philostratus offers a different date for the introduction of boys' events, 596 BCE, and another winner of the first *stadion* race for boys (Philostr. *Gym.* 13). Moreover, while the games of the classical *periodos* awarded all winners wreaths, boys, *ageneioi* and men alike, and statutory rewards from their home communities, such as the free meals and grants of money at Athens, were (as far as we know) distributed without regard to age class, other games made distinctions in the prizes they provided. At the Greater Panathenaea in the early fourth century, members of the winning group in each age class in pyrrhic dancing were rewarded equally – here they were representatives of their tribes – but individual boys in other events did less well than youths (*IG* 2² 2311 = S.G. Miller 1991: no. 84, about 380). Thus, the winner of the boys' *stadion* received fifty Panathenaic amphoras of olive oil, the second place finisher ten, while the *ageneios* who won this event got sixty and the runner-up twelve. The triumphant boy pancratiast won forty amphoras, his leading rival eight; the *ageneioi* who came in first and second perhaps fifty and ten (these lines are missing). In the other athletic contests, boy winners and those in second place got thirty and six amphoras respectively; for *ageneioi*, the relevant figures are forty and eight. Unfortunately, our only possible evidence on prizes for men, an epigram for the Corinthian pentathlete Nicolaidas, is much earlier, from the late sixth or early fifth century, and controversial in interpretation. According to one emendation of the text, he won sixty amphoras of olive oil – half again as many as an *ageneios* and double the prize for a boy. The fragmentary fifth-century inscription from Salamis provides awards for men who come in second (and probably for winners too) twice as large as those for runners-up among boys and *ageneioi* (*IG* i³ 1386, 450–440).[5]

Another kind of distinction operated at Coressia on the island of Ceos in the third century. Here adult victors in archery and throwing the javelin win weapons and money while boys compete for pieces of meat. It is likely that boy winners are alone in their age class in receiving meat from the festival sacrifice and that 'by giving these boys meat the city effectively promotes them to the citizen body before their time' (Osborne 1987:181). But the distinction in prizes also highlights the present reality, that the boys are not yet fighters themselves or competent to manage their own affairs, and so in no immediate need of the quivers, arrows, spears, helmets and cash the men take away. (Young Autolycus attends the drinking party to celebrate his Panathenaic victory, but he sits upright like any boy rather than reclining like the men: Xen. *Symp.* 1.8.) The place of *paides* on festival programmes might produce a like tension. At Olympia, their events were held on the day after the great sacrifice in the early fifth century (Bacch. 7.2–3), but had moved up to the afternoon of that day by Plutarch's time (Plut. *Mor.* 639a; Lee 1992). The Pythian festival, however, alternated boys' with men's competitions in each athletic event. This was convenient for officials, who could (for example) leave the track undisturbed while both sets of competitors ran the *stadion* or *diaulos*, and for those athletes who intended to enter more than one event and would be able to rest a little longer than at Olympia. It also integrated boys more fully into the men's programme while bringing attention to the differences in their capacities and at times their very challenges: boys threw a smaller discus in the pentathlon (Paus. 1.35.5) and perhaps ran a shorter *dolikhos*.[6]

---

[5] Nicolaidas: Simonides, *Anth. Pal.* 13.19 = 43 Page, *FGE*. For a different reading of the text, see E. Maróti 1990:133–4.

[6] Coressia: *SIG*³ 958.27–34. For such differences elsewhere, see Gauthier and Hatzopoulos 1993:100–1. Shorter *dolikhos*: three age classes – boys, youths and men – are to take part in the athletic exercises preparatory for war in Plato's ideal Cretan city. The youths race a distance two-thirds as long as men, the boys one-half: Pl. *Leg.* 8.833c.

PRECOCIOUS *PAIDES* AND ATHLETIC CAREERS

Thus, we should neglect neither the initiation rituals often detected to underlie Greek competition nor the reminder that boys can rarely compete on even terms with men; it is the latter belief which fuels the fuss when they do manage to rival them and makes compliments to that effect meaningful. We find the theme in Pindar – Alcimedon outwrestled four boys at Olympia, and did not betray his manliness, *anoreas* (Pind. *Ol.* 8.69) – and it lived on to add lustre to the reputation of P. Cornelius Ariston of Ephesus, who displayed a man's strength and valour in winning the Olympic *pankration* though he was only a boy. The Greeks did not expect boys to take on men successfully. 'What if Theodorus were praising you for your running', Socrates asks Theaetetus, 'and saying he'd never met any other so good among the young (*neoi*) – and then you raced a very fast man in his prime and were defeated? You wouldn't say his praise was untruthful, would you?' (Pl. *Tht.* 148c). Theaetetus need hardly respond. Who would expect a youth to win against odds like that? The same assumption informs Antigonus's response to the defeat of Demetrius by Ptolemy – he has conquered *ageneioi*, but must now fight with men (Plut. *Demetr.* 6.1) – and Rebekah's to Jacob. 'She addresses him as "My boy" because he is young compared to a fully grown man . . . Such a one is able to win the prizes boys compete for, but not yet capable of winning men's' (Philo, *De fuga et inventione* 40). Hence the temptation for men to try to pass as *paides* or *ageneioi*. One who yielded, the Samian Pythagoras, arrived at Olympia in 588 dressed in a purple robe and wearing his hair long, in order, it seems, to make his entry into the boys' boxing more credible. Ridiculed and rejected, he had the last laugh in the end, prevailing among the men. Pythagoras is sometimes seen as a boy who was pushed into the men's class because of his size, but the tradition that he was the first to box with technical skill is more compatible with his being a small man who was doubtful of his chances against his larger coevals (Papalas 1991:174).[7]

We are now in a better position to appreciate the detail Philostratus records about Aurelius Felix (mentioned above), that he won among the men when he was barely past boyhood. Athletes who did

[7] Ariston: *IVO* 225 = Moretti 1953: no. 64, 49 CE. Pythagoras: Diog. Laert. 8.47–8, Afric. p. 17 Rutgers (on Olympiad 48).

come out on top despite competing out of their age class were predictably proud, others impressed. Such feats include four victories in one day as a *pais* and *ageneios* at Nemea, victories as a *pais Puthikos* and *pais Isthmikos* on the same day at Thessalonica and as a *pais Ptolemaikos* and *ageneios* in the Egyptian Basileia, winning as *ageneios* and *anēr* on the same day at Ephesus, on successive days at Cyzicus, during the same celebration of the Isthmia and the Pythia at Thessalonica. Beaten at Olympia because he was too young, the pancratiast Artemidorus of Tralles was so much stronger at the Ionian games at Smyrna that he now overcame not only his Olympic opponents but *ageneioi* and grown men as well. Victory lists boast that a long distance runner from Tralles (?) and a pancratiast/ boxer from Sardis moved directly from the boys to the men without competing in intermediate classes. In a variation, a pancratiast is called the first and only athlete to fight as *pais*, *ageneios* and adult within a *trietia*, two years by our reckoning; he can have competed only a very short time as an *ageneios*.[8]

These athletes were exceptional. How common was it for boy winners who moved up to older age classes in the usual progression to achieve success in them as well? Not at all, says Aristotle (*Pol.* 8.1338b9–1339a10):

At the present time, some of the states thought to pay the greatest attention to children make them athletic at the expense of the form and development of their bodies. The Spartans have avoided this error, but make their boys like animals through laborious exercise, believing this contributes most to a man's bravery (*andreian*). However, as is often said, it is not right to manage the care of children with any one virtue in mind or this one in particular . . . Even the Spartans were superior to others only as long as they alone took to strenuous exercise. Now they are left behind in both warfare and athletics . . . Those who let boys exercise too hard turn them out untrained in what matters and make them like common labourers, to tell the truth. They are useful to the community for one task only, and even for this worse than others . . . Until puberty we should bring to bear lighter exercises,

---

[8] Nemea: a boxer and pancratiast from Alexandria, first century BCE, Afric. p. 81 Rutgers (on Olympiad 178), Euseb. *Chron.* I p. 212 Schoene. Thessalonica: *IG* 7 1856, undated. Basileia: Koenen 1977:4–5, 267 BCE. Ephesus: Michaud 1970:949 no. 2, undated. Cyzicus: a combat athlete from Smyrna in the second century CE, 'the first and only one' to do this, Petzl 1987:149–50 no. 661. Isthmia: a boxer from Sicyon in the third or early second century, *IG* 4 428 = Moretti 1953: no. 40, about 260–220. Pythia at Thessalonica: a pentathlete from Adramyttion, 252 CE, Robert 1938:53–4. Artemidorus: Paus. 6.14.2–3, 67 CE; other possible examples in S.G. Miller 1975b, Francis and Vickers 1981. Tralles: Moretti 1953: no. 78, after 180 CE. Sardis: Moretti 1953: no. 84, late second century CE. Pancratiast: Moretti 1953: no. 72, Aphrodisias, about 165 CE.

forbidding stringent diets and tough training, in order that nothing may stand in the way of growth. That training too hard can have this consequence is shown by the fact that only two or three athletes have won as both men and boys: when young men train, they lose their strength through severe exercise. But when they spend the three years after puberty otherwise, then they may turn to hard exercise and a strict diet for the next period of life (i.e., from about age seventeen).

As it turns out, however, we know of six or seven boys who had gone on to win again at Olympia by Aristotle's time, and of perhaps five more afterwards; there must have been more of whom we hear nothing, maybe as many as twenty (Crowther 1989:210). Young champions who went on to win at other games include the youngest of all, Damiscus, who later won the pentathlon at both Nemean and Isthmian games. To win as a boy, youth and man was unquestionably worth boasting about: Marcianus Rufus of Sinope crows that he is the sole winner in all three age classes at Nicomedeia, and another boxer is said to have been the only citizen of the Italian colony of Laodicea to match that feat. Such a record is one of the charms a matchmaker recommends in Gryllus (Herod. 1.50–3). But it was not all that unusual, at least in late antiquity, the period of most of our longer agonistic inscriptions. Aristotle has not let facts – facts he must have known from his work on Olympic and Pythian victors (Spoerri 1988) – get in the way of his theories of education.[9]

These impressionistic remarks reflect the nature of our evidence. Just so it is difficult to make much of the occasional indication that some athletes changed their competitive focus over time. We must recall to begin with that we generally have evidence of victories only; that these can represent nothing more than the relative performance of the winner and the field at a particular moment; that the absence of a victory does not necessarily stand for a defeat. Furthermore, my earlier observations on the programme for *paides* may be misleading if taken to imply that missing events can always be easily explained. Why (for example) did older and younger age classes run the *diaulos* at the Coan Asclepieia, or the *diaulos* and *dolikhos* at the Pythia in Thessalonica, when *ageneioi* didn't (Robert 1938:53–4)? And festivals without a *pankration* for boys admitted them as boxers, though 'the

---

[9] Marcianus Rufus: Moretti 1953: no. 64, second century CE. Boxer: *IGRom.* 3.1012 = Moretti 1953: no. 85, 221 CE; cf. the claim to have trained athletes of all age classes, Afric. p. 68 Rutgers (on Olympiad 118), 308 BCE. Late antiquity: e.g., Moretti 1953: nos. 50, 60, 61, 65, 67, 68, 75, *SEG* 37 (1987) no. 712, 41 (1991) no. 1407, all after 150.

Greeks quite accurately viewed boxing as the most physically punishing and damaging of all athletic contests' (Poliakoff 1987a:68). All the same, it is interesting to find instances of athletes who won in more disciplines as boys or youths than as men. This is consistent with the finding that events for young athletes, boys in particular, tended to be more limited to local fields and so less competitive. In one further case, a boy's multiple successes may have occurred at the end of his period as a *pais*, when he was nearing full growth and older than many of his rivals. But other career paths are on record too; M. Aurelius Heras won only in the *stadion* as both boy and youth and then, as an adult, races at all three distances and also the race in armour.[10]

Changes of event are also intriguing. Theogenes of Thasos is said to have won 1300 or even 1400 times in the early fifth century as a boxer and pancratiast – and once in the long race at Phthia in Thessaly, in order to win a prize for running 'in the homeland of the swiftest of heroes', Achilles (Paus. 6.11.5). This may say something about the speed of the other competitors at Phthia or about their prudence: it would take a fast man indeed to risk thwarting the best fighter in Greece. As Theogenes emulated Achilles, so perhaps Aurelius Septimius Irenaeus did Theogenes; also a boxer and pancratiast, he won foot-races as well. Here too, unfortunately, the evidence will not support generalizations about athletes' careers. Whereas Damatrius of Tegea followed his victory in the Olympic *stadion* for boys (208) with another in the long race for men, Parmeniscus of Corcyra won the *diaulos* and *dolikhos* at Oropus before becoming men's champion in the *stadion* at Olympia in 96. One athlete's victory list may illustrate the development of speed before strength, triumphing in the pentathlon as both boy and man, but winning individual foot-races when young and wrestling matches as an adult.[11]

---

[10] Absence of victory: illness or inability to travel might prevent a young athlete from ever gaining a victory as a boy at the Olympic or Pythian games, since he would normally be eligible only once. This must go a long way towards accounting for the fact that we know of only one boy *periodonikēs*, the wrestler Moschus of Colophon, winner at Olympia in 200. Athletes who won in more disciplines as boys or youths: e.g., *SIG*³ 1065 = Moretti 1953: no. 60, 1061 = Moretti 1953: no. 61, *IG* 7 415+417, *IG* 2² 3152+3153+*SEG* 38 (1988) no. 179. Nearing full growth: *IG* 4 428 = Moretti 1953: no. 40, about 260–220; Sève 1991:233 n. 8. Heras: *SEG* 37 (1987) no. 712, Chios, soon after 161 CE.

[11] Irenaeus: *IGRom.* 3.1012 = Moretti 1963: no. 85, 221 CE; other examples below in Chapter 5. One athlete: *SEG* 37 (1987) no. 298, Epidaurus, later third century.

THE QUICK AND THE OLD

How long could an athlete compete? Philostratus mourns the good old days, when athletes used to contest eight Olympiads or even nine (Philostr. *Gym.* 43). It is true that philosophers and physicians recommended lifelong exercise, and prescribed special regimes for the elderly (Crowther 1990a). In *Laws*, Plato stipulates that the young men (*neoi*) of his ideal city should build gymnasia for themselves and their elders – these last specially catered for with hot baths (Pl. *Leg.* 6.761cd, cf. Plut. *Mor.* 789f); Aristotle prefers separate establishments for young and old (Arist. *Pol.* 8.1331a36, *Rh.* 2.1390b9). Some followed this advice: Socrates himself supposedly practised wrestling with Alcibiades (and disappointed his young admirer with his sexual continence) when he was in his late thirties (Pl. *Symp.* 217bc); Lycon, a philosopher of the third century, was very well trained, fit in his body and altogether athletic, with battered ears, skin covered with oil and all, though we are not told that he maintained his fitness right up to his death at seventy-four (Diog. Laert. 5.67). Old men, *gerontes*, are among the beneficiaries of a gymnasiarch's generosity at Magnesia near Mt. Sipylus; these are probably men over thirty, like the *presbuteroi*, 'elders', we hear of in Hellenistic gymnasia. Some cities did indeed have separate places for older men to work out – Hellenistic Samos, perhaps fourth-century Athens. Macedon's oldest soldiers are (so Plutarch says) real 'athletes of war' (Plut. *Eum.* 16.4.); if the metaphor, echoing Polybius, is not dead, it intimates what Plutarch thought plausible – the men are all at least sixty, some seventy and up (cf. Polyb. 1.6.6, 1.59.12, 2.20.9). On the other hand, older men with athletic pretensions might appear ridiculous and many, like Lycon in Xenophon's *Symposium*, probably preferred to quit (Xen. *Symp.* 2.3–4). It was older men who made up the majority of the victims in the massacre at Corinth in 392: they were in the agora, while younger men, *hoi neoteroi*, remained quietly in a gymnasium (Xen. *Hell.* 4.4.4, cf. Plut. *Nic.* 12.1).[12]

Anyway, exercise is not competition. Philostratus exaggerates. Milon of Croton won six (conceivably seven) times at Olympia, once as a boy (Maddoli 1992); the Spartan Hipposthenes won the first wrestling competition for boys and then, after an interval, five

---

[12] Magnesia: *TAM* 5.2 1367, Imperial period. *Presbuteroi*: Blümel 1985:40 no. 23 (Iasus), Gauthier and Hatzopoulos 1993:163 n. 4 (Amphipolis). Samos: Robert 1935:476–7 no. 2, *gerontikēi palaistrai*. Athens: Antiphanes fr. 298 KA = Poll. 2.13 mentions *geronteiai palaistrai*, quite without context. Ridiculous: Pl. *Resp.* 5.452ab, *Tht.* 162bc, Xen. *Symp.* 2.17–20, Theophr. *Char.* 27.4, Plut. *Luc.* 38.4.

Olympics in a row as a man. Their careers spanned say twenty-five years, as must Theogenes' have done if he really won 1300 (*SIG*³ 64a) or even 1400 (Paus. 6.11.5) crowns and was unbeaten in boxing for twenty-two years. These extraordinary archaic and early classical combat athletes may therefore have competed until their early forties; danger and envy induced M. Aurelius Asclepiades to retire from the *pankration* at twenty-five, only to return (seemingly under duress) and win again many years later, when he was perhaps going on forty. An Alexandrian boxer was less fortunate despite his name – Agathos Daimon, 'good luck'. After winning in the Nemean games, he died at thirty-five trying to repeat the feat at Olympia. Few runners would persevere so long; no known career outlasts that of Leonidas of Rhodes, triple winner in four successive Olympics from 164, though an Argive runner of the *diaulos* matched it. ('I can't argue with Protagoras', Socrates tells Callias. 'It's as if you asked me to keep up with Crison of Himera in his prime, or with one of the long distance runners or the professional couriers. I'd like to, but I can't'; Pl. *Prt.* 335e.) Athletes who did go on would eventually risk humiliation (cf. Xen. *Hell.* 6.3.16); even the most gifted athletes are likely to slacken their regime and fall behind their rivals (Xen. *Mem.* 3.5.13, cf. 1.2.24). Yet the competitive drive and desire for the benefits of success would often outlast athletic prowess. Some were no doubt content merely to watch younger men train or perhaps to pace them (Plut. *Mor.* 593d); some were less resigned – Cicero rather unsympathetically tells a sad story about Milon, long past his prime, bewailing his lost strength while others exercise, and the pancratiast Timanthes is said to have burned himself alive when his strength slackened (Cic. *Sen.* 9.27; Paus. 6.8.4). Athletes might also choose to compete vicariously, like Melesias, Nemean wrestling champion as youth and man and later a renowned trainer (Pind. *Ol.* 8.54–9 with Schol.). The feisty Isidorus was probably unique, a regular habitué of the palaestra, now ninety-one – though not looking a day over sixty – and still sufficiently imbued with the drive to excel to take on younger men in eating and drinking bouts. For the wealthiest athletes, however, there was an alternative: equestrian competition.[13]

As so often, Homer may supply a model, the Gerenian horseman

[13] Early forties: cf. the pancratiast Ephoudion, 'old and grey' (Ar. *Vesp.* 1190–4, 1381–7). Asclepiades: *IG* 14 1102 = Moretti 1953: no. 79, about 200 CE. Agathos Daimon: *SEG* 22 (1967) no. 354, Imperial period. About to take on Odysseus in the boxing match discussed above in Chapter 3, Irus asks him, 'How can you fight a younger man?' (Hom. *Od.* 18.31).

Nestor. He was once a great athlete, winner of four contests in the funeral games for Amarynceus; 'there was no man like me then' (*Il.* 23.629–37). Now his old age presses hard upon him and his competitive days are over. Yet he can still help his son Antilochus, providing ample and prescient advice on the tactics for charioteers at Patroclus's games, and at the end of the chariot race Achilles recognizes the strength of his competitive spirit and the present manner of its expression by a special prize (*Il.* 23.615–23; Kyle 1984a:4–5). Historical athletes who moved from running or combat sports to equestrian competition on their own behalf include a citizen of Thebes, Melissus, whose chariot triumphs at Isthmia and Nemea follow (according to the most convincing reading of two obscure poems by Pindar) those in the *pankration* at local festivals; the Olympic *stadion* champion of 408, Eubotas of Cyrene (Xen. *Hell.* 1.2.1), pre-eminent forty years on in the four-horse chariot race as well (Paus. 6.8.3, 364); Sosibius, Callimachus's patron, both runner and wrestler before he owned chariot champions (Callim. fr. 384, 384a Pfeiffer); the Sicyonian leader Aratus, a successful pentathlete in his youth and then a chariot winner at Olympia (Plut. *Arat.* 3.1–2, Paus. 6.12.6); perhaps Alcibiades and (?) Sostratus. The so-called Damonon stele, a long inscription from Sparta detailing the athletic and equestrian prowess of a father and son, offers the best evidence for this trajectory. In his youth, Damonon was a runner, often the winner among the *paides* at Sparta. He then went on to drive his own horses to other local victories, while his son Enymacratidas followed – rapidly – in his footsteps as a victorious runner as both boy and man. We are left to imagine that Enymacratidas will one day emulate his father's equestrian excellence too, perhaps when he inherits his share of the family's stables and the wealth to maintain them.[14]

These examples are instructive. But it is probably better to think of the pattern in a broader context, in class terms: equestrian competition gave the Greek elite access to honour and rewards after

---

Isidorus: Arr. fr. 113 Domingo-Forasté, cf. Plut. *Mar.* 34.3–4 (a hostile account of the Roman general Marius), *Pomp.* 64.1 (on Pompey).

[14] Melissus: Pind. *Isthm.* 3 and 4; Privitera 1978–9, cf. Willcock 1995:72. Alcibiades: associated with wrestling in the story recounted above and in other sources ([Pl.] *Alc.* 1 106e, Plut. *Alc.* 2.2, 4.4. Sostratus: Kyle 1987:225, P108. If Lycinus, winner of the Olympic race in armour in 448, were the Spartan of the same name whose four-horse team is sometimes thought to have triumphed in 432 (Moretti 1957: no. 324), we would have another example, but as the ethnicity of the earlier winner is unknown and the later victory should probably be dated to 384 or sometime after, this is improbable. Damonon: *IG* 5.1 213, 450–431 or (more likely) early fourth century; Hodkinson forthcoming.

age and its concomitants denied them to most athletes. Of course young men too might race horses. (The *Iliad*'s Antilochus is an athlete as well as a charioteer.) The competitions called *apobatēs* and *heniokhos ekbibazōn* involved some combination of dismounting from, running alongside, and entering a moving chariot; they were probably too demanding for anyone else. And what horseman could be more enthusiastic than young Pheidippides in Aristophanes' *Clouds*? In general, however, we hear of older men as equestrian competitors – successful ones at least. (Parents of adolescents might fear that their inexperience would lead them into danger; Pl. *Lys.* 208a, cf. *Grg.* 516e.) When Lichas entered his Spartan team under the colours of the Thebans in 420, and was then struck by the stewards as he garlanded his victorious charioteer, he was an old man (*andra geronta*) – perhaps, if Xenophon is using the term quasi-technically, a member of the *gerousia*, and so over sixty (Xen. *Hell.* 3.2.21; Cartledge 1984:99). Pindar's poem for Psaumis of Camarina, winner of the Olympic mule-car race in about 460, refers to his old age (Pind. *Ol.* 5.22). In what is probably a companion piece for the same occasion, the poet recalls an anecdote about Erginus, first among the Argonauts in a legendary race in armour on Lemnos (Pind. *Ol.* 4.19–27). The Lemnian women jeered at his grey hair. 'Grey hair often grows on young men too, and belies their real age', Erginus retorted – likely a compliment to the vigour revealed by Psaumis's victory. Table 5 identifies the better attested winners of equestrian events at the Olympic (O), Pythian (P), Nemean (N), Isthmian (I) and Panathenaic (Pan) festivals down to about 100 BCE, along with the date of their first known victory, their birthdate, and their approximate age when that victory was won. The frequent resort to question marks will establish the surest conclusion, that it is very insecure in detail. But the data are consistent enough to seem reliable, all the more since dates of birth and victory (however uncertain they may be) are arrived at independently.[15]

We must not forget that these ages are skewed upward, referring

---

[15] Demanding: the addressee of Demosthenes' *Erotic Essay*, Dem. 61, is young enough to be the focus of respectable homoerotic attention and Phocus, another participant in the *apobatēs* (in the 320s), is termed *neaniskos* and *meirakion* (Plut. *Phoc.* 20.1–2; cf. Xen. *Eq. Mag.* 1.17). Pheidippides: cf. *SEG* 39 (1989) no. 1418, Lycaonia, second century CE and *P Oxy.* 664, a fragment of a dialogue of Hellenistic date in which Thrasybulus, a youth (*meirakion*) in love with the daughter of the sixth-century Athenian tyrant Peisistratus, is described as surpassing everyone in horse-breeding, hunting and other ways of spending money (Col. 1.18–19, 26).

Table 5. *Ages of equestrian victors*

Victor	Date, Event, Festival	Birth date	Age	Notes
Cleisthenes (Sicyon)	582,4,P	?	35+?	tyrant from (?) 595
Callias (Athens)	before 564,4+h,P	?shortly before 590	25?	
Miltiades (Athens)	?560/?548,4,O	before 585	25+?/35+?	
Cimon (Athens)	536,4,O	?585	50?	
Peisistratus (Athens)	532,4,O	?605–600	65+	proclaimed in place of the actual victor, Cimon
Damaratus (Sparta)	?504,4,O	about 550	45?	
Xenocrates (Acragas)	490,4,P	about 530	40+?	son a young man
Gelon (Gela)	488,4,O	about 530	40+	
Megacles (Athens)	486,2 or 4,P	?530–510	25–45	
Hieron (Syracuse)	478,h,P	?about 530	50+	younger brother of Gelon
Theron (Acragas)	476,4,O	about 530	50+	tyrant from 488
Chromius (Aetna)	?476,4,N	?	35+?	warrior as young man, 492
Arcesilaus (Sparta)	448,4,O	?510–500	50+?	son a *gerōn* in 420
Megacles (Athens)	436,4,O	about 480	50+	
Alcibiades (Athens)	421–416,4,P,N,Pan	before 451	30	councillor, 422/1. One or all of his victories preceded that at Olympia in 416
Lichas (Sparta)	420,4,O	?480–470	50+	*gerōn*. Victory proclaimed in name of the Thebans
Teisias (Athens)	416,4,O	?	30+	general, 417/6. Victory proclaimed in name of Alcibiades
Archelaus (Macedon)	?408,4,P	?450–445	35+?	
Timon (Elis)	?400,4,O	?	40+?	son won horse race, around 400
Chabrias (Athens)	374,4,P	before 420	45+	
Eubotas (Cyrene)	364,4,O	before 425	60+	
Philip II (Macedon)	356,h,O	383 or 382	26 or 27	
Timarchus (Athens)	?352,2,O	before 400	45+?	
Phocus (Athens)	320s, *apobatēs*, Pan*	?340s	under 25	*meirakion, neaniskos*
Demades (Athens)	?328,?,O	before 380	50+?	
Demetrius (Athens)	?320,2 or 4,Pan	before 355	35+?	
Ptolemy I Soter (Egypt)	310,2f,P	about 367	55+	
Glaucon (Athens)	?272,4,O		30+	hoplite general, 282/1
Aratus (Sicyon)	?232,4,O	271	35+	

Table 5. *contd*

Victor	Date, Event, Festival	Birth date	Age	Notes
Polycrates (Argos)	?198,4,Pan	?	40+	three daughters also won
Ptolemy V (Egypt)	?182,4 *diaulos*,Pan	210	28?	
Micion (Athens)	182,4 sprint,Pan	about 245?	60+?	
Mnesitheus (Athens)	?178,4f sprint,Pan*	after 201	under 23?	
Attalus (Pergamum)	?178,2,Pan	220	42?	
Eumenes II (Pergamum)	?178,4,Pan	before 220	40+?	
Philetaerus (Pergamum)	?178,4f,Pan	220–215	35+?	
Athenaeus (Pergamum)	?178,h,Pan	before 215	35+?	
Socrates (Athens)	170,pair sprint,Pan*	195	25	
Hagnias (Athens)	170,pair *diaulos*,Pan*	195	25	
Theophilus (Athens)	170,H *diaulos*,Pan*	before 200?	30+?	
Ophelas (Athens)	170,H sprint,Pan*	about 200	30?	
Philocrates (Athens)	170,2 sprint,Pan*	soon after 195?	under 25	
Eucles (Athens)	166,4w,Pan*	after 200	under 35	
Seleucus (Athens)	162,pair *diaulos*, Pan*	after 201	under 40?	
Ptolemy VI (Egypt)	162,2w,Pan*	186 or 184	22 or 24	
Ptolemy VI (Egypt)	?158,hf,Pan	186 or 184	26 or 28?	
Alexander Balas (Syria)	?150 or 146,4,Pan	about 173	23 or 27?	

KEY:
4=*tethrippon* 2=*synoris* h=*keles* f=foal(s) sprint=*akampion*
pair=*zeugos* H=*hippos* w=war chariot
*competition open to Athenian citizens only

as they do to known victories instead of first entries. Even at that, some younger men appear on the list: Philip II, the Athenian *hippeis* who won at the Panathenaea in the 170s, Alexander Balas, Ptolemy VI. Still, older winners predominate. One factor must be the expense of equestrian competition, beyond the reach of sons of any but the most indulgent fathers until they came into control of their family's wealth (but of course not beyond the reach of reigning monarchs like Philip and the Ptolemies). Few games offered prizes as munificent as those at the Panathenaea, so athletic success alone would rarely be sufficient to allow a man of moderate means to take up horse-racing. A second factor is the pattern traced above, of athletes moving on to horse-racing as they aged. This is not to assume that all or any of the men on this list had previously run or fought in festival competition. But the very fact that some young men could and did so compete influenced others who were unable or unwilling to match them to delay their entry into equestrian events. Otherwise, the contrast between the athlete's active struggle for distinction and its indirect pursuit by horse owners and breeders who generally relied on others to ride and drive might be too stark. Equestrian victors would risk being regarded not just as gifted men who surpassed others in wealth but as physically inferior. Such considerations need not concern Mnesitheus and his fellow *hippeis*, who made up a distinct subset of victors at the Panathenaea: those marked with an asterisk competed only against other Athenians, used their own cavalry horses and equipment – cheaper than special racing stock and chariots – and likely rode and drove for themselves. (Mnesitheus was fit enough to win one of the races which involved running as well as riding too.) Nor would they sway young men in a hurry like Alcibiades. It provokes thought to find that his hippic successes began when he was about thirty, and so eligible for Athens's most important elective office, as general. He was still fit (see Plut. *Alc.* 23.5). Yet he was then just old enough, perhaps, to legitimately avoid the competition with athletes 'of lowly birth, from small towns, poorly educated' which his son disdained (Isoc. 16.33–4), and still be a success on the racecourse earlier than most – part of his appeal to younger Athenians (cf. Thuc. 6.12–13).[16]

ON THE TRACK OF WOMEN'S SPORT

If we begin our discussion of gender with two pieces of fiction, it is partly to indicate how little we can establish as fact. When Theseus first comes to Athens, Apollo's sanctuary, the Delphinium, is still unfinished (Paus. 1.19.1). He wears a long tunic and neatly braided hair, and the roofers mockingly hail him as a marriageable girl. Catcalls and construction seem to go back a long way; but if men on the top of a building can't get their comeuppance, who can? Theseus responds by hurling a brace of nearby oxen higher than the roof: no one can say he throws like a girl. How wrong those roofers are; Theseus is not only a he-man and a hero but a great athlete, credited

---

[16] Ptolemy VI: if Tracy and Habicht (1991:221) are right to restore Ptolemy's name, rather adventurously, at *IG* 2² 2314.56, his first victory was even earlier, in (?) 182, when he was still an infant. But no parallel comes to mind. Timon's son Aegyptus need not have been a minor, let alone an infant, when his horse won at Olympia (Paus. 6.2.8); cf. above, Chapter 3.

with the development of wrestling technique – a tradition known to Pausanias himself (1.39.3) – and the *pankration*. The corollary, of course, is that we cannot expect such feats of strength and athleticism from a woman. Indeed, for an athlete to dream that he has milk in his breasts or is actually nursing a child is a bad omen, since women's bodies are weaker (Artem. 1.16, 1.50, 5.45). 'The male is larger and stronger than the female, and the extremities of his body are stronger, sleeker, better conditioned and better in respect to everything worth doing' ([Arist.] *Phgn.* 2.806b33). Now, Pausanias (like Artemidorus and, very likely, the author of *Physiognomics*) is a late writer, from the second century of our era. But the assumption that exercise and the abilities associated with it characterize males already informs Aristophanes' *Thesmophoriazusae* (411), much taken up as it is with transvestism and other travesties of gender. When Euripides' in-law asks Agathon, dressed in drag, 'What's an oil flask doing with a breast band? . . . What partnership can there be between a mirror and a sword?', he adduces pairs of incongruous objects (Ar. *Thesm.* 139–40). The flask, *lekuthos*, is one of the accessories of the athletic lifestyle, the oil used to prepare the body for exercise or to anoint it afterwards. Another accessory, the strigil, scrapes it off. The in-law refers to this too later in the play, when it is he who seeks to pass as a woman: it is used, he says, by women . . . but illicitly, as a burglar's tool (Ar. *Thesm.* 556–7). Its proper place, it seems, is in a man's hands, women's is outside the palaestra and gymnasium.[17]

Our second story is found among the works of Pausanias's contemporary Lucian, though its authorship is disputed. A young man recalls an encounter with a woman with the unusual name Palaestra – a training session in which the technical terminology of wrestling doubles for vigorous and imaginative sexual activity. Once again the metaphor has a long history, reaching back to Old Comedy. What adds to its effect here is the author's play with gender roles. Palaestra maintains the pretence that she is offering tactical advice even during intercourse, using the masculine pronoun *autos*, 'he', throughout, though in fact it is she who is the object of her young pupil's grapplings and thrusts. This linguistic deadpan

---

[17] Women outside: See, e.g., Ar. fr. 214 KA, *Dissoi Logoi* 2.3 Robinson, Pl. *Resp.* 5.452ab. The remarkable respect the Greek warriors pay to Polyxena's corpse – they throw leaves on it as if she were a victor in the games (Eur. *Hec.* 573–4) – brings out the exceptional nature of her courage, as unexpected in a young girl as athletic success.

depends on the titillation of a woman playing an athlete's role, as the opponent of a man in particular.[18]

All this, of course, is representation. What really happened? One answer is that, despite Aristophanes, Greeks sometimes painted women with strigils on pots and buried them with strigils in graves. Representation was itself multifarious. But we need not stop there; some access to women's activities is available. As before, we want to distinguish exercise and competition. First, then, did Greek women compete against each other? And did they compete with men?[19]

Olympia, main stage for men's athletics, also yields our best evidence for competition among women. Our sole literary source is Pausanias (5.16.2–4; Scanlon 1984b):

> Every fourth year the Sixteen Women weave a robe for Hera. These also hold a competition called the Heraea, which consists of foot-races for unmarried girls (*parthenois*). Not all who compete are of the same age; the youngest run first, then the next oldest, and finally the oldest girls of all. They run as follows: their hair is let down, a tunic (*khitōn*) reaches to a little above the knee, and their right shoulder is bare to the breast. The Olympic stadium is reserved for their competition too, but the track is shortened by about one-sixth for the girls. The winners receive crowns of olive leaves and a portion of the cow sacrificed to Hera. They may also dedicate inscribed likenesses of themselves. Those who work under the Sixteen Women who hold the competition are, like them, married women. The competition is traced back to ancient times; they say that Hippodameia was grateful to Hera for her marriage with Pelops, and so assembled the Sixteen Women and inaugurated the Heraea with them.

In the absence of other testimony from Olympia, conclusions on the antiquity, function and perception of these foot-races for girls must await a survey of women's athletics in other parts of Greece. We may start with Athens, for most subjects our best documented community. Claude Bérard has urged that Attic vases showing women at or after exercise, generally referred to real life elsewhere (Sparta) or myth, may be based on the activities of some women at Athens itself (Bérard 1986, cf. 1989:92–4). The vases subtly differentiate the women's setting from the gymnasium – they are perhaps in a private home – and concentrate on the paraphernalia of exercise (including strigils) and its concomitants rather than competition because (according to Bérard) female athletics had a different

---

[18] Lucian: *Asin.* 8–11; Poliakoff 1982:101–27. Old Comedy: Ar. *Ach.* 271–5, *Eccl.* 964–5, *Pax* 894–6b.

[19] Strigils: see, e.g., Kotera-Feyer 1993:6, 95 and cf. Massa-Pairault 1991.

ethos than men's, of health and beauty rather than rivalry. In the eyes of another scholar, a large Athenian water jug dated to 440–430 looks like a prize for pyrrhic dancing among *hetairai* (Liventhal 1985); acrobatic and warlike, such dances pitted tribal teams of boys, youths and men against each other at the Panathenaea.[20]

Still other pots, small bowls now called *krateriskoi*, show girls, clothed and naked, generally in animated motion. Found mainly at Brauron on the east coast of Attica, but also at other sites sacred to Artemis, these vases (from about 510 to 420) appear to be precious supplements to our meagre and contradictory literary sources on the *arkteia*, a ritual complex involving young girls, *arktoi*, associated with bears, as well as firm evidence for their athletic competitions in a cult context: running races under the supervision of older girls or women. However, despite and due to a flurry of publications, much remains obscure. Were the *arktoi* from five to nine years old (as suggested by late sources and some readings of the iconography) or somewhat older, say ten to fourteen (Ar. *Lys.* 641–7 and other readings of the iconography)? Disagreement on the relevance of Plato's Cretan city, which is to hold races (the *stadion, diaulos, ephippos* and long race) for girls, naked up until age thirteen and modestly attired until eighteen and (at the oldest) twenty, compounds the uncertainty as to age and costume (Pl. *Leg.* 8.833cd; Perlman 1983). Did all daughters of Athenian citizens take part? If so, did all go to Brauron, or might their service as *arktoi* take place in other Attic sanctuaries of Artemis as well? If not, were the 'bears' an elite few or representatives of their tribes? Though most students accept that the *arkteia* was a prenuptial rite of initiation, the possibility that the girls were so young dissuades others. Scanlon even argues that the vases do not depict races at all, but rather a chase. 'The analogy is to the hunt, not to the agonistic battle which is more suited to the imagery of male competition' (Scanlon 1990:106); the connection of such a rite with one of Artemis's main spheres of influence is seductive. But we are unlikely to reach consensus until all the pottery, as yet only partially published, is available, and even then that may be too much to ask. Hamilton, after all, casts doubt on the very link of *krateriskoi* and *arkteia* from which other recent investigations begin. In such

---

[20] Women's athletics: see especially Arrigoni 1985 and, for a survey and a bibliography of recent historical research on gender, women and sport, Vertinsky 1994a, 1994b.

circumstances, parallels with the Heraea must be sought in other communities.[21]

Our ignorance of the nature and context of their role (an entertainment, a ritual, a competition?) forces us to pass over the women who assist in the 'bull leaping' shown on frescoes from Minoan Crete. Elsewhere, an inscription from Chios records the dedication of a statue to Leto by the parents of a girl who had won in a contest (not necessarily athletic) we cannot identify. L. Castricius Regulus of Corinth introduced poetry contests and an unspecified competition for girls, *virginum certamen*, at the Isthmian games in 23 CE. John Malalas, a Byzantine chronicler of limited reliability, says that Antioch bought the Olympic festival from the Pisatans of Elis for 360 years in the early third century CE, and goes on to allege that well-born young girls competed there, wrestling in linen shorts or trousers, running, reciting tragedies and Greek hymns (Jo. Mal. *Chron.* 12.10.288–9); the winners became priestesses and vowed to remain chaste until they died. Her husband proudly honoured Seia Spes, winner of the *stadion* for daughters of magistrates at Naples, as her brother did Nicegora, who outran other *parthenoi* at Patras sometime in late antiquity. Meagre gleanings indeed, but a fuller harvest is at hand for Sparta (Scanlon 1988c).[22]

There, unlike other *poleis*, girls as well as boys underwent a community-organized and -administered course of socialization, which stressed physical fitness and group activities. These included competitions. 'Lycurgus insisted on physical training for females no less than for the male sex; moreover, he instituted races and tests of strength for women as for men, in the belief that if both parents are strong their children too will be stronger.' Lycurgus was a legendary lawgiver; but the competitions themselves are widely attested, from Euripides' *Andromache* in the 420s – Peleus castigates Spartan women who share the running tracks and wrestling schools with young men – to Theocritus, who has Helen's companions run by the Eurotas oiled down like men (Theocr. 18.22–5), to Hesychius five hundred years later. Plutarch adds discus and javelin to Lycurgus's programme and the Augustan love poet Propertius envisages naked girls working

---

[21] *Arkteia*: see most recently Kahil 1988, Sourvinou-Inwood 1988 and 1990, Dowden 1989:9–47, Hamilton 1989, Scanlon 1990, Lonsdale 1993:171–93, Demand 1994:7–14.

[22] Women: but see Marinatos 1989. Chios: *SEG* 35 (1985) no. 933, third century. Regulus: Kent 1966:70–3 no. 153, restored. Seia Spes: *SEG* 14 (1957) no. 602, 154 CE. Nicegora: Schol. Paus. 5.16.2 = vol. 3 p. 221 Spiro.

out in the presence of male wrestlers, playing ball, rolling hoops, throwing the discus, running on Mt Taygetus with their fathers' hounds (3.14.1–20). The poet's Spartan girl stands dust-spattered at the end of the stadium, wounded in the *pankration*, or boxes (with Roman equipment, mind you) – like the warlike Amazons with breasts on view, or Helen, shamelessly bearing arms and baring breasts before her brothers (cf. Ov. *Her.* 16.149–52). Another exercise, *bibasis*, involved leaping to bring the heels up to the buttocks; both girls and boys did this in competition – an epigram celebrates a girl who had once jumped 1000 times, the most ever (Poll. 4.102).[23]

Some of these authors are more reliable than others; Propertius, for one, seems to need a cold dip in the Eurotas as much as any Spartan athlete. And the tradition fed on itself. Fortunately, the content of the literary sources is in general confirmed by independent evidence. First, a series of unusual bronze statuettes of young girls, most naked, some wearing the *perizoma*, often found in Laconia and likely the product of local workshops in the sixth and fifth centuries (or of craftsmen influenced by them). These probably do not depict *hetairai* (despite the fact that many were attached to mirrors as handles or supports) or dancers, but athletes. We have in addition epigraphical evidence, a dedication for Livia, winner in the *diaulos*. We are therefore inclined to accept the historicity of the nearest match to the Heraea, mentioned by Pausanias himself, a foot-race for eleven Dionysiades, 'daughters of Dionysus', a custom said to have come from Delphi (perhaps, that is to say, validated by an oracle; Paus. 3.13.7, cf. Hsch. δ 1888). Scanlon points out 'striking formal and structural parallels with the Heraea at Olympia which characterize both as prenuptial rites' (Scanlon 1988:201); these include the link with Dionysus, since the Sixteen Women also looked after a chorus for Physcoa, a local lover and devotee of the god (Paus. 5.16.6). The restriction of competition to unmarried girls seems indeed to be the rule everywhere we have evidence. The sole exception, Seia Spes, bears a name more Roman than Greek and may besides have won at Naples before she married. Yet we should not elide local variation too eagerly. However important Dionysus may be for Spartan and Elean women, he is not ubiquitous in this

---

[23] Lycurgus: Xen. *Lac.* 1.4, cf. Plut. *Lyc.* 14.2, *Mor.* 227d, Philostr. *Gym.* 27 and, for the motive, Critias DK 88B32. Peleus: Eur. *Andr.* 595–602, cf. *Dissoi Logoi* 2.9, 25 Robinson, Pl. *Leg.* 7.805e–806a. Hesychius: ε 2823; his enigmatic entry s.v. *triolax*, a girls' race of three lengths (?), may also refer to Sparta.

context; when similar rites take place for different gods, should we privilege congruence or contrast? Moreover, it is only at Sparta where girls seem to have performed in front of young men. Their 'races and tests of strength' were not just prenuptial but meant to bring marriage on, to pique potential husbands' interest, and they were as focused on the end of marriage, childbirth, as on marriage itself. We might call them preparturitive. Arrigoni opposes ritual athletics at Sparta, a transition rite leading to marriage, in which girls competed among themselves, to political athletics, with childbirth in mind, before men (Arrigoni 1985:74–6). So tidy a scheme imposes more order than our evidence deserves, but captures a tension between cult tradition and community need which is an outcome of Sparta's distinctive social and demographic regime. Such an appeal to specificities of place must lead us back to Olympia: the most meaningful parallel with the Heraea may be none other than the men's games there.[24]

The priority of the contests is uncertain. Offerings associated with Zeus may go back to the early tenth century, sometime before the first archaeological traces of the cult of Hera (Mallwitz 1988:89–99); however, cult, festival and competitions are only related phenomena, not synonymous. Pausanias says the Heraea's races are ancient, and the link with Hippodameia may express contemporaneity with Pelops's games for men. But Pausanias also knows a variant version, that the Sixteen Women go back only to a process of peacemaking between Pisa and Elis in the 580s – when each represented one of the cities of Elis – with their responsibility for the foot-races a little later (Paus. 5.16.5–6, 6.22.3–4). In this chronology, the Heraea (at least in the form Pausanias knows it) is younger than the Olympic festival, but of an age with the other games of the classical circuit and the Panathenaea, and like them (perhaps) a product of the reordering of pre-existent cult. Such a date is a few years after the construction of the first temple to Hera at Olympia and a few years before the manufacture of a bronze figurine of a female runner dressed very much like the girls Pausanias describes. Was it, too, panhellenic? This may be the implication of another titbit in Pausanias: a winner at the first Heraea (Hippodameia's) was Chloris, a daughter of Amphion of Thebes (Paus. 5.16.4). This would separate

---

[24] Propertius: he may in fact be satirizing contemporary debates on the links between Sparta and Rome; Kennell 1995:81. Livia: *SEG* 11 (1954) no. 830, second century CE.

Plate 6. Female runner dressed as for the Heraea. Bronze statuette, probably from
a Laconian workshop, about 560.

off the Heraea from festivals at Sparta and Athens, but bring it into
closer contact with the Olympics. Whatever the case, there is no
mistaking other similarities between the festivals at Olympia. The
limitation of the Heraea to foot-races recalls the first Olympiads; the
olive wreath, the sacrificial portion, the right to an image, the men's
festival in its maturity. The use of the stadium, and especially the
shortening of the race by one-sixth (from six to five hundred feet)
warrants further thought. It may well be that the discrepancy arises

from the use of the shorter foot of the Temple of Hera as the basis of measurement (Romano 1983:12–14). But the use of a shorter distance must invite comparisons with the boys and men who ran in the same stadium; these would inevitably show up female shortcomings (cf. des Bouvrie 1995:68). Yet another parallel may be apposite here, this time with modern sport.[25]

Baron Pierre de Coubertin long opposed women's participation in public competitions like his reinvented modern Olympics. 'At the Olympic Games', he said, 'their primary role should, as in the ancient tournaments [!], be to crown the (male) victors with laurels' (quoted in Simri 1980:189). Women did not contest track and field events until the Amsterdam games of 1928, after de Coubertin's retirement as president of the International Olympic Committee. Their longest run was 800 m. That race ended with a world record and several finishers sprawled on the track, a sight that so upset traditionalists that the IOC voted to drop women's track and field from the 1932 games, and only relented in the face of threats of a boycott of men's events. But long races were abandoned, not to return until 1960 at Rome. Even then, a French commentator could call on his compatriots to 'take account of the natural suppleness and fragility of the feminine organism. It is necessary' (he went on) 'to respect the role of the future *maman* so that sports do not become the occasion for suppressing or damaging this role' (Y. Brossard, *Sport* (Paris 1961) 103, as quoted in Guttmann 1991:191). So much for prenuptial races! Today, of course, women run races as long as the marathon, just like men though slower. But only men race-walk as far as 50 km, and the road race for male cyclists is more than twice as long as women's. Moreover, while men swim 1500 m, the longest women's race in the pool is 800 m. And neither women nor men swim very long distances – distances at which women, with their greater resources of body fat and ability to metabolize it, would likely excel (Dyer 1982:74–5). This has every appearance of a discourse (conscious or not) of male supremacy, informed by the allocation of the virtue of endurance or toughness to men. Women are excluded on the grounds of their perceived weakness, then admitted to contests at which they (predictably) do less well than men. Neither sex competes in those events in which women's

---

[25] Figurine: London, British Museum inv. 208; Arrigoni 1985:157 and plate 3. Heraea and Olympia: cf. Angeli Bernardini 1986–7:20–1, 1988:166–70, stressing ritual resemblances in particular.

physiology provides a natural advantage (or at any rate one long established culturally). The Heraea too might figure in such a discourse. I should add that this reading, far from requiring us to reject the popular hypothesis that the Heraea was initiatory in function, gains support from it. Nancy Serwint calls attention to the resemblance of the runner's dress and the *eksomis*, often worn by men engaging in vigorous activity, including *apobatai* (Serwint 1993). Mimicry of the attributes of the opposite sex is regular in rites of initiation; at the Heraea, it would bring into clearer focus the comparison of the racing girls with men, and so too their predetermined failure to measure up to them.

COMPETITIONS AGAINST MEN

So much for oblique comparison. What about our second question, on the direct confrontation of male and female? Lucian's Panthea affects ignorance about the regulations on statues at Olympia – it's something only a man would know (Luc. *Pr. Im.* 11, second century CE). We have the word of his contemporary Pausanias that a law required the Eleans to hurl any woman who attended the Olympic festival, or even crossed the Alpheius on forbidden days, from Mt Trypaeum. As it happens, only one was ever caught, and she lived to have the tale told about her: Peisodorus's mother attended her son disguised as his trainer, but, excited by his victory, jumped out of the trainers' enclosure and so revealed her sex. Her family connections saved her. But from then on, Pausanias says, trainers too had to strip (Paus. 5.6.7–8). However, when mentioning the special seat set aside for a woman, *gunē*, the priestess of Demeter Chamyne, Pausanias expressly states that unmarried girls, *parthenoi*, may watch the men's competitions (Paus. 6.20.8–9). Some have been sceptical; Mouratidis, one of the latest, puts more weight on the restrictions and prohibitions on women in cults of Heracles, whom he regards as the original patron of the games (Mouratidis 1984). Those who reject Pausanias should at least retract the charge that his account is contradictory (levelled, e.g., by Harris 1964:183). His reference to women, *gunaikes*, in 5.6.7 does not include girls. We learn a little later that girls and likewise women too are allowed up to the outer circle of the altar of Zeus on days when they are not excluded from Olympia (*parthenois kai hosautōs gunaiksin*, Paus. 5.13.10). This passage establishes that *gunaikes* make up a set separate from girls and suggests that it is their presence which is remarkable. If the qualification about days of exclusion is to be taken literally, it may allude to some time other than the Olympic competitions, but I expect that the expression is loose, and that only married women are meant. A clause of a late sixth-century Olympic law, as yet unpublished, reportedly forbids judges to favour a man of the Eleans or their alliance or a woman; the following lines apparently deal with deception, corruption and their punishment (Siewert 1992a). Unfortunately, the law does not seem likely to settle the issue of women's presence, since their influence need not be exerted at the sanctuary itself.

Olympia was in any case unusual. Women fulfilled a number of functions in other competitions for men. In later antiquity, when the infrastructure, cult and cultural life of the *polis* came more and more to depend on the beneficence of the elite, women as well as men served as gymnasiarchs. Some forty or so were known by the early '80s and new examples have turned up since. Some women served with their husbands, not all. Women could establish games on their own too, like the mother from Asia Minor who financed a festival in honour of her three sons, and act as *agonothetai*. We do not know how hands-on female gymnasiarchs and founders were; it may be significant that almost all our attested female gymnasiarchs come from Roman Asia Minor, where the office was largely limited to supplying oil. Even competition was possible at a distance: inability to attend the festival did not bar women from equestrian events at Olympia. Cynisca, daughter and sister of Spartan kings, was the first woman to win there, triumphing twice, in 396 and 392 (Paus. 3.8.1). Her victories were well publicized; Pausanias saw two dedications at Olympia, both bronze chariot teams, and a heroine's shrine back home in Sparta (Paus. 5.12.5, 6.1.6, 3.15.1). She had many successors at Olympia according to Pausanias, Spartans in particular; we know of one other, Euryleonis, of uncertain date (Paus. 3.8.1, 3.17.6). Besides these, we have the names of Bilistiche, who won the Olympic four-horse chariot race for foals in 268 and then, in 264, the first running of the foals pairs (*P Oxy.* 2082, Paus. 5.8.11), and of two women from an Elean family of equestrian champions in the early first century (*IVO* 201, 203). Other festivals provide more; at panhellenic competitions, many were members of the Hellenistic royal families or the wives and daughters of their senior officials. Horse-racing was not just the sport of kings; queens include Berenice II, an

entrant at Olympia and a victor at Nemea, and Cleopatra II. At a
level only slightly less exalted, Polycrates of Argos, governor of
Cyprus and chancellor of the Ptolemaic kingdom in the late third
and early second centuries, was joined as a hippic winner at the
Panathenaea by his wife and three daughters.[26]

Equal opportunity among the super-rich? Sure. But there are
traces of the play of gender in this arena too. In Pausanias, Cynisca
is said to have been very ambitious to win at Olympia, the first
woman to breed horses as well as the first Olympic champion, and
the epigram which accompanied one of her dedications sounds
proud enough (*IG* 5.1 1564a = *Anth. Pal.* 13.16). But Xenophon, who
knew him well, says that her brother Agesilaus put her up to both
horse-rearing and racing, in an attempt to show that such victories
are won merely by wealth, not by merit (Xen. *Ages.* 9.6, cf. Plut. *Ages.*
20.1, *Mor.* 212b). Who would want a prize a woman could win? One
wonders about Bilistiche too. She was a girl-friend of Ptolemy
Philadelphus and the subject of dispute in our sources, who present
her as everything from a descendant of the Atreids (Ath. 13.596a) –
apparently a compliment – to a barbarian slave (Plut. *Mor.* 753f). No
doubt she caused controversy in life as well. It would be nice to know
something about the impetus behind her equestrian career. Was it a
means to enhance her own status, a way for Ptolemy to show her off
as a Hellenistic trophy wife? Or did Ptolemy hope to indicate that he
was above such displays himself while also advertising that he could
excel if he chose? It would also be good to learn whether that
energetic and unconventional king played any part in putting the
pairs race for foals on the Olympic programme.

For athletic competition between males and females, we must for
the most part be content with the realm of myth, with stories about
Atalanta above all (outlined conveniently in Apollod. 3.9.2). In less
compendious sources, she is sometimes a hunter, sometimes a
wrestler or a runner. Her most glorious exploit in the chase comes
as odd woman out in one of the great testosterone tests in Greek
mythology, the hunt of the Calydonian boar. She draws first blood,
wounding the beast with an arrow before Meleager finishes it off.
She wrestles with Peleus, later Achilles' father, at the funeral games
of Pelias and is sometimes said to have defeated him. This was a

---

[26] Gymnasiarchs: Casarico 1982, Hagedorn 1996:157–9. Mother: *SEG* 41 (1991) no. 1249,
Selge, undated. *Agonothetai*: Mantas 1995:136–40.

Plate 7. Atalanta wrestles Peleus. Attic black-figure hydria, Atalanta Group, about 560.

favourite subject in archaic and classical vase painting, where her size and powerful body, revealed in a short tunic or *perizoma*, mark her as a worthy opponent for a hero; here too, more often than not, she seems well on her way to a win (Ley 1990:37–46). Her career as a runner reverses a common motif, the race for a bride. Icarius, the father of Penelope, Libyan Antaeus, Danaus – all hold foot-races for their daughters' suitors; Danaus, with forty-eight to marry off after they've murdered their previous husbands on the wedding night, rewards losers too, allocating his girls to the racers in the order of finish. Atalanta, on the contrary, is no passive prize. She gives her suitors a head start and puts to death all she overtakes in her disdain for marriage. Only one defeats her, Melanion or Hippomenes, with the aid of Aphrodite and the golden apples he drops on the track.[27]

Other details of Atalanta's biography are as unclear as the name of her husband – her father's identity, her home region – and even in antiquity mythographers used to wonder whether there were two girls of that name, one a Boeotian runner, the other an archer from Arcadia, skilled in the hunt. This would be an embarrassment of riches. We have already seen reason to connect hunting and racing in the *arkteia* for Artemis, a connection stronger still in the case of a girl who runs against men who become her prey. And one of our earliest depictions of the Calydonian boar hunt, the great François vase painted by Cleitias around 570, shows Atalanta together with all three of the men in her life, Meleager, Peleus and Melanion. This last stands beside her, painted black to her white, just after she has let loose her arrow. Atalanta is the only figure in the scene to wear a wreath, a winner again. Surely there is one Atalanta story at the core of these tales, about a girl who competes with men to their ruin. When Meleager rewards Atalanta's achievement in wounding the boar, with the animal's skin, his uncles object. He kills them both, and is himself victim of his mother's vengeance soon after. Suitors who lose a race to Atalanta are doomed, and Melanion/Hippomenes no less; forgetful of what is due to Aphrodite, he makes love with Atalanta in a sanctuary, with the result (according to late sources) that both are turned into lions. Peleus, it is true, suffers no direct harm from his match with Atalanta. But he is a rather deficient hero anyway, mocked in comedy as sexually unsatisfying for his wife Thetis (Ar. *Nub.* 1067–70) and destined through her to father a son who is his better, as much the swiftest of men as he is an indifferent wrestler against a woman. Though his failure to defeat Atalanta is not the cause of his shortcomings, it is obviously a measure of them. The Atalanta story, then, is reminiscent of the saga

---

[27] Defeated him: as probably in Ibycus 282A (viii) fr. 11 Campbell = S176 *SLG*, cf. Apollod. 3.9.2. Race for a bride: see Weiler 1974:256–8. Allocating girls: when Nearchus ascribes a similar custom to the Indians, he brands them as old-fashioned: *FGrH* 133 F 11, cf. F 23.

of the Amazons, another warning of the consequences of a world turned upside down, in which women compete with men and, worse yet, may come out on top.[28]

The theme receives more playful treatment in one of the satirical epigrams of Lucillius (*Anth. Pal.* 11.79, first century CE).

Cleombrotus left the ring. But when he married he had at home all the blows of Isthmia and Nemea – a pugnacious old woman, who hit like an Olympian. He fears to see his own house more than he ever did the stadium. Whenever he catches his breath, his hide gets a tanning, blows of all kinds, to make him do his conjugal duty. And if he does, he is hit again.

The name of the hen-pecked – or hen-punched – boxer, Cleombrotus, is designed to recall the Spartan king who lost to the Thebans at Leuctra in 371. That debacle put an end to the Spartan hegemony of the early fourth century, an unexpected outcome which parallels the wife's surprising supremacy on the home front.

Such cautionary tales were superfluous. The closest our Athenian evidence comes to mixed athletic competition is a child's rattle in the form of a terracotta ball, a gift to Myrrhine at the end of the sixth century (Immerwahr 1967). This is decorated by images of youths at the palaestra, throwing the discus, practising with javelins (and being accosted by older men). It bespeaks a belief that girls like Myrrhine were interested in the athletic (and other) pursuits of young men, a belief that would be confirmed if an added inscription, 'the boy is beautiful', is in Myrrhine's hand. But interest, however keen, is a far cry from taking part in competition. Though there are plenty of references to girls' exercise in the presence of Spartan males, none unequivocally makes them antagonists. Even Peleus's complaint – insofar as it is more than another element in his portrayal as a prude – need point to nothing more than girls and youths exercising at the same time and place. We have the word of one of Athenaeus's symposiasts, an enthusiast for beauty, that the gymnasia of Chios were enhanced by wrestling bouts between girls and youths (Ath. 12.566e, second century CE). This is not inconceivable; Chian women are among those we know as gymnasiarchs and hippic

---

[28] One Atalanta: cf. Detienne 1979:26–52, R.A. Howell and M.L. Howell 1989:127–8. François vase: Cleitias, Florence 4209, Beazley, *ABV* 76 no. 1, Beazley 1986: plate 26. Atalanta as athlete and Amazon: Barringer 1996:66–74.

victors. But it seems to be envisaged outside the context of a regular agonistic festival.[29]

There we could let the matter rest if it were not for an extraordinary inscription from Delphi on the competitive career of Tryphosa, Hedea and Dionysia, daughters of Hermesianax of Tralles in Asia Minor, a community which proudly (if falsely) claimed Spartan ties. Tryphosa won the *stadion* at the Pythian games twice and at the Isthmian once in a four year period, 'first of the girls'. Hedea was an all-round competitor, victorious in the *stadion* at the Nemean games and Sicyon, in the armed chariot race at the Isthmian games, and against boy singers at the Sebasteia at Athens. Dionysia was a multiple victor too, but only her *stadion* win at Epidaurus is legible on the stone. This inscription adds to our other evidence that girls and women could sponsor winning entries in equestrian events; Hedea's success in the chariot race in armour is unprecedented as far as we know, but of course chariots had not been a force on the battlefield for a very long time. Nor is her musical triumph in mixed company unique. But both raise questions about the races she and her sisters won. These are almost certainly for girls alone, important supplements to our dossier on female athletic contests. It is particularly welcome to learn of girls' events at prestigious sites like Delphi and Nemea, and to find corroboration for the conjecture that the contest introduced by L. Castricius Regulus at the Isthmian games was a *stadion* race and one that endured for a time. (Hermesianax, then, eager though he no doubt was to see his girls succeed and willing to let them travel abroad to do so, did not go so far as to found new festivals or lobby for new events on their behalf.) Yet it is disconcerting that the (admittedly partial) Isthmian victor list of 137 CE, about one hundred years later, shows no sign of female events (*SEG* 11 (1954) no. 62). Tryphosa's distinction is odd too – 'first of the girls'. On the face of it, this refers to her feat in winning consecutively at Delphi, the Isthmian games, and Delphi again. But just how impressive was this, given the multiplicity of combinations of this kind and how recently the girls' race had been established at the Isthmian games? It is barely possible, in the end, that Tryphosa was the first girl to win a regular male *stadion* race – against boys? – at the great games of the circuit.

---

[29] Sparta: it is worth pointing out that the contests (of whatever kind) which Agesilaus is said to have attended at Sparta seem to have involved either boys or girls, not both together: Plut. *Ages.* 21.3.

However, the odds against this possibility, like those against Tryphosa herself, are formidable.[30]

Greek athletes invariably competed in groups defined according to age and sex. Age categories were sometimes simple – boys and men. They might also be elaborate, adding divisions, especially for boys, multiplying their designations. Many of these are mysterious; few, given the variety of methods used to calculate ages, could be exact. Their prevalence testifies to underlying assumptions about the capacity of the young to compete against their elders, assumptions which might be expressed explicitly or (more often) indicated by the attention paid to those exceptional instances in which they were belied.

Why did the Greeks insist on the distinction of age, when they ignored others, notably weight classes in combat events? One motive might be the avoidance of intergenerational rivalry: age categories combined with the practice of deferring marriage for men until twenty-five or thirty and the natural limitations on athletic careers to ensure that fathers would not compete against their sons and risk losing to them. (Here we may see another reason for the Greeks' failure to keep records which might be broken.) Contrariwise, the special role reserved for older men in horse-racing was only a matter of practice and practicality. No formal rules kept young men, boys even, from taking them on. Rich young men only, to be sure. And fathers could largely control their sons' opportunity to rival them in this kind of competition, so that formal distinctions may have seemed unnecessary. It was generally a father's decision whether or not to settle property on his sons during his lifetime and how much to give them. Without significant wealth, no one could raise let alone race horses. Women too were kept from competitive comparisons which might challenge prevailing hierarchies. Indeed, in their nearest regular contact with men in panhellenic athletics, they used the same stadium at Olympia but ran a shorter race. The implication is that they themselves must fall short. For them too horse-racing was exceptional, open to their participation and victory both because they competed only indirectly, through their animals, riders and charioteers, and because superiority might be represented as reflecting resources alone.

Of course, while boys would grow into men, women could not

---

[30] Inscription: *SIG*³ 802 = Moretti 1953: no. 63, S.G. Miller 1991: no. 106, 45 CE; Lee 1988b.

change their category. We move on now to another distinction, social rather than biological in its basis, that between rich and poor. Did athletic and equestrian competition afford a means for poorer winners to transcend their origins (as boys became men)? Or did it reassert distinctions, as between men and women? These questions will supply the starting point for the next chapter.

CHAPTER 5

Class difference, dissent, democracy

Plutarch offers the following account of the origins and early career of Eumenes, later secretary to King Philip II of Macedon and ruler of Cappadocia (Plut. *Eum.* 1.1–2).

Duris says that the father of Eumenes of Cardia was a poor man who worked as a wagoner in the Thracian Chersonese; nevertheless, Eumenes got a liberal education in literature and athletics (*peri palaistran*). While he was still a boy (Duris goes on), Philip visited and took the time to watch Cardian youths practising the *pankration* and boys wrestling. Eumenes was so successful a wrestler and so clearly intelligent and brave that Philip, pleased, had him join his retinue. But I find those who say that Eumenes was favoured by Philip on account of friendship with his father to be more plausible.

Two versions. As so often, we cannot say which (if either) is true. It is clear that Duris, a younger fourth-century contemporary of Eumenes, thought it unusual for a poor wagoner's son to get training in athletics, that he did not regard this as impossible, and that athletic ability, even among boys, could plausibly catch the eye of a king and lead on to fortune. Yet Plutarch (writing perhaps four hundred years later) is not convinced.

This divergence of opinion among our sources neatly mirrors modern debates on the class backgrounds of ancient Greek athletes. Learned and lively books by E.N. Gardiner and H.A. Harris popularized the view that archaic Greek sport was marked by the love of competition for its own sake. The great panhellenic festivals were the crowning glories of this spirit of amateurism because their well-born winners were satisfied with a wreath as a reward; prizes of value and the predominance of lower class professionals who wanted to win them were later developments, causes of corruption and symptoms of decline. But this picture was 'conceived by partisans of the nineteenth-century Anglo-American amateur movement' (Young

1983:45). Gardiner, Harris and the many who followed them supplied ancient precedent to legitimize, consciously or not, the ideology of the modern Olympic movement, committed from the outset to restricting competition to a leisured elite (see especially Young 1984:7–88). An ancient amateur is an anachronism.

Success at the great contests required extraordinary effort and expense. It also brought very real rewards. True, the crown games of the original *periodos* offered symbolic prizes only. But there were only a few of these and, besides, Greek cities made substantial material benefits available for their victors from the early sixth century at least (see above, Chapter 3). Prizes at other games – including the Heraea at Argos, a late addition to the *periodos* – could be very valuable. For example, the winner of the boys' *stadion* race at the Panathenaea at Athens received fifty amphoras of olive oil, worth perhaps the equivalent of US $45,000 today. What is more, there was no barrier to competing at both crown and prize games. The irony is that the ancient Olympics do provide a prototype for the modern, but for the late-twentieth-century Olympics of tennis pros and basketball's Dream Teams, of Samaranch and Sony, not for de Coubertin's and Avery Brundage's (cf. Pleket 1992:147). Take official bonuses. The United States Olympic Committee awarded US $15,000 for each gold medal at the 1996 games and payments for second, third and fourth finishers, sums often supplemented, and much exceeded, by individual sports federations. The boxer who won Thailand's first ever gold medal did better, the equivalent of about US $1.7 million; a lifetime subway pass was only one of the benefits for a Hong Kong windsurfer.[1]

However, while the decline of the ideology of amateurism has made it easier to recognize the role that money and other material benefits always played in Greek athletics, another element of the world conjured up by Gardiner and Harris – the early monopoly of aristocrats and their displacement by poorer competitors – remains controversial. David Young, whose work has done so much to clarify the relationship between the modern Olympic movement and

---

[1] Effort and expense: see, e.g., Antiph. DK 87B49, Xen. *Hiero* 9.11. Panathenaea: *IG* 2² 2311 = S.G. Miller 1991: no. 84, about 380; for the calculation, see Young 1984:115–27 and further below. Bonuses: one effect of such guaranteed pay-offs has been to prolong competitive careers. In 1996, the US Olympic team was about five years older on average than in 1984, and track and field athletes included Mary Slaney at thirty-eight and Carl Lewis, long jump champion again at thirty-five. Might such incentives have encouraged the older Greek athletes discussed in Chapter 4 as well?

scholarship on ancient sport, has pressed the case for the involvement of poorer athletes from the earliest days of organized festival competition in Greece, pointing to a cook, a goatherd and a cowherd among early Olympians. Unfortunately, our information on these athletes usually dates from many years after their deaths, and is not invariably self-explanatory. (Was Coroebus, the first Olympic victor, a cook or a cult functionary involved in sacrifice?) Significantly, Aristotle (perhaps writing as a contemporary) notes that one such Olympic champion, a fishmonger, was exceptional. We may also wonder how poorer athletes could afford the time and expense of training and travel to competitions; these were greatest at Olympia, not only distant and hard to reach but (as we saw above, Chapter 1) requiring athletes to spend thirty days on the site before competition began. Cities might honour victory and even recruit champions – one likely explanation for the fact that Crotoniates won twelve of twenty-seven Olympic *stadion* races for men between 588 and 484 and once made up the first seven finishers (Young 1984:134–47). But they were less willing to subsidize competitors before their success (Crowther 1996). Private patronage is known from Egypt in the third century, but its extent is impossible to ascertain.[2]

Young argues that poorer boys might win local events – natural ability would count for most at this age – and use their earnings to finance careers. Yet few local games can have been as generous as the Panathenaea, itself on offer only every four years. About 300 BCE, a coach (*epistatēs*) approached the city council of Ephesus for funds to help a young athlete train and make a festival trip (Robert 1967:28–32). The boy had already won at least one victory. Allowing for another practice with modern parallels, the tendency of the wealthy to avail themselves of the public purse, this suggests that in this instance a young winner had not yet earned enough to compete abroad without help. Furthermore, local games with valuable prizes attracted entrants from afar. In fact, attracting them might be a priority, important enough for an ex-archon to seek the emperor Septimius Severus's assistance when athletes passed by the Panhellenia at Athens in the early third century CE (Oliver 1970:107–9 nos. 21–2). One solution (at least in later antiquity) was appearance fees:

[2] Controversial: see especially Pleket 1974, 1975 and 1992, Young 1983, 1984:89–176, Poliakoff 1987a:129–33. Fishmonger: Arist. *Rh.* 1.1365a20,1367b18; Biliński 1990 identifies him as the winner of the *pankration* in 352. Patronage: *PZenon* 59060 = S.G. Miller 1991: no. 147, 257 BCE.

Dio Chrysostom speaks scornfully about local dignitaries who spend five talents – a considerable sum – to bring in an Amoebeus or Polus (a cithara player and a renowned actor) or an Olympic victor (Dio Chrys. *Or.* 66.11, about 100 CE). Of course, boys travelled less (see above, Chapter 4), and the rise of the gymnasium in the sixth century levelled the playing field to some degree, making facilities available to those outside the elite. Still, better-off boys could afford more food and the private trainers Pindar praises. As for public trainers, *paidotribai*, the Athenian ephebate is attested only from the later fourth century and may not have included the *thetes*, the poor majority of the population (see further below); its Hellenistic descendant was an unequivocally exclusive institution. Young has established the possibility of poorer athletes taking part in archaic and classical competition, but we cannot say that their involvement in any significant numbers was probable.

The proportion of elite and other athletes at later periods is beyond our reach and likely to remain so. We know of many athletes whose careers were studded with distinctions – multiple citizenships, magistracies, priesthoods, service on embassies. Do these testify to their origins among the elite for which such honours were usually reserved? Or are they concomitants of victory? We can rarely be sure. An important but puzzling piece of evidence is Artemidorus's discussion of dreams in which a mother gives birth to an eagle (Artem. 2.20). In a poor family, this portends a son who will rise in the ranks to command a military camp; among the rich, an emperor. A third boy, from the moderate or middling class (*metrios*), will become a famous athlete. What does Artemidorus intend by *metrios* here? Clearly not the top stratum of the population of the Roman empire. Pleket understands the term to include the most successful artisans and intellectuals, doctors and lawyers, as well as members of local councils who did not hold high office (Pleket 1974:75–6, cf. Aigner 1988:215). Artemidorus's explanation of dreams in which a father eats a son's shoulders or feet – he will profit from the boy's earnings as a wrestler or runner – seems consistent with this (Artem. 1.70). However, it is possible that the group he has in mind extends as high as the 'curial order', the local elites of the many small and medium-size cities of the Roman east, who had not yet produced claimants to the imperial throne in Artemidorus's day, the late second century CE (Langenfeld 1991:12–13).

For groups of athletes outside the elite, we may adduce third- and second-century victors in local contests at Sicyon, who make up a group quite distinct from the wealthy citizens who contributed to fund-raising campaigns (Shipley 1987:213–16). Individuals include an Olympic champion in *pankration* in (?) 129 CE, whose cognomen hints at servile origin for his family, and an Egyptian boxer and priest of an athletic guild, nicknamed 'the dummy', who was illiterate. Further up the social scale, almost all the known victors in the Meleagria at Balboura in Asia Minor in the mid-second century CE belonged to prominent local families (Milner 1991). Two, remarkably, won both the *stadion* race and the wrestling or *pankration*. Perhaps the fields were small – only citizens were eligible – or poorer Balbourans did not care to oppose the sons of influential families. Either way, members of the elite evidently thought such victories worth winning and commemorating. So too at nearby Oenoanda, where 'the social status of the local participants was high' (Hall and Milner 1994:28). Indeed, one of our latest ancient texts, the epitaph for a member of a well-off family at Gaza who died at sixteen, makes a point of his athletic activities. As Pleket concludes, 'From Pindar's time until Roman Imperial times members of the upper class were never absent in sport (neither in the running events nor in the body-contact sports)' (Pleket 1975:71–2).[3]

Pleket goes on to argue that the prevailing ideology of Greek sport, the outlook articulated so partially and persuasively by Gardiner and Harris, was always a product of the elite, an inheritance of the period in which the wealthy unquestionably predominated (Pleket 1975:74–89, cf. 1992:147–9). Though victors were eager to claim distinctions of every kind, as first of their city or among Ionians to win an event, or first of all competitors to win in three age classes, or twice on one day, none advertises himself as the first of his family or social class. On the contrary: 'it is human nature to set a higher value on abilities that have been handed down from father to son. Therefore, the Olympic victor who comes from a family of Olympic victors is more glorious' (Philostr. *VS* 611). An aristocratic sentiment. In the remainder of this chapter, I outline some reflections of the elite domination of athletic and equestrian competition in ancient Greece and some reactions to it in the most democratic of Greek communities, classical Athens.

---

[3] Olympic champion: M. Ulpius Domesticus; West 1990:85. 'The dummy': *P London* 3.1158, 1178, 194 CE. Gaza: *SEG* 37 (1987) no. 485, 569 CE.

HERACLES, WAGE-LABOUR AND SPORT

Let us begin with aristocratic ideology. We have already met (above, Chapter 1) the pre-eminence of the crown games among Greek competitions. Both Herodotus and Lucian, writing some six hundred years apart, depict barbarians' amazement at the Greek custom of competing for a mere crown (Hdt. 8.26, Luc. *Anach.* 9–10, 16); the implication is that such contests for symbolic rewards are both distinctively Greek and especially admirable. I regard this judgement as a reflection of elite attitudes, and argue that it is expressed within the myth of the greatest of legendary athletes, Heracles. The Heracles myth contains a contrast between sport and wage-labour, especially wage-labour in its most demanding form, manual labour. Implicit in the myth is a definition of sport which recalls the idealized image of the great panhellenic games: a physical contest, from which the winner took away no material reward, only immortality. In wage-labour, on the other hand, the worker exerts himself physically as a dependant and inferior, for the sake of pay; but he may fail to gain even the money he has contracted for. The myth contains an analogy between wage-labour and those games which awarded money or value prizes, and so denigrates them.

What I call 'the Heracles myth' is in fact a complex collection of stories of different genres, from different periods, with different purposes, in both Greek and Latin, from all over the ancient world. Nevertheless, I follow one source: the collection of Greek myths which has come down to us under the name Library of Apollodorus (though we do not know who its author was) and which may be as late as the first century CE (Apollod. 2.4.8–2.7.8). To be sure, much of Apollodorus's material on Heracles may come directly from much earlier writers such as Panyassis and Pherecydes. But his main advantages for my purposes are simply that his is the fullest connected account of Heracles' life we have, and it thus allows us to speak of recurring motifs with more confidence than more episodic or allusive treatments do. I then compare Apollodorus's account to some references to Heracles' story in Pindar. I believe that the incidents I focus on were essential elements of the story early on, part of the original myth, and I cite early references to some of them. But I do not know how to prove this. So, while my argument is based on the assumption that Pindar and Apollodorus tell sections of the same story, the reader is free to conclude that I have done no more than offer a partial commentary on two literary texts.

My starting point is Greek attitudes towards labour, wage-labour in particular. Who built the Seven Gates of Thebes? Brecht's question is famous. The answer is less well known today, but the names of Amphion and Zethus were celebrated in antiquity. Twin sons of Antiope and Zeus, they were abandoned at birth and reared by a shepherd. Amphion became a musician; Zethus a worker, a herdsman. And when, after an involved and implausible series of events, they founded the city called Thebes after the name of Zethus's wife, each used his special skill in building its wall. The Hellenistic poet Apollonius of Rhodes gives a nice description of their efforts. 'Zethus was shouldering a mountain peak – he seemed to find it heavy work. Amphion walked behind, singing to a golden lyre; and a boulder twice as large as that of Zethus came trundling after him' (Ap. Rhod. *Argon.* 1.738–41). Zethus's toil, his manual labour, is largely in vain; Amphion, aided by the lyre he had from the hands of Hermes, does most of the work with far less effort. In this story, manual labour is set against cultural activity and devalued; the contrast was an explicit theme of the *Antiope* of Euripides. Produced about 410 BCE, this tragedy (of which only fragments remain) featured Amphion and Zethus in debate on the value of music and poetry as compared to war and agriculture; brain, argued Amphion, is better than brawn.[4]

The denigration of physical labour is an element of myth's depiction of Hephaestus, the god of the forge who is associated with technical skill and handicrafts in general. Hephaestus makes wonderful things, such as the tripods with golden wheels which of their own motion roll to and from the gatherings of the gods. Yet he himself is lame. Whatever the myths' explanations for his misshapen limbs – they are usually said to have resulted from his fall when Zeus cast him out of Olympus – the ideological content is clear: Hephaestus's involvement with labour prevents him from enjoying the bodily beauty of the other gods, who live *rheia*, 'easily', free from toil. More than this, his deformity, his bustle and his sweat bring him the derision of his fellow Olympians (as at the end of *Iliad* 1) and the contempt of his mate Aphrodite. Hephaestus stands outcast midst the wonders he has made. Daedalus, Hephaestus's human counter-

---

[4] *Antiope*: Eur. fr. 183–202N.²; Webster 1967:205–10.

part in myth, is flawed as well. He is a great craftsman and inventor; the products of his hands do well. But his technology is responsible for the death of his son Icarus, and he himself for that of a kind of son surrogate, his young nephew and pupil Talos or Perdix. Daedalus's success in creating inanimate objects is contrasted with his inability (or in the case of his nephew, his unwillingness) to nurture and protect the living.

The denigration of those who work with their hands in Greek myth reflects the attitudes of ancient Greek society in general. Of course, those attitudes were more complex than the stories I have cited may suggest. Physical labour in itself was not always shameful. In the *Odyssey* the suitor Eurymachus mockingly offers Odysseus, disguised as a beggar, a job as a *thēs*, working for a wage on his farm. Odysseus responds, not by protesting that physical labour is beneath him – he made his own marriage-bed and a raft, after all – but by challenging his tormentor to a contest in haying or ploughing. And he goes on to say that if Zeus arranges a battle, he will demonstrate his prowess in war. Greek hero though he is, Odysseus is not ashamed of knowing how to work in the fields; the notion he resists is that he work for a wage, as another's dependant (Hom. *Od.* 18.356–80). Achilles too expresses horror at the life of a *thēs*, a dependent wage-labourer. It is not a fate worse than death for this best of the Achaeans, but it is second worst (Hom. *Od.* 11.489–91). Already in Homer, then, we see wage-labour contrasted unfavourably with physical activity in the context of a contest freely entered, whether in peacetime or in war.[5]

In general, we may say that the lot of the landed aristocrat, who didn't need to work, was the ideal; everyone else, compelled to work, was looked down on. This prejudice was not restricted to the elite; it was shared, it seems, even by those who themselves suffered from it. Particularly revealing is a passage from Demosthenes' speech *On the Crown*, delivered in 330. Addressing an Athenian jury, Demosthenes contrasts his own background with the origins and early career of his great rival Aeschines. Demosthenes went to good schools and was well enough off to avoid doing anything shameful (*aiskhron*) due to poverty. But Aeschines was poor; he had to do chores like a slave in the school where his father worked and then served as a subordinate to minor officials of the state. In sum, says Demosthenes, 'You were

---

[5] Attitudes: see, e.g., Garlan 1980, Balme 1984.

a teacher, I a pupil . . . You were a clerk, I addressed the Assembly.'
Many of us would react badly to Demosthenes' rhetoric: he is a
pampered product of privilege, who learned to enunciate by
speaking with a silver spoon in his mouth; while Aeschines is a poor
boy who made good, the shameful activities mentioned here
amounting to helping out his father and working for the govern-
ment. But we must assume that Demosthenes knew his audience,
and that a jury made up at least in part of more-or-less ordinary
Athenians, and meant to represent the citizen body as a whole, was
open to his approach (Dem. 18.257–65; Dyck 1985:42–8).

Thus, it was of compulsory, dependent labour, rather than labour
itself, that the Greeks were contemptuous. But of course the term
'dependent labour' in turn covers a broad range of activities as well
as the mass of the population. Again, distinctions must be made.
Some Greeks were directly dependent on others for their livelihood
(they hired themselves out for a wage), others only indirectly, such as
the craftsmen and merchants who made and obtained articles for
sale and so needed customers or patrons. Some were highly
accomplished doctors or artists, others unskilled men doing dull but
demanding labour. Any might work alongside slaves and for a slave's
wages; all would share his low social status to some degree. But of all
the forms of dependent labour, physical work – brute labour, as we
say – was the most slavish. At Athens at least, the most difficult and
dangerous manual labour, in the mines at Laureion, was also the
only peacetime activity virtually reserved for slaves; Aristotle defined
the slave's function as the use of the body; and *soma*, 'body', came to
mean 'slave' at least as early as the third century. Dependent physical
work was thus the most degrading.[6]

Heracles is the greatest of the Greek heroes and at the same time
the most prominent and most prodigious manual worker in myth.
He may at first sight appear to provide an exception to the tendency
of Greek myths to denigrate workers and their work. After all, in
many accounts Heracles' famous labours lead directly to his immortality (Pind. *Nem.* 1.61–72, cf. Hes. *Th.* 950–5); the son of Zeus and a
mortal woman, Alcmena, he rises from earth to Olympus, from hero
to god. However, in Heracles' activities, especially the labours and
the events which surround them, two elements are opposed. As a
group, Heracles' labours, undertaken not for material gain, but in

---

[6] Aristotle: *Pol.* 1.1254b18, cf. 1252a33 (reading *diaponein*), 1254b26.

expiation of blood pollution, do indeed win him immortality. In this way they are like the great panhellenic athletic festivals from which winners took away only a wreath and undying glory. In support of this comparison, we may note that Heracles' labours are called *athloi*, 'contests', from the time of Homer and win him (along with Theseus) the appellation 'athlete on behalf of human life' (Isoc. 10.23); they usually take the form of a struggle with a human or monstrous animal opponent; and Heracles himself is shown as a founder and patron of games. But at the same time certain details of the individual labours emphasize Heracles' connection with dependent work, and a recurring motif suggests that work undertaken for material gain, wage-labour, is not only demeaning but futile (and so doubly devalued).[7]

Heracles is connected with labour from an early age. As a young man, he kills his music teacher, and his father Amphitryon, wishing to curb his temper, sends him outside Thebes to work as a herder of cattle. It is while he is still a herdsman at Amphitryon's command that he performs his first great exploit, killing the lion of Cithaeron. On his way home, he meets heralds sent by king Erginus of Orchomenus to collect tribute from the Thebans; Heracles kills these envoys – his temper has not improved – and then leads a Theban army which captures Orchomenus and kills Erginus (Apollod. 2.4.9–11). Erginus we may regard as another link between Heracles and work. Though the name itself does not occur as a Greek word, its first element, *erg-*, recalls *ergon*, 'work', *ergatēs*, 'workman', and a number of related words, and this Erginus (or other men of Orchomenus with the same name) is associated with Hephaestus, the craftsman god, in other stories.

According to Apollodorus's account, Heracles' valour in the victory over the Orchomenians earns him Megara, the daughter of the king of Thebes, as his wife; they have three sons. Then, disaster. Jealous Hera, the wife of Zeus, has hated Heracles from his birth. She drives the hero mad, and he kills his children. Seeking to expiate his crime, Heracles goes to Delphi, where Apollo orders him to serve Eurystheus, king of Mycenae, and to perform labours Eurystheus will impose on him. In this way, says the priestess, Heracles will win immortality (2.4.12). I will have more to say about this reward later.

---

[7] *Athloi*: Hom. *Il.* 8.363, 19.133, perhaps 15.639, *Od.* 11.622; Pavese 1996.

What needs stressing now is the debased moral and social position in which Heracles finds himself as he sets out on his labours. He is a wrongdoer of the most terrible kind, and he is forced to work at the bidding of Eurystheus, a king to be sure but a coward and a weakling. Eurystheus emphasizes Heracles' degradation by refusing to communicate with him directly. Instead, he relays his commands through an underling, one Copreus, himself a murderer, and a man whose name is formed from *kopros*, a Greek word for excrement (2.4.1).[8]

To move on to the labours themselves: the first task Eurystheus lays on Heracles is to bring him the skin of the Nemean lion, and it is on his return with that terrifying prize that the cowering king appoints Copreus as his intermediary. One detail is worth noting here: on his way to attack the lion, Heracles stays with Molorchus of Cleonae, a poor man, one who works with his hands (2.5.1). In the second labour appears a motif which will recur. Heracles kills the many-headed Hydra; but he has the help of Iolaus, and as a result Eurystheus refuses to count this feat as one of Heracles' labours (2.5.2). Eurystheus's arbitrary action is of course a reminder of his power and of the impotence to which Heracles has been reduced. But now the king has added injury to insult; Heracles has worked for nothing. We may recall an earlier Theban hero – Zethus, who carried a mountain peak to little avail. Heracles' physical labour is as difficult and more demeaning, as it is done at another's bidding. Like Zethus's, it is apparently futile as well. Apollodorus draws no conclusions about dependent labour in general. But what a devastating denunciation the story is all the same! A similar incident, in which this motif is expressed more explicitly, occurs in the fifth labour of Apollodorus's series, the cleansing of the stables of Augeas, king of Elis. This is dirty work indeed – again Heracles is associated with excrement – and Heracles wants to make it worth his while. He tells Augeas that he will clean the stables of manure in just one day in return for one-tenth of the royal cattle. Augeas agrees; Heracles keeps his side of the bargain by diverting nearby rivers, but Augeas reneges on his and refuses to pay. He orders Heracles out of Elis; and when the hero returns to Mycenae, Eurystheus again refuses to count this labour, on the grounds that Heracles did it for profit (2.5.5). Once more wage-labour, here of a particularly unpleasant kind, gains the worker nothing.

---

[8] Copreus: already linked with Heracles in Hom. *Il.* 15.638–40.

This motif also appears in the story of Laomedon. On his way back from his ninth labour with the girdle of the amazon Hippolyta, Heracles puts in at Troy. That city is suffering from a plague and a sea monster, sent by Apollo and Poseidon respectively in anger at King Laomedon. The cause of the gods' anger is significant: hiring themselves out as labourers, they had built the walls of Troy, but Laomedon cheated them of their pay. Now an oracle offers the Trojans a terrible release: the city will be free of the sea monster if Laomedon's daughter Hesione is sacrificed to it. It is at this point, with Hesione chained to a rock and the sea monster starting to think about supper, that Heracles intervenes. He offers to rescue the girl in return for some of the mares for which Troy was so famous. 'Of course', says Laomedon; Heracles kills the monster; and Laomedon reneges (2.5.9).[9]

So far I have been discussing the motif of wage-work without wages within the frame of the labours. It appears in another important story involving Heracles as well. After completing his labours, and after many other adventures – including a stint as a slave of Omphale, queen of the Lydians, which is an echo of his service to Eurystheus – Heracles marries Deianira and settles in Calydon. But Heracles accidentally kills a young Calydonian and, contrite, decides to go into exile at Trachis. Accompanied by Deianira, he reaches the river where Nessus the centaur is working as a ferryman. Heracles crosses the river by himself, but when asked for the fare allows Nessus to carry Deianira. During the passage, the semi-bestial Nessus tries to rape her, and Heracles shoots him with an arrow as he emerges from the river (2.7.6). No more than he deserves? But consider the situation from the point of view of Nessus the worker. He has been given no chance to earn his livelihood by ferrying Heracles. Deianira he has carried; and in killing him (for whatever reason) Heracles has again prevented the ferryman from getting his wages. Nessus works for money; but all he gets is the wages of his sin, death.

So much for the presentation of wage-labour in Apollodorus; despite Heracles' accomplishments, workers and their work are denied their due. What about sport? I have already said something about Heracles' labours as athletic contests. There is much more to say about his ties with sport in general. Heracles is celebrated as the

---

[9] Laomedon: hinted at in Hom. *Il.* 5.638–42, cf. 21.441–57.

Plate 8. Heracles fights Antaeus: the hero as pancratiast. Attic black-figure eye cup,
Leagrus Group, 515–500.

first pancratiast in poetry (Bacch. 13.46–57), depicted as a pancratiast and wrestler in art; one of his cult epithets is Palaimon, 'the
wrestler'. He is already 'an athlete in miniature' on a famous vase
depicting his strangling of the serpents as an infant. Other areas of
athletic activity – boxing, horse-racing, a chariot race for a gold
tripod – are shown on his shield (Hes. *Scut.* 301–13). An athlete
himself, Heracles is also a patron of athletes. His statues (often
accompanied by those of Hermes) adorned gymnasia and palaestrae;
a race in armour on Chios began from one. His shrines had sports
fields and buildings attached or nearby, and were the sites of games
(such as the Heracleia at Marathon: Vanderpool 1984). Individual
athletes took him as a model: the great wrestler Milon of Croton is
said to have worn a lion skin and brandished a club when leading an
army against Sybaris in 510 (Diod. Sic. 12.9.5–6). The pancratiast
Pulydamas killed a lion in emulation of Heracles' Nemean feat
(Paus. 6.5.5). A later pancratiast, Callicrates of Aphrodisias, prides
himself on taking the road to virtue – a reference to Heracles'

famous choice. A dream of the white poplar, associated with Heracles, was interpreted as an omen of victory (Artem. 2.25, 5.7.4). Athletes who won both the wrestling and *pankration* competitions on the same day at Olympia styled themselves 'successors of Heracles'; others took Heracles as a nickname (Ameling 1987). Indeed, associations of athletes invoked Heracles in their official designations in late antiquity. It has even been argued that Heracles' story is just one of a series of similarly structured tales involving athletes who become heroes or gods (Fontenrose 1968:86). But none of these stories (discussed briefly above, Chapter 3) includes the hero's ascension to Olympus or an accompanying victory procession and feast, as Heracles' does (Slater 1984:242, 250).[10]

There is little of this in Apollodorus. We are given a list of Heracles' teachers in various subjects, including chariot-racing, wrestling, and fighting in heavy armour (2.4.9), all of them events in various games; this is just Hellenistic antiquarianism. We hear of several adversaries who challenge him to a wrestling match: Polygonus and Telegonus (2.5.9), Eryx (2.5.10), Menoetes (2.5.12). Each he defeats, Eryx in three falls in succession, the number needed for an Olympic victory. But there is nothing here for our theme. However, another story is both relevant and important. After his labours (says Apollodorus) Heracles goes to Thebes and gives Megara to Iolaus, his helper in the conquest of the Hydra. He now needs a wife. So, learning that Eurytus, king of Oechalia, has offered his daughter Iole as a prize in an archery contest, Heracles travels to Oechalia, surpasses Eurytus and his sons as a bowman – and then finds that Iole is not to be his after all. The losers in the contest have heard of the fate of Megara's children, fear the same for Iole's, and renege (2.7.2). This story is a variant of a tale told in a number of widely separated cultures; Ingomar Weiler notes examples of archery contests for a bride from Japan, from the Iroquois of North America, and from India, in addition to the most famous Greek version, the competition between Odysseus and the suitors (Weiler 1974:294–8). It is interesting to note that it has clearly been shaped

---

[10] Heracles and sport: see Gruppe 1918:1007–9, Mouratidis 1984, Emmanuel-Rebuffat 1985, Poliakoff 1987:137–9, Boardman *et al.* 1988:796–7. Palaimon: Lycoph. *Alex.* 663 (with Tzetzes' note), *Etym. Magn.* 511.29. Serpents: Berlin Painter, Louvre G 192, Beazley, *ARV²* 208 no. 160, 480/470; Moret 1992:86–7. Statues: see Paus. 4.32.1 and, e.g., Woodford 1971 (Attica), Fraser 1972:2.353 n. 149 (Egypt). Race in armour: *SEG* 35 (1985) no. 930, about 100 CE. Callicrates: *MAMA* 8 417; Merkelbach 1970. Associations: *IG* 14.1054, 1055, 1105, 1107, 1109.

to fit the context of the Heracles myth. A common feature in many variants is the use of guile or deception by the winning archer (Odysseus again). Deception is in evidence in Apollodorus's story too, but in this case it is the sponsor of the contest who is guilty. The usual form of the story has been varied to make it conform to the pattern of incidents involving a refusal to pay.

In this instance Heracles is involved in what seems to be a completely different activity – not wage-labour, but a contest, sport. But it is crucial to the argument to recognize that this is a sporting contest of a certain kind: a contest for a prize. Not, it is true, a money prize (although Apollodorus himself may assume a dowry would go with Iole, as was generally the custom in the Greek world after the earliest period), but not a mere token either; Heracles would not have come to Oechalia for an olive wreath. In the context I have outlined, the recurrence of this motif suggests that such contests for a prize of value are to be linked with wage-labour, and are in the end just as unrewarding. The analogy denigrates value prizes, the festivals which honour them, and the athletes who compete for them. But what of other prizes and other festivals? Here we must return to a greater artist: Pindar provides the pole of comparison missing in Apollodorus, the presentation of sport for its own sake in the Heracles myth.

Heracles was sometimes said to have inaugurated the Nemean games (see Doffey 1992), but his ties are closest with Olympia, where the metopes of the great Temple of Zeus commemorated his labours. He was widely regarded as the founder of the Olympic games, a long-delayed result of Augeas's refusal to pay for the cleansing of his stables. So in Apollodorus (2.7.2). But Apollodorus's account is very brief, too allusive this time to bear the weight of analysis. Fortunately, the story was a favourite of Pindar's (he refers to it six times) and the elaborate centrepiece of one poem in particular, the tenth Olympian ode.[11]

The tenth Olympian was written for Hagesidamus of Epizephyrian Locri in the toe of Italy, winner of the boys' boxing at the Olympics of 476. It falls into three divisions. In the first (1–21), Pindar apologizes to Hagesidamus for being tardy in fulfilling a commission to write him a victory ode. He had reneged on a contract he says – terms from commerce and book-keeping abound

---

[11] Six times: Pind. *Ol.* 2.3–4, 3.9–38, 6.67–70, 10.24–30, *Nem.* 10.32–3, 11.27–8.

– and this poem is his payment, with interest. In the second part (22–77), the poet tells the story of the origin of the games in which his patron has triumphed. After the arrogant Augeas had sent Heracles away unpaid, the hero led an army looking for revenge; the king's nephews, the Moliones, lay in ambush and drove it off. But in the end Heracles paid back his enemies. He set a trap in his turn, killed the Moliones, ravaged Elis, and did away with its ruler. He then established the Olympic festival there, its terms, its events, and its prizes – victory wreaths – and presided over its first celebration. Pindar gives a list of the victors in this first festival. His intent, it seems, is to demonstrate that their names are still remembered, that the wreath is not their only reward; they have won the immortality of fame.

Immortality is the subject of the poem's third and final section (78–105). Here Pindar moves back into the present. First, a general reflection: an aging father dotes on a late-born son who will inherit his estate, for a dying man hates to see his property pass outside the family. To pass on one's goods is one kind of immortality. Pindar now addresses Hagesidamus, who has no such family concerns as yet, and speaks again of the immortality of fame. 'Great deeds are forgotten without poetry', he tells him; they are labours undertaken in vain (like the labour Heracles did for Augeas, we may think). But Pindar's poem will ensure that Hagesidamus's prowess will not be without fame, that his name will live on. In just this way, Pindar concludes, young Ganymede's beauty preserved him from death.

To sum up: Heracles works for Augeas, seeks a material reward, and gets nothing. They fight – not as equals precisely, for Heracles, as Pindar says, is much stronger, but with some success on each side; and from Heracles' victory come the Olympic games. In the games too there is physical effort and struggle, *ponos*, this time in sporting contests among equals (see Szastyńska-Siemion 1971, 1981). These contests hold no material prizes, only tokens, the products of nature, not human handiwork; a later writer says Heracles set wreaths as prizes because he had benefited mankind (in his labours) without thought of pay (Diod. Sic. 4.14.1). But the winner may gain something better, certainly something more durable than anything made by man: undying fame. So far is sport superior to wage-labour. In Apollodorus's retelling of the Heracles story, contests for a value prize are assimilated to wage-labour; in Pindar's poem, contests for a symbolic prize are presented as very much better. I conclude that there was more of a stigma involved in value prizes than the realities of Greek competition might suggest. Money certainly spoke to ancient athletes, but some, it seems, might condemn those who listened.

ELITE ATHLETICS AT ATHENS: ASSENT AND ANIMOSITY

We move on to classical Athens and the social status and standing of its athletes. These certainly made up a distinctive group, even an identifiable one. The tragic poet Achaeus of Eretria, a rival of Euripides, describes athletes 'naked, their arms swelling with youthful power, going about their activities with their strong shoulders glistening in youthful bloom' (20 F 4, cf. Ar. *Nub.* 1002–19). In Euripides himself, Dionysus's hair is said to be too luxurious for wrestling; wrestlers kept their hair close-cropped. Aeschines refers to the bodily vigour which permits us to recognize those who exercise even if we don't visit the gymnasium (1.189, cf. Plut. *Dion* 1.4). Much of this vigour, and much of the air of self-indulgence Achaeus describes (and probably ridicules), were the result of the athlete's distinctive diet; for combat competitors at least, this was richer and more dependent on meat than the Greek norm. 'Are you speaking to spectators or competitors?', asks a character in one of Achaeus's plays, likely the same drama already quoted (20 F 3). 'To men who eat a lot, as is the way of men in training.'[12]

The passages from Achaeus are known to us from a long section of Athenaeus devoted to gluttony (10.412d ff.). Among the most spectacular specimens are the famous heavy athletes Milon and Theogenes, along with others whose feats of food consumption are no less noteworthy: Titormus of Aetolia, who ate an ox at breakfast (Milon's presence spurred him on), and Astyanax of Miletus, thrice victor in the Olympic *pankration*, who came to a dinner party given by Ariobarzanes the Persian and ate all the food for nine male guests. We hear of no such heroic Athenian trenchermen, but the tendency itself was certainly known at Athens. To eat meat without bread is acceptable in training, says Xenophon's Socrates, but

---

[12] Wrestlers: Eur. *Ba.* 455–6, cf. *El.* 517–29, Simon. fr. 507 Page, *PMG.* Athletes of the Roman period wore the *cirrus*, a topknot of hair, like sumo wrestlers today or wrestlers in New Kingdom Egypt, but this is not attested in classical times: Suet. *Nero* 45; Gąssowska 1966. Meat: Bažant 1982. But runners might prefer to lose weight: Artem. 5.79, cf. Arist. *Cael.* 2.292b17.

otherwise greedy (Xen. *Mem.* 3.14.3, cf. Pl. *Resp.* 1.338cd). Less tolerant, the more intellectual of the pair of rivals in the Platonic *Amatores* dismisses an athlete's interests as nothing but quarrelling, stuffing himself and sleeping. Speaking as a scientist, Aristotle cautions about the potential perils of an athlete's diet, evident to all. 'Owing to their great bulk of nourishment, Nature cannot master it in order to bring about well proportioned growth. So the parts turn out ill-assorted, and sometimes bear little resemblance to what they were like before.' Athletic activities gave individuals an identity too. Among a group of beautiful men with many suitors, Aeschines mentions Timositheus the runner. Even young men might earn recognition of this kind, like Anticles the *stadion* runner, one of the youths and those still boys (Aeschin. 1.156); so too foreigners such as Diodorus the Chalcidian ambassador, said to have been a long distance runner (Aeschin. 3.91). Herodotus often makes a point of mentioning a man's athletic accomplishments; the feats and fates of victors at the great games are perhaps of special interest, but others appear as participants only.[13]

So: a recognizable and recognized segment of society. What can be said of its class origins? 'At Athens, athletics demonstrably were related to wealth and social prominence' (Kyle 1987:123). Smarting over Demosthenes' attacks on his allegedly lowly origins, Aeschines announces that his aged father Atrometus had been an athlete as a young man, before losing his property in the Peloponnesian war (2.147). He later helped restore the democracy, served bravely as a soldier in Asia Minor, and besides was a member of a group using the same altar as the aristocratic Eteoboutadae – all claims to status on a par with an athletic past. Similarly, his eldest brother Philochares, far from being addicted to ignoble pursuits, spends his time in the gymnasia when he is not on campaign with Iphicrates or serving as general. It is presumably the elite overtones of athletic activities that lead Aeschines to lard this and other speeches with references to the world of the gymnasium, to call himself and his allies fellow-competitors for the Athenians' peace and security, to refer to the effort required for victory in the crown games, to appeal

---

[13] Athlete's interest: [Pl.] *Amat.* 132c, cf. Eur. *Autolycus* fr. 282N.², Theophilus fr. 8 KA. Aristotle: *GA* 4.768b29, cf. *NE* 2.1106b2 and, for similar sentiments in the Hippocratic corpus, Visa 1992b. Timositheus: Aeschin. 1.156, cf. Dem. 17.11, 21.71, 59.121, 124, Hyper. *Lyc.* 5–6. Victors: Hdt. 5.47, 102, 6.92, 8.47. Participants: Hdt. 9.75, 105, cf. Xen. *An.* 5.8.23, *Hell.* 7.1.33.

to the image of boxers manoeuvring for position. And such associations provide the bite for his question at the end of the speech against Ctesiphon: 'Look to see who among you purposes to aid Demosthenes. Fellow huntsmen of his youth or men who exercise with him? But no, for he hasn't spent his time hunting wild boars or cultivating bodily vigour, but in hunting down men of property' (3.255, cf. 216). Plutarch's biography offers a belated defence: Demosthenes' guardians defrauded him of his father's estate, and he was besides sickly – these facts explain this seeming failure to engage in suitable pursuits (Plut. *Dem.* 4.3–4).[14]

In a less tendentious (but comic) context, Syrus, a slave charcoal burner, hesitates to raise a foundling who may grow up to despise his humble adoptive parents and revert to true type: hunting lions, running in competitions (Men. *Epitr.* 320–5). Socrates remarks that the rich know more of boxing than they do of war (Pl. *Resp.* 4.422b); when he cites criticisms of Pericles for the pay which let poorer Athenians participate in public life, Callicles accuses him of listening to men with cauliflower ears, reactionaries who go in for Spartan fashions in exercise and other matters (Pl. *Grg.* 515e, cf. *Prt.* 342c). Isocrates speaks of the good old days when Athens was well governed, poor men farmed and traded and those who had sufficient means devoted themselves to riding, the gymnasia, hunting and philosophy (7.44–5). Particularly revealing is a passage in Euripides' *Electra*. Struck by the nobility of character of Electra's peasant husband, Orestes opines that birth and wealth are no warrant of a man's worth; character is all (366–85). It is such men who manage cities and houses well. But pieces of flesh empty of sense are merely adornments – literally, 'statues' – in the agora. 'For a strong arm does not even await the spear in battle better than the weak; this is a matter of character and courage' (386–90). The lines often echo Euripides' *Autolycus*, and, like it, must aim at athletes. But the transition has been found abrupt, and the lines are sometimes excised as an interpolation – Diggle's standard text rejects 373–9 and 386–90. No need: the empty bodies are specific instances of Orestes' generalization, rich and well-born men who turn out to be of little use (cf. Goldhill 1986:169).

Aristotle mentions states where the prosperous are fined if they

---

[14] Philochares: Aeschin. 2.149; for the connection of athletes and the office of general, cf. 1.132. Fellow-competitors: Aeschin. 2.183 (*sunagonistas*). Crown games: Aeschin. 3.179–80. Boxers: Aeschin. 3.205–6; Poliakoff 1982:28–31, Ober 1989:281–3.

don't exercise (or possess hoplite weapons), in an attempt to mono-
polize physical fitness for the elite (Arist. *Pol.* 4.1297a32). That was
not the Athenian way. The opportunity cost, the need to earn a
living, probably kept most Athenians away from the gymnasia long
enough to preclude athletic success; someone aiming to win at
Olympia or Delphi had no time for other pursuits (Pl. *Leg.* 7.807c).
The expense of a skilled trainer would be a further hurdle. An
anecdote about the hetaera Gnathaena, renowned for her wit,
provides (unreliable) evidence on the cost (Ath. 13.584c). 'Is my
daughter like Hippomachus the trainer (*paidotribēn*)?', she is said to
have asked a penniless young man. 'Do you think you can keep
visiting her for a *mina*?' The *mina* contained one hundred drachmas,
and so amounted to about fifty or seventy-five days' wages for a
labourer at the dramatic date of this story, in the fourth century. As
Plato's Protagoras notes, it is those who are best able who go on to
take instruction from the *paidotribēs* and so 'perform the orders of
their minds with their bodies improved'; and those best able are the
richest (Pl. *Prt.* 326bc). No doubt there were some poorer Athenians
who took part in athletic competitions, perhaps most often in the
foot-races, as it was these in which natural ability would count for
most; long before Syrus, citizen charcoal burners in comedy prided
themselves on quickness in youth, when they could keep up with
Phayllus (Ar. *Ach.* 211–18). (Of those archaic and classical Olympic
victors traditionally said to be of poor backgrounds – none of them
Athenian – two were runners, two and perhaps three heavy athletes.)
But in general athletics, and familiarity with athletics – jock talk –
were a part of the elite milieu into which Aristophanes' Bdelycleon
seeks to introduce his untutored father (Ar. *Vesp.* 1190–213, 1381–9).
All Philocleon can do, of course, is reminisce about how he too
chased after Phayllus – and in the end convicted him of using
abusive language. The pun on *diokō*, both 'pursue' and 'prosecute',
brings together the two very different worlds of the gymnasium and
the democratic law-courts, just as Philocleon later bridges fantasy
and reality in knocking his son down during a lively account of an
Olympic *pankration* long ago.

Furthermore, there was a powerful preference among the elite to
compete only against their own kind. Take Alexander the Great.
Asked if he would enter the dash at Olympia – he was a swift runner
– he replied that he would – if he could have kings as his competitors
(Plut. *Alex.* 4.5, cf. *Mor.* 179d, 331b). The motif appears already in

Xenophon's *Hiero*. Here we learn that athletes get no pleasure from proving their superiority to the untrained, but are mortified to be defeated by their peers. So a tyrant has no joy of possessing more than private citizens, but is vexed to have less than his fellow rulers (Xen. *Hiero* 4.6). This general reflection is later translated into the arena of the great games. It is not fitting, says Simonides in that dialogue, for a ruler to compete with private citizens, for his great resources will bring him more envy than admiration if he wins, and ridicule if he loses. Hieron must compete only against other leaders of their cities, 'and to cause his state to surpass theirs in prosperity would be the greatest victory of all, proclaimed not by one herald's voice (as at the games) but by the whole world' (11.5–8). Again, Xenophon's Agesilaus says that a victory over private citizens would add nothing to his renown; he prefers to be first in the noblest and most splendid of contests, to stand first in his people's affections, to serve his country and his comrades best, and to punish his enemies (Xen. *Ages.* 9.6–7).

I would be surprised if these sentiments were Xenophon's alone or confined to the likes of kings and tyrants; indeed, there is the example of Alcibiades (to which we will turn a little later) to show that they were not. Unfortunately, the common man's point of view is provided, as usual, only by our upper-class sources – and in a non-Greek, fictional context besides. Xenophon portrays Pheraulas, one of the private soldiers in the army of the great Persian conqueror Cyrus, as welcoming the king's proposal to distribute war prizes according to merit. The fighting they face, says Pheraulas, favours courage over skill, Cyrus is a fair judge, commoners have more endurance and capacity to bear hunger and cold. He urges other soldiers to join this competition, 'for now they [the Persian elite] are trapped in a democratic contest' (Xen. *Cyr.* 2.3.7–15). This sounds as if Xenophon thought such an equal or even favourable competition between members of different classes was unusual – and would be to the liking of ordinary men. But another story with a military setting implies that such men were content to compete against those similar in status to themselves (Hdt. 5.111).

Finally, more than the backgrounds of the participants marked athletic competition as a minority pursuit. Athletic activities were carried out under an ethos significantly different from that of the democratic polis. The athletic programme itself, involving as it did contests of individual strength, speed and skill essentially unchanged from those narrated in the great heroic epics, recalled and reinforced an aristocratic milieu far from the cooperation and group solidarity required to fight in a hoplite battle line, row a trireme or serve on a democratic board or council. (The greater, quadrennial, Panathenaea featured a torch race, boat race and competitions in *euhexia* and *euandria* for tribes, but did not award the distinctive oil-filled amphorae as their prizes.) Xenophon's Socrates, conversing with Critobulus, draws the distinction. 'Even in athletic competitions it is clear that stronger competitors would win all the events and carry off all the prizes if they were allowed to join forces against the weaker. They are not allowed to do this there. But in politics, in which the elite dominate, no one prevents anyone from benefiting the community with whomever he pleases' (Xen. *Mem.* 2.6.26). At the same time, however, gymnasia, palaestrae and the competitions themselves were run with an arbitrary authority which, once again, seems out of tune with democratic mores. We know next to nothing about the administration of Athenian public gymnasia in the classical period; Sally Humphreys suggests, hesitantly, that they were managed by priests (and paid for from cult funds), or, alternatively, leased out to contractors who ran them on their own (Humphreys 1974:91). A story in the Platonic corpus does at least suggest that they could be kept under a tight rein: the gymnasiarch of the Lyceum threw Prodicus out on the grounds that he was talking about matters unsuitable for the young ([Pl.] *Eryx.* 399a, cf. [Pl.] *Ax.* 367a). Prodicus, of course, was not an Athenian citizen. Even citizens, however, were accustomed to obey the officials (*tois epistatais*) in athletic contests, as they did their naval commanders and their choir trainers (Xen. *Mem.* 3.5.18, cf. 21). This might involve rough justice. Adeimantus, the Corinthian admiral at Salamis, reminded Themistocles that those who false start in the games are struck (and disqualified) by the officials. Xenophon says the power to punish lawbreakers on the spot was one officials held in common with despots, *turannoi*, and the ephors at Sparta.[15]

What we may call a civic critique of Greek athletes and their honours runs from Tyrtaeus to Isocrates and beyond. This denigrates the contribution of athletic training and achievement to the

---

[15] Themistocles: Hdt. 8.59, cf. Plut. *Them.* 11, *Mor.* 185b, Ael. *VH* 13.40. Power to punish: Xen. *Lac.* 8.4; for an example, the case of the Spartan Lichas at Olympia, see Thuc. 5.50.4, Xen. *Hell.* 3.2.21, Paus. 6.2.2.

Plate 9. An official strikes a boxer for a foul. Attic black-figure Panathenaic amphora, Painter of Munich 1519, about 510.

community in favour of those who stand fast in the front lines or fall in battle, or understand the art of poetry. Generals and tyrannicides, the reasonable leader of the city, the man who toils in private for the public good and to help his fellow citizens – it is these who enrich the city in peacetime and keep it safe in peril. As Aristotle puts it, 'Men do not claim office on the ground of every kind of superiority: if one group of men are slow and another swift, this is no claim to political preferment, but a distinction which will win honour in athletic competitions' (Arist. *Pol.* 3.1283a12). Was there also a democratic critique, hostility to athletes or their activities on class grounds? We might pose another question in response: Why should there be? If the elite chose to be pushed around by officials at athletic venues, to break each others' ears – why should the *demos* care? All the less in that some at least of the expense of public athletics at Athens was borne by the rich themselves. An unknown critic of the democracy known as the Old

Oligarch speaks of gymnasiarchies in the same breath as providing choruses and trierarchies ([Xen.].[16]

But there is some misrepresentation here. The torch race, the boat race and the *euandria* at the greater Panathenaea were indeed tribal contests requiring ten sponsors each; so too annual torch races at the Prometheia and Hephaesteia and perhaps the lesser, annual, Panathenaea were funded by gymnasiarchs, and two men per tribe paid for the *eutaxia*, which may be athletic. The sums involved range from modest – 50 or 100 drachmas for the *eutaxia* (IG 2² 417)– to considerable, the 1200 drachmas with which the speaker of Lysias 21 won a victory in the torch race at the Prometheia at the end of the fifth century, the 1500 drachmas he contributed to the Panathenaic boat race (Lys. 21.3, 5). He says he spent much more than he needed. However, even these compare tellingly to others: even at the upper end, they run somewhat less than the same man's expenses as comic choregus (Lys. 21.4); dithyrambic and tragic choruses and trierarchies might cost still more. Nor do these gymnasiarchies provide all the funding for Athenian athletics.[17]

We are hardly better informed on the expenses of Athenian festivals than we are on the management of athletic facilities. Still, some idea of costs can be obtained from two inscriptions recording payments from the treasury of Athena during the Peloponnesian War. One, dated to 410/9, lists a sum of five talents, 1000 drachmas paid to the *athlothetai* for the greater Panathenaea, as well as an additional 5114 drachmas to other officials towards the sacrifice (*IG* 1³ 374.5–8 = 84 ML). The other is more mysterious, since a payment of nine talents for the *athlothetai* in 415/4 is simply said to be for the Panathenaea (*IG* 1³ 370.66–8 = 77 ML). This seems a lot for the lesser Panathenaea in relation to the sum for the quadrennial celebration five years later, and envisages an otherwise unheard of role for the *athlothetai* at the annual festival during this period. There is some reason, then, to sympathize with the suspicion that the sum is an instalment paid towards the greater Panathenaea of 414

---

[16] Civic critique: see Marcovich 1978:16–26, Angeli Bernardini 1980:84–92, Kyle 1987:127–41. Stand fast: Tyrtaeus 12 West, *IE²*. Fall in battle: Solon in Diog. Laert. 1.55–6, cf. Diod. Sic. 9.2.5. Understand: Xenophanes DK 21B2. Generals: Lyc. *Leocr.* 51. Leader: Eur. *Autolycus* fr. 282N.² Man who toils: Isoc. 4.1–2, cf. 15.250, 301–2, *Ep.* 8.5. Old Oligarch: [Xen.] *Ath. Pol.* 1.3, cf. Xen. *Oec.* 2.5–7, Plut. *Nic.* 3.3.

[17] Sponsors: see J.K. Davies 1967, Crowther 1991a for these and other contributions possibly required of the rich and, for gymnasiarchies in the demes, Isae. 2.42, *IG* 2² 3109 (early third century).

(Davison 1958:29–33); but on balance the discrepancy is better explained as a consequence of Athens's changed circumstances, from the expansive optimism of the Sicilian adventure to the poverty which was one of its sequels. These are of course significant sums, but not staggeringly large, even for a city at war. The accounts for 415/4 mention something over 350 talents of expenditure in all, and those for 410/9 at least 180 talents, paid from Athena's annual revenues. Most poorer Athenians would probably support such expenditures even if it was their wealthier fellow citizens who took part in the competitions and bore away their prizes.[18]

These prizes were themselves costly. In the early fourth century, athletic and equestrian winners and runners-up were awarded at least 1423 Panathenaic amphorae, each filled with olive oil for their own use or for resale without the usual restrictions on export (Johnston 1987). Individuals at the time could win as many as 140, the first prize for the chariot race. Following the conservative calculations of David Young, which are based on the cheapest known price for olive oil, twelve drachmas per amphora, the oil component of the prizes alone would amount to about three talents (Young 1984:116); using a more common price, from sixteen to eighteen drachmas, we arrive at a figure of four or five talents – forgone income rather than expense, to be sure, since the oil came from the community's own trees. As for the amphorae in which the oil was contained, large lots of used examples fetched from about two to four obols in the auction of the property confiscated from those convicted of sacrilege in 415 (Amyx 1958:178).

However, resentment at these outlays would be tempered by two factors. First, individual prizes at the Panathenaea were of such a scale that even a boy winner in the wrestling, say, would earn the equivalent of eight or nine months' wages for a skilled worker – enough to pay for the training to launch a successful athletic career (Young 1984:120, 159). It remains the case nevertheless that we know of no classical Athenian athlete who followed this trajectory; given the number of athletes we can identify – Kyle lists 78 definite and 116 possible individuals (Kyle 1987:194–228) – this silence is surprising, all the more since Athenians might choose to advertise an improvement in status (Arist. *Ath. Pol.* 7.4). Second – perhaps a more

---

[18] Better explained: cf. Rhodes 1981:669, Meiggs and Lewis 1988:236 and, for the *athlothetai* at the lesser Panathenaea in the Hellenistic period, B. Nagy 1978.

important consideration – many prizes did not go to Athenians at all, poor or rich. The substantial rewards for athletic and equestrian events, like the lavish prizes for musicians and singers, were probably meant to attract the best and best-known competitors from all of Greece. Consistent with this conclusion, the prizes for equestrian events for all-comers on *IG* 2² 2311 (= S.G. Miller 1991: no. 84) are much greater than those available to Athenians only. Of extant inscriptions recording athletic and equestrian victors in Athenian games, *IG* 2² 2312 (early fourth century) has been restored to show only one Athenian victor among others from Erythrae, Troezen and Zacynthus at an unknown festival. Of the 200–odd victories listed on six accounts of the Panathenaea from the second century (*IG* 2² 2313–17, *Hesperia* 60 (1991) 188–9), about half – including most boy victors – are not Athenian. The great majority of Athenian wins come in events restricted to citizen competitors, a much expanded part of the programme in the Hellenistic period. Otherwise, 'most of the known winners in all categories are foreigners' (Tracy and Habicht 1991:197, cf. Tracy 1991:138).

This pattern was probably long established. Finds at the sanctuary of Athena Chalkioikos and the Menelaion at Sparta include fragments of sixth- and fifth-century prize Panathenaics, and early dedications of Panathenaics were made at other sanctuaries outside Attica, especially at the Theban Cabeirion, surely by local victors. Poorer Athenians were apparently willing to countenance and support athletic and equestrian activities which brought enjoyment to themselves as spectators and credit to their city as sponsor without undue concern for the dominance of the elite or even of foreigners in those activities and their unequal access to their rewards. Demosthenes puts it plainly: 'from earliest times, Athens has given its richest honours to those athletes who have won at the crown games, and not begrudged them on the grounds that they are naturally won by only a few' (Dem. 20.141). And of course if only a few won, many lost. There may well have been some pleasure to be had in the defeats and debacles of the privileged (see below). So it is, no doubt, that we find no classical Athenian curse tablets directed at athletes, and that no ostrakon yet reported identifies its target as an athlete. Nor were contemporary athletes prominent among the targets of Athenian comic playwrights (cf. Sommerstein 1996:331). The apparent exception is Autolycus, whose victory in the Pan-athenaic *pankration* for youths occasioned at least one of the two plays by Eupolis bearing his name (Ath. 5.216cd). Yet even in his case the extant fragments (48–75) of the comedies do not refer to athletic pursuits, and his father and mother too come in for abuse in these and other plays. Autolycus, it seems, attracts interest in the main as a member of a prominent family rather than as an athlete.[19]

Yet the case is not quite closed. 'We Athenians' (says the chorus leader in Aristophanes' *Frogs*) 'mistreat those citizens we know are well-born, wise and just, Nature's noblemen raised in palaestrae and choruses and the arts – and entrust all our affairs to those less worthy' (Ar. *Ran.* 727–30). Sometime later in the same play, Aeschylus complains that no one these days can carry a torch because of lack of exercise. 'You're right', agrees Dionysus. 'In fact, not long ago at the Panathenaic torch race, the inhabitants of the Ceramicus beat up a slow runner, hitting him with open hands in the stomach, the ribs, the flanks and the rear end. So he farted, made his torch flare up, and got away' (Ar. *Ran.* 1089–98). An ancient commentator on line 1093 cites another reference to something similar in Aristophanes (fr. 459 KA, cf. perhaps fr. 470), and then notes, on the authority of the Alexandrian scholar and specialist in Attic comedy Euphronius, that the slowest runners among the youths in the torch race were struck by the common people (*hupo tōn agoraiōn*), and that these were called 'blows of the Ceramicus', *Kerameikai plegai*. Hesychius adds that they struck those who weren't running, and the other competitors, to get a laugh.[20]

We can count on some guesswork and confusion here – the scholion speaks of a torch race within the Ceramicus, and Hesychius makes the competition itself of little value, not the onlookers. Still, the repeated comic references must show that this is not simply a matter of a one-off joke but rather the representation (or misrepresentation) of something ongoing at Athens. But what? Much depends on the identity of the runners. If they were drawn from the same circles as other athletic competitors, the practice afforded an opportunity for ordinary Athenians to abuse the kinds of athletic youths who had gained prominence and prizes on the preceding

---

[19] Sparta: Dickins 1906–7:150–3, Catling 1976–7:7–41. Local victors: Valavanis 1986:459–60, cf. Hamilton 1996:142–3. Curse tablets: some are known from Roman Athens however; Jordan 1985:213–22 nos. 1–6. Father and mother: Ameipsias fr. 22 KA (from Schol. Ar. *Vesp.* 1169, where the reference to the pentathlon is presumably a slip), Eupolis fr. 58, 295 KA.

[20] Hesychius: κ 2263, cf. ε 3280, ρ 2482, Pherecrates fr. 258 KA.

days. A parallel: the procession which preceded the public proclamation of honours at the City Dionysia featured ritual verbal abuse,
which 'allowed those with less status to mock those with more' in a
safe, sacralized context (Cole 1993:34). But the torch racers may not
have been like other athletes. The interpretation I have just offered
implies that the Panathenaic torch racers are among the city's best
who can't get no respect these days. It might be easier, however, to
see them instead as examples of the unworthy who have supplanted
them, those (as Aeschylus laments) who do not go to the gymnasia.
N.V. Sekunda has argued that only the torch race at the Hephaestia
was run in relays of selected youths; in the other festivals, including
the Panathenaea, all a tribe's ephebes ran as a compulsory part of
their training (Sekunda 1990:154–5). It is often assumed that only
those of hoplite status served as ephebes (e.g. Rhodes 1981:503). Even
at that, something like half or a little more of the male citizen
population could qualify as hoplites in the late fifth century, the time
of the play (Strauss 1986:81). Hoplite torch racers would thus include
many youths outside the athletic and equestrian elite. Furthermore,
there is also a compelling demographic argument for the inclusion of
some if not all of the lowest census group, the *thetes*.[21]

This may help elucidate a difficult section of the Old Oligarch's
pamphlet already referred to. We read that the demos has destroyed
respect for those who exercise, *tous gumnazomenous*, as for those who
are concerned with the arts, knowing that they themselves can't
succeed in such activities ([Xen.] *Ath. Pol.* 1.13). On the other hand,
when it comes to funding choruses and gymnasiarchies and providing ships, the rich pay and command, while the poor obey. So
money is what the people need when singing and running and
dancing in a chorus and sailing in ships. The pamphleteer distinguishes between *tous gumnazomenous* and runners; the reference to
gymnasiarchies specifies the kind of running he has in mind – torch
races. Now, we have already seen that this author is prone to
exaggeration; a little further on, he observes that the *demos* builds
many palaestrae for its own use (2.10) – he must define the *demos*
more inclusively than most, sharing, it may be, the vantage point of
the very rich who could afford the private gymnasia he mentions.
Nevertheless, the parallel to Aeschylus's complaint is intriguing. We

---

[21] Ritual abuse: cf. the analysis of sport as carnival in, e.g., Blake 1996:46–53. Inclusion of *thetes*: Hansen 1985:47–50, 1988:5–6, Sekunda 1992:330–1; *contra*, Sallares 1991:121.

should entertain the possibility that those who ran in the Panathenaic torch race, in relays or not, were truly representative of
their tribes, selected (as so often at Athens) by lot from all its young
adults. The possibility is made more palatable by the race's ritual
overtones, as by its likely siting in the Panathenaic programme, after
the individual and tribal competitions and before the procession and
sacrifice (Neils 1992b:15). On one level, the openness of the race to
all who cared to compete would presage the distribution of meat
which reasserted the democratic nature of the polis, and thus act as
a counterweight to the Panathenaic procession, displaying as it did
magistrates and other segments of the community and its allies by
group. On another level, the *Kerameikai plegai* parody the discipline
of the *rhabdoukhoi*, the rod-wielding umpires, and challenge the
ordered and severe ethos of Greek athletic competition. We have
returned, by this reckoning, to the playfulness and subversion of
hierarchy which marked the games of the '10,000' at Trapezus (see
Chapter 1).[22]

EQUESTRIAN COMPETITION AND POLITICAL LEADERSHIP
DURING THE DEMOCRACY

With horses the stakes were higher. Teisias sued Alcibiades for either
five or eight talents – sources differ – the value of the team which
won the Olympic four-horse chariot-race in 416 (Isoc. 16.46, Diod.
Sic. 13.74.3). Even the smaller sum represents around seventy years
of wages at the time, say US $2,000,000 today. This is just the yearly
take of a modern superstar, or rather of a midistar – the top athletes
earn six times as much. But of course Alcibiades had to stable and
feed his horses, buy a chariot and its appurtenances, arrange for a
driver. Whatever the numbers, raising horses was a rich man's game,
the business of 'the most fortunate'. Everyone knew it, not everyone
approved. Silent though they may be on athletic activities, one
ostrakon does reproach Megacles, the head of the illustrious Alc-
maeonid family in the 480s, for raising horses (Siewert 1991:10); a
four-horse Thessalian chariot – the most beautiful kind (Poll. 7.112) –
comes into Eupolis's *Autolycus* (fr. 66 KA); and the reference by
Aristophanes' chorus of cavalrymen to the chariot crashes of the

---

[22] [Xen.] *Ath. Pol.* 2.10: see now Lapini 1994:134–5. Procession: one of the groups which took
part may have been made up of competitors at the games: Tracy 1991:149–51.

gilded youth may be meant to raise a laugh. Victories in horse-racing (according to Lycurgus) are evidence of wealth and nothing more, of less value than trierarchies or building the city's walls (Lyc. *Leocr.* 139–40, cf. Dem. 18.320).[23]

Yet a defendant includes among his father's services which brought honour to the city his racehorses; with them he won at Isthmia and Nemea, so that Athens was proclaimed by the herald and he himself crowned (Lys. 19.63). For another speaker in another case, keeping horses, including a racing team, is a respectable, even expected, way for a rich man to spend a lot of money. The best example of this kind of claim, of course, is Alcibiades himself – or Thucydides' portrayal of him – entering a record seven chariots at Olympia, finishing first, second and fourth; in this way he earned honour on his own behalf and displayed Athens's power. Other sources say Alcibiades was third, not fourth, but are as insistent on the scope of his achievement. Isocrates, of course, is an advocate for Alcibiades' son; his presentation of Alcibiades, disdaining athletic competition because of the presence of some athletes of low birth and little culture, living in small cities, is meant to place him beyond the reach of the vulgar theft of which Teisias charged him, just as the account of his ancestor Alcmaeon, first to win the Olympic *tethrippon* for Athens, elides the origins of his wealth, ignobly rooting about in Croesus's vaults.[24]

An invective, no less skewed, provides balance: not only is Alcibiades to be deemed guilty of horse theft, but their owner (here called Diomedes) is said to be of merely moderate means, a man like the audience rather than a figure of awe ([Andoc.] 4.26). Nor do Alcibiades' successes impress Thucydides' Nicias (Thuc. 6.12.2). Indeed, Thucydides himself supplies a critical commentary on Alcibiades' speech, preceding it with the observation that he spent more than he could afford (6.15.3) and following it, as often, with an instructive and ironic narrative. The armada was marked by competition among the soldiers in respect to their weapons and equipment;

---

[23] 'The most fortunate': Isoc. 16.33, cf. Herod. 6.125, cf. Xen. *Ages.* 1.23, *Eq.* 2.1, Arist. *Pol.* 4.1289b35, 8.1321a11. Chariot crashes: Ar. *Eq.* 556–68, cf. *Pax* 899–904 and the report of popular enthusiasm for such mishaps at [Dem.] 61.29; Crowther 1994a:50–1.

[24] A respectable way: Isae. 7.43, cf. 11.41, Xen. *Eq.* 11.8–9, Hyper. 1.16. Alcibiades: Thuc. 6.16.2–3; cf., for claiming credit for the number of entries, Xen. *Hiero* 11.5. Third: Eur. 755 Page, *PMG* in Plut. *Alc.* 11, Isoc. 16.34, cf. Dem. 21.144–5. Alcmaeon: cf. Too 1995:213–21 and, for the notion that *hippikē* is more pleasurable and less toilsome than athletics, Xen. *Eq. Mag.* 8.5–6.

it was more like a show of wealth and power before the rest of the
Greeks than a military expedition. It put to sea in a single column,
and then the ships competed to reach Aegina first (6.31.3–4, 32.2).
The echo of Alcibiades' speech is no accident; his pursuit of glory,
like the sailors', is futile in the historian's eyes, another example of
the peril of ambition for private ends.[25]

Yes, Alcibiades was an especially controversial figure. But this
controversy does not arise with him. We have seen reasons to believe
that disputes over the worth of equestrian events affected even the
history of the Olympic programme. It was perhaps Athens's fifth-
century tragedians who were most responsible for the unfavourable
version of the original chariot race at Olympia, featuring Pelops's
plot and the treachery of Myrtilus (Moreau 1987). Sophocles'
Oenomaus was well enough regarded to be revived in fourth-century
productions (Dem. 18.180, 242 with Hsch. α 7381). Yet we can hardly
suppose that hostility to hippic competition was the cause. Is there
better evidence for widespread popular resentment of or opposition
to this most costly of competitions and its wealthy participants?
Some has been seen in the Prytaneion Decree, an inscription from
the 430s or early 420s awarding *sitesis*, free meals in the city hall, to
victors in the four crown games of the festival circuit. Athletic and
equestrian victors (at least) are specified separately. The result of
'democratic opposition towards the granting of *sitesis* to hippic
victors', necessitating a restatement of their rights (Morrissey
1978:124)? A means to give them something extra, fodder for their
horses (Thompson 1979)? The inscription is too fragmentary to tell.
We should remember, however (as Thompson does), that the
rewards were extended to the winners of the Olympic two-horse
chariot race, first run not long afterwards, in 408. And Socrates: he
asked his peers to grant him *sitesis*, as this was more suitable for a
poor man than for someone who won a horse or chariot race and
could afford to buy his own meals, but they preferred to condemn
him to death.[26]

It remains to explore an attractive hypothesis of John Davies
(J. K. Davies 1981:97–105). Struck by the drop in the number of
known chariot entries in the crown and other panhellenic games in

---

[25] Ambition: cf. Thuc. 2.65.7, 3.83.8, 8.89.3; Whitehead 1983:58.

[26] Prytaneion Decree: *IG* i^3 131.11–19; for other references to *sitesis* and discussion, see S.G.
Miller 1978:4–13, Schmitt Pantel 1992:147–63 and (on the date) Mattingly 1990:114–15.
Socrates: Pl. *Ap.* 36de; Kyle 1987:145–7.

Table 6. *Athenian equestrian competitors and victors, 600–300 BCE*

generation[a]	propertied Athenians[b]	chariot entries[c]	chariot entrants	hippic victors at Olympia[d]	Athenian hippic victors at Olympia[d]	Athenian athletes/ equestrians[e]
A	2	2	2	2	1	3/1
B	10	7	3	6	3	1/7
C	3	5	3	8	2	1–3/4–7
D	16	5 or 6	3+	16	0	7–8/4–6
E	32	5 or 6	3	12	1	10/5
F	71	12	2	7	1	8/7
G	154	3	2	9	0	12–13/2
H	334	10	9	7 or 8	1	16–18/9
I	206	5	3	4	1	4–5/3

Notes:
(a) A, 600–567/6; B, 566/5–534/3; C, 533/2–501/0; D, 500/499–467/6; E, 466/5–434/3; F, 433/2–401/0; G, 400/399–367/6; H, 366/5–334/3; I, 333/2–301/0. See J.K. Davies 1971:xxvii.
(b) J.K. Davies 1971:xxvii.
(c) J.K. Davies 1981:167–168 (with the addition of chariot competitors at the panhellenic Amphiaraei at Oropus, 366–338).
(d) Moretti 1957, 1970, 1987 (with the omission of the three victories attributed to Callias in 500, 496, 492).
(e) Kyle 1987:104–9 (including both attested and possible competitors until 322/1 only).

the fourth century (see Table 6, columns 3 and 4), a drop more startling still in light of the contemporaneous explosion of information on the propertied Athenians listed in his register (Table 6, column 2) and of the doubling of opportunities for victory with the addition of six new equestrian events at Olympia and Delphi from 408 to 314, Davies drew the 'tentative inference that for much of the fourth century spending of this sort did not have its former political importance' (103). Some have been sceptical – Rhodes thinks chariot racing never paid political dividends (Rhodes 1986:138–42), and it is disconcerting for generalizations that over half the entries of two- and four-horse chariots were made by three famous families (Davies 1981:100–1). Of course, such scepticism suits the scarce and scattered nature of our data, which could take on a completely different cast with the discovery of a single inscription. But in general Davies's view prevails. The issue is important for our purposes because heightened sensitivity to this form of elite display among the *demos* provides one obvious explanation. It is easy enough to sketch a plausible context: Alcibiades' performance at Olympia in 416 was a hard act to follow, and his subsequent career alone would dissuade most from following it; for those still so inclined, the alignment of the cavalry with the dictatorship of the Thirty Tyrants at the end of the Peloponnesian war and their complicity in some of their worst outrages much reduced the appeal of a political persona based on equestrian competition, given the likelihood that the cavalry was purged after the restoration of the democracy and reorganized to bring in new members from outside the traditional horseraising families (Spence 1993:216–24, Németh 1994).[27]

Nevertheless, some doubts remain. First, Chabrias, Timocrates and Demades: three fourth-century political figures who won Olympic or Pythian chariot victories. In maintaining that horse-racing was 'no longer viable as a claim to leadership', Kyle dissociates their political and competitive activities (Kyle 1987:166–7). But why? True, Chabrias's Pythian victory in 374 did come some fifteen years after he served as general in 390/89, but his political and military career continued into the 350s. Timocrates was important enough to warrant an attack by Demosthenes in 353/2, about the time of his triumph at Olympia, and appeared as a witness for Meidias in 348. And if chariot racing were unpopular or inappropriate for political leaders, Demosthenes' failure to so much as mention Timocrates' activities would be very odd. As for Demades, Kyle simply labels him a *parvenu* and asserts that it was oratory, not horse-racing, which gained him influence. For his part, however, Demades must have thought that competing, and winning above all, consolidated and enhanced his position. The case for distinguishing these men from their few fifth-century counterparts is not compelling (cf. Hamilton 1996:140).

Second, Davies's hypothesis envisages an Athenian elite out of step with their peers in other Greek cities, who presumably continued to enter the established hippic contests of the crown games

---

[27] Davies's view: cf. Kyle 1987: 160–1, 167–8. Cavalry: I have the impression – imprecise dating precludes more – that *hippos* names, personal names incorporating the Greek word for horse, were less frequent among propertied Athenians born during the early fourth century than among their fifth-century fellows.

(though in what numbers we cannot tell) and may well have encouraged the introduction of the new ones. (It is a pity that we know nothing about the process by which the equestrian programme at the greater Panathenaea had become so elaborate by the 380s.) This is not impossible. Courting a boy by extolling his ancestors' triumphs with chariots and racehorses is made to appear laughable in Plato (Pl. *Lys.* 205bd). Still, others (we hear) told similar tales, and Plato was a crank anyway, happy to exclude chariot racing from his Cretan city (Pl. *Leg.* 8.834b). Besides, the Athenian record in equestrian events at Olympia does not fully bear it out (see Table 6, columns 5 and 6). There are no fewer Athenians known to have won in the fourth century than the fifth; and even at that Alcibiades won in the enforced absence of the Spartans, who had dominated the four-horse event for a generation. The downturn in Athenian fortunes seems to occur 100 years or so earlier, between generations C and D. Similarly, owners of horses make up a larger proportion of the known and possible competitors in the fifth century than the fourth, but here again the difference from the sixth to the fifth seems as great or greater (see Table 6, column 7). We might have expected that the continual growth of the cavalry wing of the armed forces during the expansion of the Athenian empire in the mid-fifth century would spur more interest in equestrian competition than we find (for that development, see Bugh 1988:39–52). The earlier period apparently saw another, perhaps related, shift, from depictions of horsemen to athletes in Attic vase painting. 'Partly this must be a change of interest and partly perhaps the increasing expense of keeping horses', writes Webster (1972:215); 'it may be that if you are rich enough to keep a horse or horses, you are also rich enough to have decorated metal symposium ware and so cease to buy special pots for the symposion'.

Neither should the impact of democracy be discounted, and not just that restored at the end of the fifth century. Cleisthenes' too may have ushered in a period in which equestrian competition and excess aroused less admiration, and more antipathy, than before (though in neither context was it utterly discredited as a path to political leadership). It is of course impossible to be sure whether the relative scarcity of known Athenian victors at Olympia which follows generation C really reflects a drop in participation, and no less difficult to pinpoint when it began. Each of Davies's generations covers a period of thirty-three or thirty-four years; any shift might be the result of a relatively small cluster of instances early in one generation or late in the next, and so dates may be sixty-odd years out either way. The earlier shift I've pointed to, then, might come near the beginning of generation C. Certainly Cimon's fate, murdered on Peisistratid orders after his third victory, might discourage imitators; and Hippias and Hipparchus, for all the equestrian overtones of their names, are associated with the arts as a means of personal expression or political propaganda. But the Alcmaeonids, at any rate, seem to have maintained their interest, racking up a notable string of successes at Delphi even before Megacles' victory in 486. We have already mentioned his *ostrakon*, with its accusation of horse breeding; Megacles was in fact ostracized just before his Pythian triumph. It is preferable, I think, to date the shift in attitudes and actions within generation D and to see opposition to equestrian display in competitive contexts as yet another delayed effect of Cleisthenes' revolution (508), spurred (like ostracism itself, first attested only in 487) by the Persian threat. It says something about the flavour of that early democracy that it did not (so far as we know) aspire to race horses on its own, despite the example of the Argive community's successes at Olympia in 480 and 472. If my hunch here is correct – a supplement to Davies's hypothesis, not a refutation – it is another sign that the Athenian *demos* was normally content to rein in its wealthy citizens and harness their resources for its own purposes, not to supplant them in their chosen pursuits, whether in athletic and equestrian competition or in political leadership.

Conclusion

Everyone knows the story about the speed reader. Challenged to prove his prowess, he read *War and Peace* in a day and even offered a book review. 'It's about Russia.'

This book is about ancient Greek sport. But it may be useful at this stage to review what sets it apart from other such books (much as Tolstoy might have wished to distinguish *War and Peace* and, say, *From Russia with Love*). The main theme has been what I call the discourse of difference in Greek sport. In the opening chapter, I reviewed a number of approaches to the subject, devoting particular attention to the links between sport and religion and sport and warfare. I affirmed that these ties were indeed strong, as is often argued. Nevertheless, these associations did not lead me to conclude that sport was to be envisioned as a kind of dependent variable, comprehensible mainly in the context of one or another aspect of Greek life. On the contrary: the singularity of Greek sport set the Greeks apart from contemporary cultures of the Mediterranean as neither religion nor warfare could do. Sport was too significant, too pervasive and (above all) too distinctive to be regarded as a reflex. It demands consideration on its own.

This is not to suppose that the practices and values of Greek sport were unique within Greek society. Sport was like religion and warfare in affording a field for the creation and reinforcement of divisions among groups and the ordering of these groups into hierarchies. Sacrifice joins and demarcates gods, animals and humans; young men conquer others while old men, women and children figure as passive victims of war. In Greek sport, this discourse of difference takes three forms. It problematizes boundaries between Greeks and foreigners and among groups of Greeks; it defines individuals as winners and losers; and it provides the framework for divisions of opinion on the value of different forms of competition.

First, sport makes boundaries. Greeks compete, non-Greeks do not. In fact, at the festival with the most prestige and the longest pedigree, the Olympic games, non-Greeks were excluded. Other games need not have imposed this formal restriction, but they too followed a practice, athletic nudity, which was foreign and even distasteful to neighbouring peoples. Again, Greek sport was for males, not females. These barriers to participation asserted a superiority which might otherwise be challenged. We may compare baseball's World Series. Originally named after a newspaper, this competition is often billed as the championship of the world, though it is open only to a restricted collection of North American professional teams. There were significant barriers within sport as well. Greek males competed in age classes, as boys (sometimes further sub-divided) or men. One motive, I have suggested, is to prevent another undesirable outcome, the defeat of a father by his son.

A second sort of difference was an inevitable result of competition itself: the creation of winners and losers. The material rewards victors earned affirmed their privileged position within the social structure of the *polis*; their excellence, and the honours that went with it, tended to exalt them above other mortals and assimilate them to the gods – a process much aided by poems in their praise and victory statues. Such stature did not come without cost; victors and their monuments might attract envy. And, since the Greeks were not much interested in establishing records for individual performances – one reason they took so little care to record times and distances or establish uniform standards for tracks, javelins or discuses – even the greatest champion might well become just another loser. Orestes is hailed as a victor for his revenge on his mother and her lover in one strain of the mythological tradition, but the imagery of athletic and equestrian competition is used to paint him as a failure in Euripides' *Orestes*.

Equestrian competition offers exceptions to much of this. Tiberius, the future Roman emperor, and his adopted son Germanicus each triumphed in the Olympic four-horse chariot race long before Nero. Women too could compete in equestrian events, even at Olympia. Sons might race against their fathers – there were no age classes for owners (though colts and grown horses came to be raced separately). Explanations abound. Who would wish to hold the most powerful men in the world to the letter of the law, especially after Elis had become part of the Roman province of Achaea? Women's competition was at a remove, since owners need not ride or drive their entries, and victory might in any case be represented as the consequence of superior resources rather than strength or skill. Living fathers could control their sons' access to such resources, and so make their rivalry impossible. Most significant for our purposes, however, is the simple fact that horse-racing was different.

Horse-racing could therefore figure prominently in the third form which the discourse of difference takes in Greek sport: debate about the relative value of various events and classes of events. The rivalry between horse-racing and athletics runs through this book, usually enveloped (explicitly or not) within antagonisms of class. If successful athletes were generally well-off, equestrian competitors came from the political and economic elite. In Chapter 1, I suggested that opposing views on the claims of equestrian and athletic competition inspired both the compilation and the content of Hippias's canonical list of Olympic victors. In Chapter 4, I demonstrated that horse-racing was the preserve of older competitors, and so prolonged the careers of the elite past the point where the less privileged had to give up the pursuit of pre-eminence. In Chapter 5, I found traces of antagonism towards the use of equestrian success as a basis for political preferment in the heady days which followed the Athenian democracy's great victory over the invading Persians.

I have tried in this book to provide the information most essential for an introduction to Greek sport. Of course, facts – these and the many others which might be supplied – take on most meaning within a framework. Many frameworks are possible. I believe that the context constructed here, the discourse of difference, is of exceptional value in illuminating the role sport played in Greek society and history.

Bibliographical essay

I have sought in the text of this book to provide references to contemporary scholarship in whatever language it is written, subject to my own limitations. (For example, I do not read Hungarian or microfilm.) Here my intention is rather different, to suggest further reading which might be accessible to students at institutions like my own, a small public undergraduate university on the Canadian prairies. I have therefore concentrated on publications in English. In doing so I necessarily slight important contributions in other languages, in German above all. J.H. Krause's work set the standard in scholarship on ancient sport for the nineteenth century (1835, 1838, 1841a, 1841b); some is still useful even now, for the Pythian, Isthmian and Nemean games in particular. (Klee 1918 does not list equestrian victors.) The German Archaeological Institute, in charge of excavations at Olympia since 1875, continues to issue its series of publications on the site. Mallwitz (1972) and Herrmann (1972) offer authoritative accounts by experts. Julius Jüthner prepared the standard edition and commentary on Philostratus's *On Athletic Exercise* (1909) and many articles on athletic subjects in *RE*. The massive collection of material left at his death in 1945, edited and published in two volumes by Friedrich Brein, is equally indispensable to scholars, especially those interested in the conduct of individual events (1965, 1968). Ingomar Weiler's books on competition in Greek myth and culture (1974) and on sport in the ancient Mediterranean (1988) are rich in comparative material, invaluable for supplying a context for Greek practices and beliefs and for full bibliographies. (I have not yet seen the new synthesis by Wolfgang Decker (1995).) Furthermore, only those who read French will profit directly from the reports on the ongoing excavations at Delphi or from Louis Robert's many magisterial (but widely dispersed) studies on the competitive culture of the Greek cities of the Roman Empire. Work in Italian includes Moretti's standard work on the Olympic victors and its supplements (1957, 1970, 1987), the fullest discussion of women in Greek sport (Arrigoni 1985), the latest book on athletic sculpture (Rausa 1994), the only commentary on Lucian's *Anacharsis or Athletics* (Angeli Bernardini 1995).

Fortunately, some access to all this (and much more) is available through the excellent bibliographies by Nigel Crowther (1985b, annotated) and Thomas Scanlon (1984a, with an introductory survey) and review articles by Kyle (1983a, cf. 1983b, 1991b) and Crowther (1990b). In addition, *Nikephoros*, the leading journal on ancient sport since its inception in 1988, publishes extensive annual bibliographies, and *Journal of Sport History* often includes the ancient world as a heading in its regular journal surveys.

Those who study Greek and Latin can find collections of ancient sources on various events in the series edited by Weiler for Böhlau in Vienna (*Quellendokumentation zur Gymnastik und Agonistik im Altertum*), each with German translations and commentary; volumes published so far treat discus, long jump, javelin, boxing, *pankration*. Agonistic inscriptions have been collected by Moretti (1953, with Italian commentary), victory epi-grams by Ebert (1972, with German commentary). Frisch has re-edited and commented (in German) on papyri which shed light on associations of athletes and other performers (1986). Three sourcebooks in English are now available. R.S. Robinson (1981, first published 1955) supplies a lot of material in chronological order, but her translations are often offputtingly old-fashioned. Sweet (1987) accompanies his texts with an introduction to Greek sport, maps, and some eighty plates of ancient sites and works of art, as well as a running commentary and questions meant to orient students towards the material; the inclusion of chapters on walking and mountai-neering, hunting and fishing, theatre, dining, situate the competitive material in a misleading context, leisure studies. S.G. Miller (1991), in an expanded version of an earlier sourcebook, includes translations of a number of important inscriptions and papyri otherwise hard to find and incorporates a handy glossary of terms in the index.

General books on sport history inevitably devote a chapter or more to the Greeks. But even the ablest scholars are unlikely to be familiar with the evidence at first hand; misjudgements on what secondary sources to follow and misunderstandings of those they choose are only to be expected. No less an authority than Allen Guttmann can speak of the Athenaic games, of Apollo as the god of Nemea, of Plato's panhellenic prizes in wrestling (attested by late and divergent sources), and of an *agonathete* (Guttmann 1978:21, 21, 23, 45). According to Richard Mandell, there were cult observances at Olympia at least a millennium before 776 BCE and boxing and wrestling bouts were so boring, lasting several days, that music was needed to amuse the spectators – good news for the barbarians who seek to justify the practice of playing rock 'n' roll at top volume between innings of baseball games (Mandell 1984:25, 58). Syntheses by specialists are more reliable. Pride of place must go to the books of E.N. Gardiner (1910, 1925, 1930) and his spiritual descendant, H.A. Harris (1964, 1972a, 1976). Both men combined learning and the love of sport with an unusual ability to communicate in print. Gardiner rowed for his Oxford college and played rugby for Devon and the Western Counties in the late 1880s. His *JHS* articles on individual events and his two major books are still worth reading, and *Athletics of the Ancient World*, a well-illustrated abridgement of his earlier work, was reprinted (with a helpful introductory updating by S.G. Miller) as recently as 1979 and remains a staple of university courses to this day. Harris taught himself to throw the discus and javelin in middle age as preparatory fieldwork for *Greek Athletes and Athletics*. That book 'at once established him as the leading authority on the subject, at least in the English-speaking world' (Barton 1976:5); its successor, *Sport in Greece and Rome* (1972a), contains the most extensive treatment of equestrian events in English. Their weaknesses are all too apparent. Both Gardiner and Harris were devotees of the contemporary cult of amateurism. (Harris dedicated the last book he completed before his death, on English sport, to 'all those who have ever enjoyed playing games not very well but as well as they could'.) Both idealized a Greek athletic ethos they had a hand in inventing at the same time as they patronized or disparaged the competitors they met in the sources. (Dubious about a claim by M. Aurelius Asclepiades, Harris commented, 'Greeks being Greeks, it is probable that this statement was not entirely true' (Harris 1962:20), and was firmly rebuked for this ethnic slur by Louis Robert (Robert 1968:183 n. 2.).) But their achievements are as real. (For an even-handed discussion of Gardiner's life and work, see Kyle 1991a.)

Among more recent comprehensive accounts in English, Yalouris 1979 (published under a number of titles) is a lavishly illustrated coffee-table book, Olivová 1984 a smaller-scale version of the same kind of thing with coverage of the ancient Near East and Rome. Tzachou-Alexandri 1989 is, like Yalouris's book, a collection of pieces with excellent pictures. Articles in *Archaeology* 49.4 (July/August 1996) 27–37 (by Kyle, Lee, Mark Rose, Scanlon, Young) bring recent research within reach of the general reader. I turn now to the major sites and festivals, Finley and Pleket 1976 (on the Olympics) represents one of the few occasions when ancient historians who have distinguished themselves in other areas have considered sport. But the book is occasionally disappointing and often frustrating in its failure to cite the evidence. Mallwitz 1988 discusses the implications of his excavations at Olympia for the early history of the games, C. Morgan 1990 combines a rigorous account of the finds with a surprising readiness to reconcile them with Pausanias and other late literary sources. Crowther 1988b builds on the work of Moretti to compile lists of Olympic victors by city, revealing the pre-eminence of Elis in the late classical and Hellenistic periods. The decline in equestrian competition is one theme of Scanlon's account of Olympia under Roman rule (1988b). The work of Young on the elitist origins of the modern Olympic movement and their effects (1984, 1988a, 1988b, 1996) is a model for the way passionate involvement with the ancient world can transform our understanding of our own. The A&E video *Blood and Honor at the First Olympics*, introduced by Leonard Nimoy, also has its uses. I have not viewed *The Ancient Olympics: Athletes, Games and Heroes* (by D.G. Romano and the Archaeological Institute of America). For an overview of the Pythian games, see Fontenrose 1988. On Nemea, we have the guide to the site and museum edited by the excavator, S.G. Miller (1990); Gebhard's article on Isthmia (1993) also comes from the hand of an expert on the site. Jennifer Neils's large-format collection of articles on the

Panathenaea (1992a) includes Kyle's excellent survey of the games (1992). This supplements his full account of the role and reputation of athletic and equestrian competition in archaic and classical Athens (1987). Kyle and others return to the Panathenaea in Neils 1996. (For the Hellenistic Panathenaea, see Tracy 1991 and for the Theseia, Bugh 1990.) Stephen Hodkinson's book on Spartan property, now in preparation, also aims to situate sport within the context of a classical Greek community. For those unable to read (or locate) the many contributions of Louis Robert, there is a useful introduction to the competitive culture of Asia Minor in the imperial period by S. Mitchell (1990); this includes an English translation of the dossier of documents on the foundation of games at Oenoanda by C. Iulius Demosthenes in 124 CE (edited and discussed in German by Wörrle 1988).

I conclude with some notes on the issues to which much of this book is devoted: the hierarchy of festivals and events, the representation of victory in literature and art, distinctions of age, sex, social class. A new translation of Pindar in the bilingual Loeb Classical Library series (by W.H. Race) appeared in 1997; D.A. Campbell translates Simonides, Ibycus and Bacchylides in the same series (*Greek Lyric* volumes 3 and 4). Among many books on Pindar, Willcock 1995 includes a short discussion of the games and their competitors in its introduction to selected poems. Kurke stresses the perils of praise, the need to reintegrate victors into family, class and community (1991), the rage of those who go unrecognized (1993). Victor statues, valued and vengeful in the stories of heroes she discusses, are examined from other perspectives too by Lattimore 1988 and Raschke 1988b. (Herrmann 1988 offers a German-language catalogue of Olympic victor statues.) Papalas 1991 deals with boy athletes, Crowther 1990a with the elderly. Harris's chapter on women in athletics (1964) seems something of an afterthought but is helpful on a subject other syntheses pass over, Guttmann's (1991) current and perceptive; Scanlon's articles on the Heraea (1984b), women's athletics at Sparta (1988c) and the Athenian *arkteia* (1990) amount to a major contribution, industrious in amassing evidence (especially from art), stimulating in interpretation. On social class, reviews of Young 1984 by Kyle, *EMC* 29 (1985) 134–44 and Poliakoff, *AJP* 110 (1989) 166–71 are excellent. John Davies has been the most industrious and insightful to chronicle the lifestyles of the rich and famous at Athens (1971, 1981).

Some important dates

BRONZE AGE

2000 BCE	Wrestlers on wall paintings, Beni Hasan, Egypt
	Shulgi's run, Sumer
1600 BCE	Boxers on fresco, Akrotiri, Thera
1500 BCE	Boxers on rhyton, Agia Triada, Crete
1200 BCE	Athletic contests (?) in Hittite festivals
	Funeral games (?) on Mycenaean larnax

DARK AGES

1100 BCE	Boxers on tomb of Rameses III, Medinet Habu, Egypt
884 BCE	Olympic games (Eratosthenes' date)
776 BCE	Olympic games (Hippias's date)

ARCHAIC PERIOD

750 BCE	Homer, *Iliad*
725 BCE	Homer, *Odyssey*
724/652 BCE	Orsippus
704 BCE	Olympic games (Mallwitz's date)
632 BCE	Boys' events at Olympia (Hippias's date)
	Cylon (Olympic victor) stages unsuccessful coup at Athens
594 BCE	Solon makes laws at Athens
586/582 BCE	Pythian games
582 BCE	Isthmian games
580 BCE	Heraea
573 BCE	Nemean games
566 BCE	Greater Panathenaea
560 BCE	Earliest evidence for gymnasium
	Ibycus
536 BCE	Milo of Croton
520 BCE	Race in armour at Olympia
510 BCE	*Perizoma* (loincloth) vases
508 BCE	Cleisthenes reforms democracy at Athens
500 BCE	*Apenē* (mule-car race) at Olympia
	Simonides
	Xenophanes

498–446 BCE	Pindar's poems
496 BCE	*Kalpē* (mares' race) at Olympia
490 BCE	Persians invade Greece (Marathon)
486 BCE	Megacles ostracized
484/480 BCE	Astylus of Croton/Syracuse
480 BCE	Persians invade Greece (Salamis)
	Phayllus of Croton
	Theogenes of Thasos

CLASSICAL PERIOD

480–450 BCE	Bacchylides' poems
470 BCE	Temple of Zeus at Olympia
	Aegisthus Painter
458 BCE	Aeschylus, *Oresteia*
450 BCE	Stadium III at Olympia
444 BCE	*Apenē* and *kalpē* dropped from programme at Olympia
431 BCE	Peloponnesian war begins
	Prytaneion Decree
425 BCE	Nemea destroyed by warfare
	[Xenophon], *Constitution of the Athenians*
422 BCE	Aristophanes, *Wasps*
421 BCE	Autolycus of Athens
420 BCE	Lichas of Sparta
	Polyclitus, *Doryphorus*
416 BCE	Alcibiades of Athens
415 BCE	Sophocles, *Electra*
408 BCE	*Synoris* (two-horse chariot race) at Olympia
	Euripides, *Orestes*
405 BCE	Aristophanes, *Frogs*
404 BCE	Peloponnesian war ends
400 BCE	Xenophon and the '10,000' reach Trapezus
	Hippias of Elis compiles list of Olympic victors
	Lysias
399 BCE	Socrates executed
396 BCE	Cynisca of Sparta
380 BCE	Prize-list from Greater Panathenaea
	Plato, *Republic*
374 BCE	Chabrias of Athens
364 BCE	Arcadians and Eleans wage war at Olympia
356 BCE	Philip II of Macedon
352 BCE	Timocrates of Athens
350 BCE	Plato, *Laws*
340 BCE	Aeschines
330 BCE	Aristotle, *Politics*
328 BCE	Demades of Athens
323 BCE	Alexander the Great dies

HELLENISTIC PERIOD

279 BCE	Ptolemaieia at Alexandria
268 BCE	Bilistiche
257 BCE	Hierocles' letters
240 BCE	Callimachus
200 BCE	*Pankration* for boys at Olympia
167 BCE	Theseia reorganized at Athens
164 BCE	Leonidas of Rhodes
146 BCE	Greece becomes a Roman province (Achaea)

IMPERIAL PERIOD

27 BCE	Augustus becomes first Roman emperor
4 BCE	Tiberius of Rome
10 CE	Philo
45 CE	Tryphosa, Hedea, Dionysia
66–7 CE	Nero competes in Greece
86 CE	Capitoline games at Rome
100 CE	Plutarch, *Lives*
	Dio Chrysostom
124 CE	Demostheneia at Oenoanda
175 CE	Artemidorus
	Lucian
	Pausanias
200 CE	Prize-list from Aphrodisias
220 CE	Sextus Julius Africanus compiles list of Olympic victors
240 CE	Philostratus
385 CE	Latest known Olympic victor
393 CE	Theodosius I bans pagan festivals
450 CE	Hesychius
569 CE	Grave epitaph of young athlete, Gaza
1000 CE	*Suda*

Note: Many dates are approximate or conjectural.

Works cited

ADELMAN, M.L. (1986) *A Sporting Time. New York City and the Rise of Modern Athletics, 1820–70.* Urbana IL

AIGNER, H. (1988) 'Zu gesellschaftlichen Stellung von Henkern, Gladiatoren und Berufsathleten,' in I. Weiler, ed., *Soziale Randgruppen und Aussenseiter im Altertum*, 201–20. Graz

AMELING, W. (1987) 'Maximinus Thrax als Herakles', in *Bonner Historia-Augusta-Colloquium 1984/5*, 1–11. Bonn

AMYX, D.A. (1958) 'The Attic stelai, part III', *Hesperia* 27:163–310

ANDRONICOS, M. (1991) *Vergina. Royal Tombs and the Ancient City.* Athens

ANGELI BERNARDINI, P. (1980) 'Esaltazione e critica dell'atletismo nella poesia greca dal VII al V sec. a. C.: storia di un'ideologia', *Stadion* 6:81–111

(1985) 'L'attualità agonistica negli epinici di Pindaro', in A. Hurst, ed., *Pindare*, 117–49. Vandoeuvres and Geneva (*Entretiens sur l'antiquité classique* 31)

(1986–7) 'Aspects ludiques, rituels et sportifs de la course féminine dans la Grèce antique', *Stadion* 12–13:17–26

(1988) 'Le donne e la pratica della corsa nella Grecia antica', in P. Angeli Bernardini, ed., *Lo sport in Grecia*, 153–84. Rome and Bari

(1992) 'La storia dell'epinicio: aspetti socio-economici', *SIFC*:965–79

(1993) 'Il mito di Oreste nella *Pitica* II di Pindaro', in R. Pretagostini, ed., *Tradizione e innovazione nella cultura greca da Omero all'età ellenistica. Scritti in onore di Bruno Gentili*, 2.413–26. Rome

(1995) *Luciano: Anacarsi o Sull'atletica.* Pordenone

ANTRICH, J. and USHER, S. (1978) *Xenophon. The Persian Expedition.* Bristol

ARAFAT, K.W. (1996) *Pausanias' Greece. Ancient Artists and Roman Rulers.* Cambridge

ARIETI, J.A. (1975) 'Nudity in Greek athletics', *CW* 68:431–6

ARRIGONI, G. (1985) 'Donne e sport nel mondo greco: religione e società', in G. Arrigoni, ed., *Le Donne in Grecia*, 55–201. Rome and Bari

BALME, M. (1984) 'Attitudes to work and leisure in ancient Greece', *G&R* 31:140–52

BARRETT, W.S. (1978) 'The Oligaithidai and their victories (Pindar, *Olympian* 13; *SLG* 339,340)', in R.D. Dawe, J. Diggle, and P.E. Easterling, eds.,

Dionysiaca. Nine Studies in Greek Poetry by Former Pupils Presented to Sir Denys Page on his Seventieth Birthday, 1–20. Cambridge

BARRINGER, J.M. (1996) 'Atalanta as model: the hunter and the hunted', *ClAnt* 15:48–76

BARRON, J.P. (1984) 'Ibycus: *Gorgias* and other poems', *BICS* 31:13–24

BARRY, D. (1995) *Dave Barry's Complete Guide to Guys*. New York

BARTON, I.M. (1976) 'Harold Arthur Harris: 27 October 1902 - 29 August 1974', in Harris (1976), 3–6

BASSI, K. (1995) 'Male nudity and disguise in the discourse of Greek histrionics', *Helios* 22:3–22

BAŽANT, J. (1982) 'On the gluttony of ancient Greek athletes', *LF* 105:129–31

BEAZLEY, J.D. (1986) *The Development of Attic Black-Figure*. Rev. edn. Berkeley and Los Angeles

BELL, D. (1989) 'The horse race (κέλης) in ancient Greece from the pre-classical period to the first century BC', *Stadion* 15:167–90

BÉRARD, C. (1986) 'L'impossible femme athlète', *AION(arch)* 8:195–202

(1989) 'The order of women', in C. Bérard, *et al.*, *A City of Images. Iconography and Society in Ancient Greece*. Trans. D. Lyons, 89–105. Princeton

BERGQUIST, B. (1973) *Herakles on Thasos. The Archaeological, Literary and Epigraphic Evidence for his Sanctuary, Status and Cult Reconsidered*. Uppsala (Acta Univ. Ups. BOREAS. Uppsala Studies in Ancient Mediterranean and Near Eastern Civilizations 5)

BERNAL, M. (1987) *Black Athena. The Afroasiatic Roots of Classical Civilization* 1. *The Fabrication of Ancient Greece 1785-1985*. New Brunswick

(1991) *Black Athena. The Afroasiatic Roots of Classical Civilization* 2. *The Archaeological and Documentary Evidence*. New Brunswick

BILIŃSKI, B. (1990) 'Un pescivendolo olimpionico (Aristoteles Rhet. 1.7 1365a – Ps. Simonides fr. 110 D.)', *Nikephoros* 3:157–75

BILLAULT, A. (1993) ' Le Γυμναστικός de Philostrate: a-t-il une signification littéraire?', *REG* 106:142–62

BIRRELL, S. (1981) 'Sport as ritual: interpretations from Durkheim to Goffman', *Social Forces* 60:354–76

BLAKE, A. (1996) *The Body Language. The Meaning of Modern Sport*. London

BLANCHARD, K. and CHESKA, A. (1985) *The Anthropology of Sport. An Introduction*. South Hadley MA

BLÜMEL, W. (1985) *Die Inschriften von Iasos* 1. Bonn (*Inschriften griechischer Städte aus Kleinasien* 28.1)

BOARDMAN, J., *et al.* (1988) 'Herakles', *LIMC* 4.1, 728–838. Zürich and Munich

BOEGEHOLD, A.L. (1996) 'Group and single competitions at the Panathenaia', in Neils (1996), 95–105

BOHRINGER, F. (1979) 'Cultes d'athlètes en Grèce classique: propos politiques, discours mythiques', *REA* 81:5–18

BONANNO ARAVANTINOU, M. (1982) 'Un frammento di sarcofago romano con fanciulli atleti nei Musei Capitolini. Contributo allo studio dei sarcofagi con scene di palestra', *BA* 67.15:67–84

BONFANTE, L. (1989) 'Nudity as costume in classical art', *AJA* 93:543–70

BOURDIEU, P. (1978) 'Sport and social class', *Social Science Information* 17:819–40

(1984) *Distinction. A Social Critique of the Judgement of Taste.* Trans. R. Nice. Cambridge MA

BOUTROS, L. (1981) *Phoenician Sport. Its Influence on the Origin of the Olympic Games.* Amsterdam

BOWMAN, J.S. (1993) 'The Minoans – a whole new ball game', in P.C. Bjarkman, ed., *Baseball and the Game of Ideas: Essays for the Serious Fan*, 65–83. Delhi NY

BOWRA, C.M. (1970) *On Greek Margins.* Oxford

BRAUER, G.C., Jr. (1974–5) 'The *kalpē*. An agonistic reference on several Greek coins?', *San* 6:6–7

BRODERSEN, K. (1990) 'Zur Datierung der ersten Pythien', *ZPE* 82:25–31

BROHM, J.-M. (1978) *Sport – A Prison of Measured Time.* Trans. I. Fraser. London (1986) 'La critique du sport. Les enjeux actuels', *Quel corps?* 11 (no. 30–1):2–17

(1992) *Sociologie politique du sport.* 2nd edn. Nancy

BRONEER, O. (1962) 'The Isthmian victory crown', *AJA* 66:259–63

BROPHY, R. and BROPHY, M.O. (1985) 'Deaths in the pan-Hellenic games II: all combative sports', *AJP* 106:171–98

(1989) 'Medical sports fitness: an ancient parody of Greek medicine', *Literature and Medicine* 8:156–65

BROPHY, R.H, III (1978) 'Deaths in the pan-Hellenic games: Arrachion and Creugas', *AJP* 99:363–90

BRULOTTE, E.L. (1994) ' "The pillar of Oinomaos" and the location of stadium I at Olympia', *AJA* 98:53–64

BRUYÈRE-DEMOULIN, N. (1976) 'La vie est une course. Comparaisons et métaphores dans la littérature grecque ancienne', *AC* 45:446–63

BUGH, G.R. (1988) *The Horsemen of Athens.* Princeton (1990) 'The Theseia in late Hellenistic Athens', *ZPE* 83:20–37

BUHMANN, H. (1972) 'Der Sieg in Olympia und in den anderen panhelle-nischen Spielen' (Dissertation Ludwig-Maximilians Universität). Munich

BURCKHARDT, J. (1902) *Griechische Kulturgeschichte* Vol. 4. Stuttgart and Berlin

BURKERT, W. (1983) *Homo Necans. The Anthropology of Ancient Greek Sacrificial Ritual and Myth.* Trans. P. Bing. Berkeley and Los Angeles

CAILLOIS, R. (1961) *Men, Play and Games.* Trans. M. Barash. New York

CAIRNS, F. (1991) 'Some reflections of the ranking of the major games in fifth century BC epinician poetry', in Rizakis (1991), 95–8

CAMPOREALE, G. (1993) 'Sull'origine della corsa armata in Etruria', in *Spectacles sportifs et scéniques dans le monde étrusco-italique. Actes de la table ronde organisée par l'Equipe de recherches étrusco-italique de l'UMR 126 (CNRS, Paris) et l'Ecole française de Rome, Rome, 3-4 mai 1991*, 7–19. Rome (Collection de l'Ecole française de Rome 172)

CAREY, C. (1991). 'The victory ode in performance: the case for the chorus', *CP* 86:192–200

CARTER, C. (1988) 'Athletic contests in Hittite religious festivals', *JNES* 47:185–7

CARTER, J.M. and KRÜGER, A. (1990) eds., *Ritual and Record. Sports Records and Quantification in Pre-Modern Societies*. New York

CARTLEDGE, P. (1984) 'A new lease of life for Lichas son of Arkesilas?', *LCM* 9:98–102

(1985) 'The Greek religious festivals', in P.E. Easterling and J.V. Muir, eds., *Greek Religion and Society*, 98–127. Cambridge

CASARICO, L. (1982) 'Donne ginnasiarco (a proposito di P. Med. inv. 64.01)', *ZPE* 48:117–23

CASHMORE, E. (1990) *Making Sense of Sport*. New York

CATLING, H. (1976–7) 'Excavations at the Menelaion, Sparta, 1973–76', *Archaeological Reports for 1976–7*, 24–42

CHUVIN, P. (1987) 'Observations sur les reliefs du théâtre de Hiérapolis. Thèmes agonistiques et légendes locales', *RA*:97–108

CLARYSSE, W. (1977) Ἀτλητός, athlete or irrigation?', *ZPE* 27:192

COLE, S.G. (1993) 'Procession and celebration at the Dionysia', in R. Scodel, ed., *Theater* and *Society in the Classical World*, 25–38. Ann Arbor

COULSON, W. and KYRIELEIS, H. (1992) eds., *Proceedings of an International Symposium on the Olympic Games (5-9 September 1988)*. Athens

CRAWFORD, M. (1983) ed., *Sources for Ancient History*. Cambridge

CROWTHER, N.B. (1977) 'Weightlifting in antiquity: achievement and training', *G&R* 24:111–20

(1982) 'Athletic dress and nudity in Greek athletics', *Eranos* 80:163–8

(1985a) 'Male beauty contests in Greece: the euandria and euexia', *AC* 54:285–91

(1985b) 'Studies in Greek athletics', *CW* 78:497–558, 79:73–135

(1988a) 'The age-category of boys at Olympia', *Phoenix* 42:304–8

(1988b) 'Elis and the games', *AC* 57:301–10

(1989) 'Boy victors at Olympia', *AC* 58:206–10

(1990a) 'Old age, exercise and athletics in the ancient world', *Stadion* 16:171–83

(1990b) 'Recent trends in the study of Greek athletics (1982–1989)', *AC* 59:246–55

(1990c) 'A Spartan Olympic boxing champion', *AC* 59:198–202

(1991a) 'Euexia, eutaxia, philoponia: three contests of the Greek gymnasium', *ZPE* 85:301–4

(1991b) 'The Olympic training period', *Nikephoros* 4:161–6

(1992a) 'Rounds and byes in Greek athletics', *Stadion* 18.1:68–74

(1992b) 'Second-place finishes and lower in Greek athletics (including the pentathlon)', *ZPE* 90:97–102

(1992c) 'Slaves and Greek athletics', *QUCC* 40:35–42

(1993) 'Numbers of contestants in Greek athletic contests', *Nikephoros* 6:39–52

(1994a) 'Reflections on Greek equestrian events. Violence and spectator attitudes', *Nikephoros* 7:121–33

(1994b) 'The role of heralds and trumpeters at Greek athletic festivals', *Nikephoros* 7:135–55

(1995a) 'Greek equestrian events in the late Republic and early Empire. Africanus and the Olympic victory lists', *Nikephoros* 8:111–23

(1995b) 'Team sports in ancient Greece: some observations', *International Journal of the History of Sport* 12:127–36

(1996) 'Athlete and state: qualifying for the Olympic games in ancient Greece', *Journal of Sport History* 23:34–43

DAVIES, J.K. (1967) 'Demosthenes on liturgies: a note', *JHS* 87:33–40

(1971) *Athenian Propertied Families 600-300 B.C.* Oxford

(1981) *Wealth and the Power of Wealth in Classical Athens.* Salem NH

DAVIES, M.I. (1969) 'Thoughts on the *Oresteia* before Aischylos', *BCH* 93:214–60

(1985) 'Ajax at the bourne of life', in *Eidolopoiia. Actes du Colloque sur les problèmes de l'image dans le monde méditerranéen classique. Château de Lourmarin en Provence: 2-3 septembre 1982*, 83–117. Rome

DAVISON, J.A. (1958) 'Notes on the Panathenaea', *JHS* 78:23–42

DECKER, W. (1982–3) 'Die mykenische Herkunft des griechischen Totenagons', *Stadion* 8–9:1–24

(1992a) *Sports and Games of Ancient Egypt.* Trans. A. Guttmann. New York and London

(1992b) 'Zum Wagenrennen in Olympia – Probleme der Forschung', in Coulson and Kyrieleis (1992), 129–39

(1995) *Griechischer Sport in der Antike. Von minoischen Wettkampf zu den olympischen Spielen.* Munich

DELORME, J. (1960) *Gymnasion.* Paris (Bibliothèque des Ecoles françaises d'Athènes et de Rome 196)

DEMAND, N. (1994) *Birth, Death and Motherhood in Classical Greece.* Baltimore and London

DES BOUVRIE, S. (1995) 'Gender and the games at Olympia', in B. Berggreen and N. Marinatos, eds., *Greece and Gender*, 55–74. Bergen (Papers from the Norwegian Institute at Athens 2)

DES COURTILS, J. and PARIENTE, A. (1991) 'Problèmes topographiques et religieux à l'Hérakleion de Thasos', in R. Etienne and M.-T. Le Dinahet, eds., *L'espace sacrificiel dans les civilisations méditerranéennes de l'antiquité. Actes du colloque tenu à la Maison de l'Orient, Lyon 4–7 juin 1988*, 67–73. Paris

DETIENNE, M. (1979) *Dionysus Slain.* Trans. M. Muellner and L. Muellner. Baltimore and London

DICKINS, G. (1906–7) 'The Hieron of Athena Chalkioikos', *ABSA* 13:137–54

DOBLHOFER, G., MAURITSCH, P. and LAVRENCIC, M. (1992) *Weitsprung: Texte, Übersetzungen, Kommentar.* Vienna (*Quellendokumentation zur Gymnastik und Agonistik im Altertum* 2)

DOFFEY, M.-C. (1992) 'Les mythes de fondation des Concours Neméens', in M. Piérart, ed., *Polydipsion Argos. Argos de la fin des palais mycéniens à la constitution de l'état classique*, 185–193. Paris (*BCH* Supp. 22)

DOUGHERTY, C. (1993) *The Poetics of Colonization. From City to Text in Archaic Greece*. Oxford

DOWDEN, K. (1989) *Death and the Maiden. Girls' Initiation Rites in Greek Mythology*. London and New York

DREES, L. (1968) *Olympia: Gods, Artists, Athletes*. Trans. G. Onn. New York.

DUNNING, E. and ROJEK, C. (1992) *Sport and Leisure in the Civilizing Process. Critique and Counter-Critique*. Toronto and Buffalo

DYCK, A.R. (1985) 'The function and persuasive power of Demosthenes' portrait of Aeschines in the speech On the crown', *G&R* 32:42–48

DYER, K.F. (1982) *Challenging the Men. The Social Biology of Female Sporting Achievement*. St Lucia, Queensland

EBERT, J. (1963) *Zum Pentathlon der Antike*. Berlin. (*ASAW* 56.1)

(1965) '*Paides Puthikoi*', *Philologus* 109:152–6

(1966) 'Zu griechischen agonistischen Inschriften', *Wiss. Zs. der Martin-Luther-Universität, Halle-Wittenberg* (*Ges. u. Sprachwiss. R.*) 15:375–87

(1972) *Griechische Epigramme auf Sieger an gymnischen und hippischen Agonen*. Leipzig (*ASAW* 63.2)

(1974) 'Noch einmal zum Sieg im Pentathlon', *ZPE* 13:257–62

(1988) 'Neues zu den Inschriften für Aurelios Heras aus Chios', *Nikephoros* 1:85–102

(1989) 'Neues zum Hippodrom und zu den hippischen Konkurrenzen in Olympia', *Nikephoros* 2:89–107

(1991a) 'Eine Textverderbnis bei Pindar, *Pyth.* 5.49', *QUCC* 38.2:25–30

(1991b) 'Neues zum Olympischen Hippodroms', in Rizakis (1991) 99–102

EMMANUEL-REBUFFAT, D. (1985) 'Hercle agonistique en Etrurie', *Latomus* 44:473–87

ENGELMANN, H., KNIBBE, D. and MERKELBACH, R. (1980) (eds.) *Die Inschriften von Ephesos 4*. Bonn (*Inschriften griechischer Städte aus Kleinasien* 14)

EVANS, A. (1935) *The Palace of Minos*. Vol. 4. London

EVJEN, H.D. (1983) 'Semitic origin of the Olympic games: a phoenix risen again', *EHEM* 2:271–8

(1986) 'Competitive athletics in ancient Greece: the search for origins and influences', *OAth* 16.5:51–6

(1992) 'The origins and functions of formal athletic competition in the ancient world', in Coulson and Kyrieleis (1992), 95–104

FIEDLER, W. (1985) 'Sexuelle Enthaltsamkeit griechischer Athleten und ihre medizinische Begründung', *Stadion* 11:137–75

(1992) 'Der Faustkampf in der griechischen Dichtung', *Stadion* 18:1–67

FINLEY, M.I. and PLEKET, H.W. (1976) *The Olympic Games. The First Thousand Years*. London

FONTENROSE, J. (1968) 'The hero as athlete', *CSCA* 1:73–104

(1988) 'The cult of Apollo and the games at Delphi', in Raschke (1988a), 121–40

FRANCIS, E.D. and VICKERS, M. (1981) 'Leagros kalos', *PCPS* 27:97–136

FRASER, P.M. (1972) *Ptolemaic Alexandria*, 3 vols. Oxford

FRISCH, P. (1986) *Zehn agonistische Papyri.* Opladen (Abh. der Rheinisch-Westfälischen Akademie der Wissenschaften, Sonderreihe Papyrologica Coloniensia 13)

(1988) 'Die Klassifikation der Παῖδες bei den griechischen Agonen', *ZPE* 75:179–85

(1991) 'Der erste vollkommene Periodonike', *EA* 18:71–3

FROST, F.J. (1997) *Greek Society.* 5th edn. Boston

FUHRER, T. (1992) *Die Auseinandersetzung mit den Chorlyrikern in den Epinikien des Kallimachos.* Basel and Kassel

(1993) 'Callimachus' epinician poems', in M.A. Harder, R.F. Regtuit, and G.C. Wakker, eds., *Callimachus*, 79–97. Groningen

GALLIS, K.J. (1988) 'The games in ancient Larissa. An example of provincial Olympic games', in Raschke (1988a), 217–35

GARDINER, E.N. (1904) 'Phayllus and his record jump', *JHS* 24:70–80

(1910) *Greek Athletic Sports and Festivals.* London

(1925) *Olympia: its History and Remains.* Oxford

(1929) 'Regulations for a local sports meeting', *CR* 43:210–12

(1930) *Athletics of the Ancient World.* Oxford

GARLAN, Y. (1980) 'Le travail libre en Grèce ancienne', in P. Garnsey, ed., *Non-slave Labour in the Greco-Roman World*, 6–22. Cambridge (*PCPS* Supplementary Volume 6)

GASSOWSKA, B. (1966) 'Cirrus in vertice – one of the problems in Roman athlete iconography', in *Mélanges offerts à Kazimierz Michałowski*, 421–7. Warsaw

GAUTHIER, P. and HATZOPOULOS, M.B. (1993) *La loi gymnasiarchique de Beroia.* Athens (*Meletemata* 16)

GEBHARD, E.R. (1993) 'The evolution of a pan-Hellenic sanctuary: from archaeology towards history at Isthmia', in N. Marinatos and R. Hägg, eds., *Greek Sanctuaries. New Approaches*, 154–77. London and New York

GLASS, S.L. (1988) 'The Greek gymnasium: some problems', in Raschke (1988a), 155–73

GOLDHILL, S. (1986) 'Rhetoric and relevance: interpolation at Euripides *Electra* 367–400', *GRBS* 27:157–71

GOMME, A.W., ANDREWES, A. and DOVER, K.J. (1981) *A Historical Commentary on Thucydides. Volume V. Book VIII.* Oxford

GRUNEAU, R. (1983) *Class, Sports, and Social Development.* Amherst MA

(1993) 'The critique of sport in modernity: theorising power, culture, and the politics of the body', in E.G. Dunning, J.A. Maguire and R.E. Pearton, eds., *The Sports Process. A Comparative and Developmental Approach*, 85–109. Champaign IL

GRUPPE, O. (1918) 'Herakles', *RE Supplementband* 3:910–1121. Munich

GUTTMANN, A. (1978) *From Ritual to Record. The Nature of Modern Sports.* New York

(1988) *A Whole New Ball Game*. Chapel Hill and London

(1991) *Women's Sports: A History*. New York

HABICHT, C. (1985) *Pausanias' Guide to Ancient Greece*. Berkeley and Los Angeles

HAGEDORN, D. (1996) 'Noch einmal: weibliche Gymnasiarchen in Ägypten?', *ZPE* 110:157–60

HALL, E. (1994) 'Drowning by nomes: the Greeks, swimming, and Timotheus' *Persians*', in H.A. Khan, ed., *The Birth of the European Identity: the Europe-Asia Contrast in Greek Thought 490–322 B.C.*, 44–80. Nottingham (Nottingham Classical Literature Studies 2, 1993)

HALL, A.S. and MILNER, N.P. (1994) 'Education and athletics at Oenoanda', in D. French, ed., *Studies in the History and Topography of Lycia and Pisidia in Memoriam A.S. Hall*, 7–47. Ankara (British Institute of Archaeology at Ankara Monograph 19)

HAMILTON, R. (1974) *Epinikion. General Form in the Odes of Pindar*. The Hague and Paris

(1989) 'Alkman and the Athenian Arkteia', *Hesperia* 58:449–72

(1992) *Choes and Anthesteria. Athenian Iconography and Ritual*. Ann Arbor

(1993) 'Archons' names on Panathenaic vases', *ZPE* 96:237–48

(1996) 'Panathenaic amphoras: the other side', in Neils (1996), 137–62

HANSEN, M.H. (1985) *Demography and Democracy. The Number of Athenian Citizens in the Fourth Century B. C.* Herning

(1988) *Three Studies in Athenian Demography*. Copenhagen (The Royal Danish Academy of Sciences and Letters. Historisk-filosofiske Meddelelser 56)

HARRIS, H.A. (1962) 'Notes on three athletic inscriptions', *JHS* 82:19–24

(1964) *Greek Athletes and Athletics*. London

(1972a) *Sport in Greece and Rome*. London and Ithaca

(1972b) 'The method of deciding victory in the pentathlon', *G&R* 19:60–4

(1976) *Greek Athletics and the Jews*, ed. I.M. Barton and A.J. Brothers. Cardiff

HEATH, M. and LEFKOWITZ, M.R. (1991) 'Epinician performance: a response to Burnett and Carey', *CP* 86:173–91

HERRMANN, H.-V. (1972) *Olympia: Heiligtum und Wettkampfstätte*. Munich

(1988) 'Die Siegerstatuen von Olympia', *Nikephoros* 1:119–83

HERTER, H. (1973) 'Theseus', *RE Supplementband* 13:1045–238. Munich

HINTZEN-BOHLEN, B. (1990) 'Die Familiengruppe – ein Mittel zur Selbstdarstellung hellenistischer Herrscher', *JDAI* 105:129–54

HOCH, P. (1972) *Rip Off the Big Game. The Exploitation of Sports by the Power Elite*. New York

HODKINSON, S. (forthcoming) *Property and Society in Classical Sparta*

HÖGHAMMAR, K. (1993) *Sculpture and Society. A Study of the Connection between the Free-Standing Sculpture and Society on Kos in the Hellenistic and Augustan Periods*. Uppsala (Acta Univ. Ups. BOREAS. Uppsala Studies in Ancient Mediterranean and Near Eastern Civilizations 23)

HÖNLE, A. (1972) *Olympia in der Politik der griechischen Staatenwelt von 776 bis zum Ende des 5. Jhs*. Bebenhausen

HOWELL, R.A. and HOWELL, M.L. (1989) 'The Atalanta legend in art and literature', *Journal of Sport History* 16:127–39

HOWIE, G. (1991) 'Pindar's account of Pelops' contest with Oenomaus', *Nikephoros* 4:55–120

HOWLAND, R.L. (1950–1) 'Phayllus and the long-jump record (Anth. Pal. Append. 297)', *PCPS* 181:30

(1954–5) 'Epeius, carpenter and athlete (or what makes the Achaeans laugh at *Iliad* XXIII, 840)', *PCPS* 3:15–16

HUBBARD, T.K. (1995) 'On implied wishes for Olympic victory in Pindar', *ICS* 20:35–56

HUDE, C. (1931) *Xenophon Anabasis*. Stuttgart

HUIZINGA, J. (1970) *Homo Ludens. A Study in the Play Element in Culture*. London (original German edition, 1938)

HUMPHREYS, S.C. (1974) 'The nothoi of Kynosarges', *JHS* 94: 88–95

HYDE, W.W. (1921) *Olympic Victor Monuments and Greek Athletic Art*. Washington

IMMERWAHR, H. (1967) 'An inscribed terracotta ball in Boston', *GRBS* 8:255–66

JACKSON, D.F. (1991) 'Philostratos and the pentathlon', *JHS* 111:178–81

JEFFERY, L.H. (1990) *The Local Scripts of Archaic Greece*. 2nd edn, rev. A.W. Johnston. Oxford

JENNER, E.A.B. (1986) 'Further speculations on Ibycus and the epinician ode: S 220, S 176 and the "Bellerophon" ode', *BICS* 33:59–66

JOHNSTON, A.W. (1987) '*IG* II² 2311 and the number of Panathenaic amphorae', *ABSA* 82:125–9

JONES, C.P. (1990) 'A new Lycian dossier establishing an artistic contest and festival in the reign of Hadrian', *JRA* 3:484–8

JORDAN, D.R. (1985) 'Defixiones from a well near the southwest corner of the Athenian Agora', *Hesperia* 54:205–55

JÜTHNER, J. (1909) *Philostratos Über Gymnastik*. Leipzig and Berlin

(1965) *Die athletische Leibesübungen der Griechen 1. Geschichte der Leibesübungen*, ed. F. Brein. Vienna (*SAWW* 249.1)

(1968) *Die athletischen Leibesübungen der Griechen 2.1. Einzelne Sportarten*, ed. F. Brein. Vienna (*SAWW* 249.2)

KAHIL, L. (1988) 'Le sanctuaire de Brauron et la religion grecque', *CRAI* 1988:799–813

KAUFFMANN-SAMARAS, A. (1988) ' "Mère" et enfant sur les lébétès nuptiaux à figures rouges attiques du Ve s. av. J.C.', in J. Christiansen and T. Melander, eds., *Proceedings of the 3rd Symposium on Ancient Greek and Related Pottery (Copenhagen, August 31 – September 4 1987)*, 286–99. Copenhagen

KENNELL, N.M. (1988) 'Νέρων περιοδονίκης', *AJP* 109:239–51

(1995) *The Gymnasium of Virtue. Education and Culture in Ancient Sparta*. Chapel Hill and London

KENT, J.H. (1966) *Corinth* 8.3. *The Inscriptions 1926-1950*. Princeton

KHANOUSSI, M. (1991) 'Ein römisches Mosaik aus Tunesien mit der Darstellung eines agonistischen Wettkampfes', *AW* 22:146–53

KLEE, T. (1918) *Zur Geschichte der gymnischen Agone an griechischen Festen.* Leipzig and Berlin

KNOEPFLER, D. (1994) 'Haltère de bronze dédié à Apollon *Hékabolos* dans la collection G. Ortiz (Genève)', *CRAI* 1994:337–79

KOENEN, L. (1977) *Eine agonistische Inschrift aus Ägypten und frühptolemäische Königsfeste.* Meisenheim (Beiträge zur klassischen Philologie 56)

KOTERA-FEYER, E. (1993) *Die Strigil.* Frankfurt am Main

KRATZMÜLLER, B. (1993) 'Synoris – Apene. Zweigespannrennen an den Grossen Panathenäen', *Nikephoros* 6:75–91

KRAUSE, J.H. (1835) *Theagenes oder wissenschaftliche Darstellung der Gymnastik, Agonistik und Festspiele der Hellenen.* Halle

(1838) *Olympia oder Darstellung der grosse olympischen Spiele.* Vienna

(1841a) *Die Gymnastik und Agonistik der Hellenen.* Leipzig

(1841b) *Die Pythien, Nemeen und Isthmien aus den Schrift- und Bildwerken des Altertums.* Leipzig

KRÜGER, A. (1990) 'The ritual in modern sport: a sociobiological approach', in Carter and Krüger (1990), 135–51

KRÜGER, G. (1990) 'Sport in the context of non-European cultural tradition: the example of Hawaii', in Carter and Krüger (1990), 87–102

KURKE, L. (1991) *The Traffic in Praise. Pindar and the Poetics of Social Economy.* Ithaca and London

(1993) 'The economy of kudos', in C. Dougherty and L. Kurke, eds., *Cultural Poetics in Archaic Greece. Cult, Performance, Politics*, 131–63. Cambridge

KYLE, D.G. (1983a) 'Directions in ancient sport history', *Journal of Sport History* 10.1:7–34

(1983b) 'The study of Greek sport: a survey', *EMC* 27:46–67

(1984a) 'Non-competition in Homeric sport: spectatorship and status', *Stadion* 10:1–19

(1984b) 'Solon and athletics', *AncW* 9:91–105

(1987) *Athletics in Ancient Athens.* Leiden

(1990) 'Winning and watching the Greek pentathlon', *Journal of Sport History* 17:291–305

(1991a) 'E. Norman Gardiner: historian of ancient sport', *International Journal of the History of Sport* 8:28–55 (abridged from 'E. Norman Gardiner and the decline of Greek sport', in D.G. Kyle and G.D. Stark, eds., *Essays in Sport History and Sport Mythology* (College Station TX 1990) 7–44)

(1991b) 'Athletes and archaeologists: some recent works on the sites and significance of ancient Greek sport', *International Journal of the History of Sport* 8:270–83

(1992) 'The Panathenaic games: sacred and civil athletics', in Neils (1992a), 77–101.

(1995) 'Philostratus, *repêchage*, running and wrestling: the Greek pentathlon again', *Journal of Sport History* 22:60–5

(1996) 'Gifts and glory: Panathenaic and other Greek athletic prizes', in Neils (1996), 106–136

KYRIELEIS, H. (1973) '*Kathaper Hermes kai Horos*', in F. Eckstein, ed., *Antike Plastik* 12, 133–47. Berlin

LACOMBRADE, C. (1959) 'En marge de Sophocle: une course de quadriges aux jeux Pythiques', *Pallas* 8.1:5–14

LAMBRECHTS, P. (1957) 'L'importance de l'enfant dans les religions à mystères', in *Hommages à Waldemar Deonna*, 322–33. Brussels (Collection *Latomus* 28)

LÄMMER, M. (1982–3) 'Der sogennante Olympischen Friede in der grie-chischen Antike', *Stadion* 8–9:47–83

(1985) 'Zum Verhältnis von Sport und Krieg in der griechischen Antike', in H. Becker, ed., *Sport im Spannungsfeld von Krieg und Frieden. Fachtagung der DVS-Sektion Sportgeschichte vom 4.-6. April 1984 an der Führungs- und Verwaltungs-Akademie des Deutschen Sportbundes in Berlin*, 17–30. Clausthal-Zellerfeld

(1992) 'Myth or reality: the classical Olympic athlete', *International Review for the Sociology of Sport* 27.2:107–12

(1993) 'The nature and significance of the Olympic oath in Greek antiquity', in D.P. Panagiotopoulos, ed., *The Institution of the Olympic Games: A Multidisciplinary Approach. Proceedings of the International H.C.R.S.L. Congress, Olympia, Greece, September 3–7, 1991*, 141–8. Athens

LAMONT, D.A. (1995) 'Running phenomena in ancient Sumer', *Journal of Sport History* 22:207–15

LANE FOX, R. (1996) 'Ancient hunting: from Homer to Polybios', in G. Shipley and J. Salmon, eds., *Human Landscapes in Classical Antiquity. Environment and Culture*, 119–53. London and New York

LANGDON, M.K. (1989) 'Scoring the ancient pentathlon: final solution?', *ZPE* 78:117–18

(1990) 'Throwing the discus in antiquity. The literary evidence', *Nikephoros* 3:177–82

LANGENFELD, H. (1991) 'Artemidors Traumbuch als sporthistorische Quelle', *Stadion* 17:1–26

LAPINI, W. (1994) 'Note testuali sulla Ἀθηναίων πολιτεία dello pseudo-Senofonte', *RFIC* 122:129–38

LASER, S. (1987) *Sport und Spiel*. Göttingen (*Archaeologica Homerica* T)

LATTIMORE, S. (1988) 'The nature of early Greek victor statues', in S.J. Bandy, ed., *Coroebus Triumphs. The Alliance of Sport and the Arts*, 245–56. San Diego

LAVRENCIC, M. (1991) 'Krieger und Athlet? Der militärische Aspekt in der Beurteilung des Wettkampfes der Antike', *Nikephoros* 4:167–75

LEE, H.M. (1976) 'The τέρμα and the javelin in Pindar, Nemean vii 70–3, and Greek athletics', *JHS* 96:70–9

(1983) 'Athletic arete in Pindar', *AncW* 7:31–7

(1986) 'Pindar, *Olympian* 3.33–34: "The twelve-turned *terma*" and the length of the four-horse chariot race,' *AJP* 107 (1986) 162–74

(1988a) 'The "first" Olympic games of 776 BC', in Raschke (1988a), 110–18

(1988b) '*SIG*³ 802: did women compete against men in Greek athletic festivals?', *Nikephoros* 1:103–17

(1992) 'Some changes in the ancient Olympic programme and schedule', in Coulson and Kyrieleis (1992), 105–11

(1993) 'Wrestling in the *repêchage* of the ancient pentathlon', *Journal of Sport History* 20:277–9

(1995) 'Yet another scoring system for the ancient pentathlon', *Nikephoros* 8:41–55

LEFKOWITZ, M.R. (1984) 'Pindar's Pythian V', in A. Hurst, ed., *Pindare*, 33–69. Vandoeuvres and Geneva. (Entretiens sur l'antiquité classique 31)

(1991) *First-Person Fictions. Pindar's Poetic 'I'*. Oxford

(1995) 'The first person in Pindar reconsidered – again', *BICS* 40:139–50

LEFKOWITZ, M.R. and ROGERS, G.M. (1996) eds., *Black Athena Revisited*. Chapel Hill

LEGAKIS, B.A. (1977) 'Athletic Contests in Archaic Greek Art'. (Dissertation University of Chicago)

LÉVÊQUE, P. (1982) 'Approche ethno-historique des concours grecs', *Klio* 64:5–20

LEY, A. (1990) 'Atalante – von der Athletin zur Liebhaberin. Ein Beitrag zum Rezeptionswandel eines mythologischen Themas auf Vasen des 6.–4. Jhs. v. Chr.', *Nikephoros* 3:31–72

LIVENTHAL, V. (1985) 'What goes on among the women? The setting of some Attic vase paintings of the fifth century BC', *ARID* 14:37–52

LLOYD, A.B. (1976) *Herodotus Book II. Commentary 1–98*. Leiden

LLOYD, G.E.R. (1987) *The Revolutions of Wisdom. Studies in the Claims and Practice of Ancient Greek Science*. Berkeley and Los Angeles

LLOYD-JONES, H.J. (1971) 'Fragments', in H.W. Smyth, *Aeschylus* vol. 2. Cambridge, MA

(1983) 'Artemis and Iphigeneia', *JHS* 103:87–102

(1994) *Sophocles: Ajax, Electra, Oedipus Tyrannus*. Cambridge MA

LÖSCHHORN, K. (1918) 'Kleine kritische Bemerkungen zu Xenophons Anabasis', *BPW* 29:694–5

LONSDALE, S.H. (1993) *Dance and Ritual Play in Greek Religion*. Baltimore and London

LORENZ, T. (1991) 'Der Doryphoros des Polyklet: Athlet, Musterfigur, politisches Denkmal oder mythischer Held?', *Nikephoros* 4:177–90

LOUDEN, B. (1993) 'An extended narrative pattern in the *Odyssey*', *GRBS* 34:5–33

MACCLANCY, J. (1996) 'Sport, identity and ethnicity', in J. MacClancy, ed., *Sport, Identity and Ethnicity*, 1–20. Oxford

MACHIN, A. (1988) 'Oreste ou l'échec glorieux: Sophocle, *Électre* (741–745)', *Pallas* 34:45–60

MADDOLI, G. (1992) 'Milone olimpionico ἑπτάκις ([Simon.] fr. 153 D e Paus. VI 14,5)', *PdP* 262:46–49

MALLWITZ, A. (1972) *Olympia und seine Bauten*. Munich

(1988) 'Cult and competition locations at Olympia', in Raschke (1988a), 79–109

MALTEN, L. (1923–4) 'Leichenspiel und Totenkult', *MDAI(R)* 38–9:300–40

MANDELL, R.A. (1984) *Sport. A Cultural History.* New York

MANTAS, K. (1995) 'Women and athletics in the Roman East', *Nikephoros* 8:125–44

MARCOVICH, M. (1978) 'Xenophanes on drinking-parties and Olympic games', *ICS* 3:1–26

MARINATOS, N. (1989) 'The bull as an adversary: some observations on bull-hunting and bull-leaping', *Ariadne* 5:23–32

MARÓTI, E. (1985–8) 'Περιοδονίκης. Anmerkungen zum Begriff Perioden-Sieger bei den panhellenischen Spielen', *AAntHung* 31:335–55

(1990) 'Zum Siegerepigramm des Nikoladas', *Nikephoros* 3:133–40

(1994) 'Zur Problematik des Wettlaufes und der Reihenfolge der einzelnen Disziplinen beim altgriechischen Pentathlon', *AAntHung* 35:1–24

MARÓTI, E. and MARÓTI, G. (1993) 'Zur Frage des Pentathlon-Sieges', *Nikephoros* 6:53–9

MASSA-PAIRAULT, F.-H. (1991) 'Strigiles féminins et idéologie funéraire (IVe-IIIe siècles av.n.è.)', *Nikephoros* 4:197–209

MASSON, O. (1994) 'A propos de Théogenès, athlète et héros thasien', *REG* 107:694–7

MATTHEWS, V.J. (1994) 'The Greek pentathlon again', *ZPE* 100:129–38

MATTINGLY, H.B. (1990) 'Some fifth-century Attic epigraphic hands', *ZPE* 83:110–22

MAUL-MANDELARTZ, E. (1990) *Griechische Reiterdarstellungen in agonistischem Zusammenhang.* Frankfurt am Main

McDEVITT, A. (1994a) 'Horses for courses. A note on Bacchylides 3.3–4', *Hermes* 122:502–3

(1994b) '"We wuz robbed": a note on Bacchylides 4.11–13', *LCM* 19:20–1

McDONNELL, M. (1991) 'The introduction of athletic nudity: Thucydides, Plato and the vases', *JHS* 111:182–93

(1993) 'Athletic nudity among the Greeks and Etruscans', in *Spectacles sportifs et scéniques dans le monde étrusco-italique. Actes de la table ronde organisée par l'Equipe de recherches étrusco-italique de l'UMR 126 (CNRS, Paris) et l'Ecole française de Rome, Rome, 3–4 mai 1991*, 395–407. Rome (Collection de l'Ecole française de Rome 172)

McGOWAN, E.P. (1995) 'Tomb marker and turning post: funerary columns in the archaic period', *AJA* 99:615–32

MEIGGS, R. and LEWIS, D. (1988) *A Selection of Greek Historical Inscriptions to the End of the Fifth Century B.C.* 2nd edn. Oxford

MERKELBACH, R. (1970) 'Herakles und der Pankratiast', *ZPE* 6:47–9

(1973) 'Der Sieg im Pentathlon', *ZPE* 11:261–9

(1987) 'Der Fünfkämpfer Nikoladas', *ZPE* 67:293–5

MEULI, K. (1941) 'Der Ursprung der Olympischen Spiele', *Die Antike* 17:189–208 (= *Gesammelte Schriften* (Basel and Stuttgart 1975) 881–906)

(1968 [1926]) *Der griechische Agon*. Cologne

MICHAUD, J.-P. (1970) 'Chronique des fouilles et découvertes archéologiques en Grèce en 1968 et 1969', *BCH* 94:883–1164

MIDWINTER, E. (1986) *Fair Game. Myth and Reality in Sport*. London

MILLER, A.M. (1991) 'A wish for Olympian victory in Pindar's *Tenth Pythian*', *AJP* 112:161–72

MILLER, S.G. (1975a) 'The date of Olympic festivals', *MDAI(A)* 90:215–31

 (1975b) 'The pentathlon for boys at Nemea', *CSCA* 8:199–201

 (1978) *The Prytaneion. Its Function and Architectural Form*. Berkeley and Los Angeles

 (1990) ed., *Nemea. A Guide to the Site and Museum*. Berkeley and Los Angeles

 (1991) *Arete. Greek Sports from Ancient Sources*. 2nd edn. Berkeley and Los Angeles

 (1992) 'The stadium at Nemea and the Nemean games', in Coulson and Kyrieleis (1992), 81–6

MILLER, STELLA G. (1988) 'Excavations at the panhellenic site of Nemea. Cult, politics, and games', in Raschke (1988a), 141–51

MILNE, M.J. (1945) 'A prize for wool-working', *AJA* 49:528–33

MILNER, N.P. (1991) 'Victors in the Meleagria and the Balbouran elite', *Anatolian Studies* 41:23–62

MITCHELL, S. (1990) 'Festivals, games and civic life in Roman Asia Minor', *JRS* 80:183–93

MOLES, J.L. (1994) 'Xenophon and Callicratidas', *JHS* 114:70–84

MOREAU, A. (1987) 'Epouser la princesse: Pélops et Hippodamie', in G. Ravis-Giordani, ed., *Femmes et patrimoine dans les sociétés rurales de l'Europe Méditerranéenne*, 227–37. Paris

MORET, J.-M. (1992) 'Iconographical appendix. The earliest representations of the infant Herakles and the snakes', in B.K. Braswell, *A Commentary on Pindar Nemean One*, 83–90. Fribourg

MORETTI, L. (1953) *Iscrizioni agonistiche greche*. Rome

 (1956) 'Un regolamento rodio per la gara del pentatlo', *RFIC* 84:55–60

 (1957) 'Olympionikai, i vincitori negli antichi agoni olimpici', *MAL* (ser. 8) 8.2:55–198

 (1970) 'Supplemento al catalogo degli Olympionikai', *Klio* 52:295–303

 (1987) 'Nuovo supplemento al catalogo degli Olympionikai', *MGR* 12:67–91 (*Studi pubblicati dell'Istituto italiano per la storia antica* 39)

 (1991) 'Dagli *Heraia* all'*Aspis* di Argo', *MGR* 16:179–89

MORGAN, C. (1990) *Athletes and Oracles*. Cambridge

MORGAN, K. (1993) 'Pindar the professional and the rhetoric of the κωμος', *CP* 88:1–15

MORRIS, D. (1981) *The Soccer Tribe*. London

MORRIS, I. (1997) 'Periodization and the heroes: inventing a Dark Age', in M. Golden and P. Toohey, eds., *Inventing Ancient Culture. Historicism, Periodization and the Ancient World*, 96–131. London and New York

MORRISSEY, E.J. (1978) 'Victors in the Prytaneion decree (*IG* I² 77)', *GRBS* 19:121–5

MOSSHAMMER, A.A. (1982) 'The date of the first Pythiad – again', *GRBS* 23:15–30

MOURATIDIS, J. (1984) 'Heracles at Olympia and the exclusion of women from the ancient Olympic games', *Journal of Sport History* 11.3:41–55

(1985a) 'The origin of nudity in Greek athletics', *Journal of Sport History* 12:213–32

(1985b) 'The 776 BC date and some problems connected with it', *Canadian Journal of History of Sport* 16.2:1–14.

(1989) 'Are there Minoan influences on Mycenaean sports, games and dances?', *Nikephoros* 2:43–63

(1990) 'Anachronism in the Homeric games and sports', *Nikephoros* 3:11–22

MURRAY, O. (1993) *Early Greece*. 2nd edn. Cambridge MA

MYRICK, L.D. (1994) 'The way up and down: trace horse and turning imagery in the Orestes plays', *CJ* 89:131–48

NAGY, B. (1978) 'The Athenian athlothetai', *GRBS* 19:307–13

NAGY, G. (1986) 'Pindar's *Olympian* 1 and the aetiology of the Olympic games', *TAPA* 116:71–88 (cf. *Pindar's Homer. The Lyric Possession of an Epic Past* (Baltimore and London 1990) 116–35)

NEILS, J. (1992a) ed., *Goddess and Polis. The Panathenaic Festival in Ancient Athens*. Princeton

(1992b) 'The Panathenaia: an introduction', in Neils (1992a), 13–27

(1996) ed., *Worshipping Athena. Panathenaia and Parthenon*. Madison WI

NÉMETH, G. (1994) 'IG II–III² 5222; 6217 und die athenische Reiterei nach dem Sturz der Dreissig Tyrannen', *ZPE* 104:95–102

NOLLÉ, J. (1985) 'Grabepigramme und Reliefdarstellungen aus Kleinasien', *ZPE* 60:117–35

NOVAK, M. (1976) *The Joy of Sports: End Zones, Bases, Baskets, Balls, and the Conservation of the American Spirit*. New York

OBER, J. (1989) *Mass and Elite in Democratic Athens. Rhetoric, Ideology, and the Power of the People*. Princeton

OKRENT, D. and WULF, S. (1989) *Baseball Anecdotes*. New York

OLIVER, J.H. (1970) *Marcus Aurelius. Aspects of Civic and Cultural Policy in the East*. Princeton (*Hesperia* Supp. 13)

OLIVOVÁ, V. (1984) *Sports and Games in the Ancient World*. Trans. D. Orpington. New York

OSBORNE, R. (1987) *Classical Landscape with Figures*. London

(1993) 'Competitive festivals and the polis: a context for dramatic festivals at Athens', in A.H. Sommerstein, S. Halliwell, J. Henderson and B. Zimmermann, eds., *Tragedy, Comedy and the Polis. Papers from the Greek Drama Conference, Nottingham, 18–20 July 1990*, 21–37. Bari

PAPALAS, A.J. (1991) 'Boy athletes in ancient Greece', *Stadion* 17:165–92

PARSONS, P.J. (1977) 'Callimachus: Victoria Berenices', *ZPE* 25:1–50

PAVESE, C.O. (1996) 'Ἄθλοι e ἄθλα', *SIFC* 14:3–9

PEISER, B. (1990) 'The crime of Hippias of Elis. Zur Kontroverse um die Olympionikenliste', *Stadion* 16:37–65

PERLMAN, P. (1983) 'Plato *Laws* 833C–834D and the bears of Brauron', *GRBS* 24:115–30

(1989) 'The calendrical position of the Nemean games', *Athenaeum* 77:57–90

PERYSINAKIS, I.N. (1990) 'The athlete as warrior: Pindar's *P.* 9.97–103 and *P.* 10.55–9', *BICS* 37:43–9

PETZL, G. (1987) *Die Inschriften von Smyrna* 2.1. Bonn (*Inschriften griechischer Städte aus Kleinasien* 24.1)

PLEKET, H.W. (1973) 'Some aspects of the history of the athletic guilds', *ZPE* 10:197–227

(1974) 'Zur Soziologie des antiken Sports', *MNIR* 36:57–87

(1975) 'Games, prizes, athletes and ideology', *Arena* (= *Stadion*) 1:49–89

(1992) 'The participants in the ancient Olympic games: social background and mobility', in Coulson and Kyrieleis (1992), 147–52

PLESCIA, J. (1970) *The Oath and Perjury in Ancient Greece*. Tallahassee

POLIAKOFF, M.B. (1980) 'The third fall in the *Oresteia*', *AJP* 101:251–59

(1982) *Studies in the Terminology of the Greek Combat Sports*. Königstein/Ts.

(1986) 'Deaths in the pan-Hellenic games: addenda et corrigenda', *AJP* 107:400–2

(1987a) *Combat Sports in the Ancient World. Competition, Violence and Culture.* New Haven and London

(1987b) 'Melankomas, ἐκ κλίμακος, and Greek boxing', *AJP* 108:511–18

(1990) 'Overlooked realities: sport myth and sport history', *Stadion* 16:91–102

POLJAKOV, F.B. (1989) *Die Inschriften von Tralleis und Nysa* 1. *Die Inschriften von Tralleis*. Bonn (*Inschriften griechischer Städte aus Kleinasien* 36.1)

POSTLETHWAITE, N. (1995) 'Agamemnon best of spearmen', *Phoenix* 49:95–103

PRAG, A.J.N.W. (1985) *The Oresteia. Iconographic and Narrative Tradition*. Warminster

PRIVITERA, G.A. (1978–9) 'Le vittorie di Melisso nelle *Istmiche* III e IV', *Helikon* 18/19:3–21

PRONGER, B. (1990) *The Arena of Masculinity. Sports, Homosexuality, and the Meaning of Sex*. New York

PUHVEL, J. (1988) 'Hittite athletics as prefigurations of ancient Greek games', in Raschke (1988a), 26–31

RADER, B.G. (1979) 'Modern sports: in search of interpretations', *Journal of Social History* 13:307–21

RAMBA, D. (1990) 'Recordmania in sports in ancient Greece and Rome', in Carter and Krüger (1990), 31–9

RASCHKE, W.J. (1985) 'Aulos and athlete: the function of the flute player in Greek athletics', *Arete: The Journal of Sport Literature* 2.2:177–200

(1988a) ed., *The Archaeology of the Olympics. The Olympics and other Festivals in Antiquity*. Madison

(1988b) 'Images of victory. Some new considerations of athletic monuments', in Raschke (1988a), 38–54

RAUBITSCHEK, A.E. (1980) 'Zum Ursprung und Wesen der Agonistik', in W. Eck, H. Galsterer and H. Wolff, eds., *Studien zür antiken Sozialgeschichte. Festschrift Friedrich Vittinghoff*, 1–5. Cologne and Vienna
   (1983) 'The agonistic spirit in Greek culture', *AncW* 7:3–7

RAUSA, F. (1994) *L'immagine del vincitore. L'atleta nella statuaria greca dall'età arcaica all'ellenismo.* Treviso and Rome

REED, N.B. (1987) 'The *euandria* competition at the Panathenaia reconsidered', *AncW* 15:59–64

RENFREW, C. (1988) 'The Minoan-Mycenaean origins of the panhellenic games', in Raschke (1988a), 13–25

RHODES, P.J. (1981). *A Commentary on the Aristotelian* Athenaion Politeia. Oxford
   (1986) 'Political activity in classical Athens', *JHS* 106:132–44

RIZAKIS, A.D. (1991) ed., *Achaia und Elis in der Antike. Akten des 1. Internationalen Symposiums Athen, 19.-21. Mai 1989.* Athens (*Meletemata* 13)

ROBBINS, E.I. (1987) 'Nereids with golden distaffs: Pindar, *Nem.* 5', *QUCC* 54:25–33

ROBERT, L. (1935) 'Inscriptions de Lesbos et de Samos', *BCH* 59:471–88 (*Opera Minora Selecta* 2 (Amsterdam 1969) 740–57)
   (1938) *Etudes épigraphiques et philologiques.* Paris
   (1939) 'Inscriptions grecques d'Asie Mineure', in W. M. Calder and J. Keil, eds., *Anatolian Studies Presented to William Hepburn Buckler*, 227–48. Manchester (*Opera Minora Selecta* 1 (Amsterdam 1969) 611–32)
   (1960) 'Inscription agonistique d'Ancyre. Concours d'Ancyre', *Hellenica* 11/12:350–68
   (1967) 'Sur des inscriptions d'Ephèse. Fêtes, athlètes, empereurs, épigrammes', *RPh* 41:7–84
   (1968) 'Les épigrammes satiriques de Lucillius sur les athlètes. Parodie et réalités', in O. Reverdin, ed., *L'épigramme grecque*, 181–291. Vandoeuvres and Geneva. (Entretiens sur l'antiquité classique 14)
   (1984) 'Discours d'ouverture', in *Praktika tou H' Diethnous Sunedriou Hellenikēs kai Latinikēs Epigraphikēs Athena, 3–9 Oktabriou 1982*, 35–45. Athens

ROBINSON, E.S.G. (1946) 'Rhegion, Zankle-Messana and the Samians', *JHS* 66:13–20

ROBINSON, R.S. (1981) *Sources for the History of Greek Athletics.* Chicago

ROJEK, C. (1992) 'The field of play in sport and leisure studies', in Dunning and Rojek (1992), 1–35

ROLLER, L.E. (1981) 'Funeral games for historical persons', *Stadion* 7:1–18

ROMANO, D.G. (1983) 'The ancient stadium: athletes and arete', *AncW* 7:9–16
   (1993) *Athletics and Mathematics in Ancient Corinth: the Origins of the Greek Stadion.* Philadelphia (*Memoirs of the American Philosophical Society* 206)

ROSE, P.W. (1992) *Sons of the Gods, Children of Earth. Ideology and Literary Form in Ancient Greece.* Ithaca and London

RYSTEDT, E. (1986) 'The foot-race and other athletic contests in the Mycenaean world. The evidence of the pictorial vases', *OAth* 16:103–16

SÄFLUND, G. (1987) 'The *agoge* of the Minoan youth as reflected by palatial iconography', in R. Hägg and N. Marinatos, eds., *The Function of the*

Minoan Palaces. Proceedings of the Fourth International Symposium at the Swedish Institute in Athens, 10–16 June 1984, 227–33. Stockholm

SAÏD, S. and TRÉDÉ-BOULMER, M. (1984) 'L'éloge de la cité du vainqueur dans les épinicies de Pindare', *Ktema* 9:161–70

SALLARES, R. (1991) *The Ecology of the Ancient Greek World*. London

SANI, E. (1982) 'Valore atletico e valore guerriero nell'iscrizione per Faillo di Crotone', *QUCC* 41:53–7

SANSONE, D. (1988) *Greek Athletics and the Genesis of Sport*. Berkeley and Los Angeles
(1991) 'Cleobis and Biton in Delphi', *Nikephoros* 4:121–32

SARIAN, H. and MACHAIRA, V. (1994) 'Orestes', *LIMC* 7.1:68–76

SCANLON, T.F. (1983) 'The vocabulary of competition: *agon* and *aethlos*, Greek terms for contest', *Arete. The Journal of Sport Literature* 1.1:147–62
(1984a) *Greek and Roman Athletics: a Bibliography*. Chicago
(1984b) 'The footrace of the Heraia at Olympia', *AncW* 9:77–90
(1988a) 'Combat and contest: athletic metaphors for warfare in Greek literature', in S.J. Bandy, ed., *Coroebus Triumphs. The Alliance of Sport and the Arts*, 230–44. San Diego
(1988b) 'The ecumenical Olympics: the games in the Roman era,' in J.O. Segrave and D. Chu, eds., *The Olympic Games in Transition*, 37–64. Champaign IL
(1988c) 'Virgineum gymnasium. Spartan females and early Greek athletics', in Raschke (1988a), 185–216
(1990) 'Race or chase at the Arkteia of Attica?', *Nikephoros* 3:73–120

SCHMITT PANTEL, P. (1992) *La cité au banquet. Histoire des repas publics dans les cités grecques*. Rome

SEAFORD, R. (1984) *Euripides: Cyclops*. Oxford

SEGAL, C. (1968) 'Two agonistic problems in Pindar, *Nemean* 7.70–4 and *Pythian* 1.42–5', *GRBS* 9:31–45

SEKUNDA, N.V. (1990) 'IGii² 1250: a decree concerning the *lampadephoroi* of the tribe Aiantis', *ZPE* 83:149–82

SERWINT, N. (1993) 'The female athletic costume at the Heraia and prenuptial initiation rites', *AJA* 97:403–22

SÈVE, M. (1991) 'Note sur la date du sculpteur Thoinias de Sicyone', *REG* 104:232–5
(1993) 'Les concours d'Epidaure', *REG* 106:303–328

SHAPIRO, H.A. (1994) *Myth into Art. Poet and Painter in Classical Greece*. London and New York

SHIPLEY, G. (1987) *A History of Samos 800–188 BC*. Oxford

SIEWERT, P. (1991) 'Accuse contro i "candidati" all'ostracismo per la loro condotta politica e morale', in M. Sordi, ed., *L'immagine dell'uomo politico: vita pubblica e morale nell'antichità*, 3–14. Milan (*Contributi dell'Istituto di storia antica* 17)
(1992a) 'The Olympic rules', in Coulson and Kyrieleis (1992), 113–17
(1992b) 'Zum Ursprung der Olympischen Spiele', *Nikephoros* 5:7–8

SIMRI, U. (1980) 'The development of female participation in the modern Olympic games', *Stadion* 6:187–216

SINN, U. (1991) 'Olympia. Die Stellung der Wettkämpfe in Kult des Zeus Olympios', *Nikephoros* 4:31–54

(1995) 'Neue Erkenntnisse zu den letzten Olympischen Spielen in der Antike – ein Neufund aus Olympia', *AW* 26:155–6

SLATER, W.J. (1979) 'Pindar's myths: two pragmatic explanations', in G.W. Bowersock, W. Burkert and M.C.J. Putnam, eds., *Arktouros: Hellenic Studies Presented to B.M.W. Knox*, 63–70. Berlin

(1984) '*Nemean One*: the victor's return in poetry and politics', in D.E. Gerber, ed., *Greek Poetry and Philosophy. Studies in Honour of Leonard Woodbury*, 241–64. Chico CA

SLOWIKOWSKI, S.S. (1989) 'The symbolic *Hellanodikai*', *Aethlon* 7.1:133–41

SOKOLOWSKI, F. (1962) *Lois sacrées des cités grecques. Supplément.* Paris

SOMERS, D.A. (1972) *The Rise of Sports in New Orleans, 1830–1900.* Baton Rouge

SOMMERSTEIN, A.H. (1996) 'How to avoid being a *komodoumenos*', *CQ* 46:327–56

SOURVINOU-INWOOD, C. (1988) *Studies in Girls' Transitions: Aspects of the Arkteia and Age Representation in Attic Iconography.* Athens

(1990) 'Ancient rites and modern constructs: on the Brauronian bears again', *BICS* 37:1–14

SPAWFORTH, A.J.S. (1984) 'Notes on the third century AD in Spartan epigraphy', *ABSA* 79:263–88

SPENCE, I.G. (1993) *The Cavalry of Classical Greece. A Social and Military History with Particular Reference to Athens.* Oxford

SPOERRI, W. (1988) 'Epigraphie et littérature: à propos de la liste des Pythioniques à Delphes', in D. Knoepfler, ed., *Comptes et inventaires dans la cité grecque. Actes du Colloque international d'épigraphie tenu à Neuchâtel du 23 au 26 septembre 1986 en l'honneur de Jacques Tréheux*, 111–40. Neuchâtel and Geneva.

STEFANIS, I.E. (1988) '*Athletōn apologia*', *Hellenika* 39:270–90

STEINER, D. (1986) *The Crown of Song. Metaphor in Pindar.* New York

STRAUSS, B.S. (1986) *Athens after the Peloponnesian War. Class, Faction and Policy 403-386 B.C.* Ithaca and London

STRUNA, N.L. (1985) 'In "glorious disarray": the literature of American sport history', *Research Quarterly for Exercise and Sport* 56:151–60

SWEET, W.E. (1983) 'A new proposal for scoring the Greek pentathlon', *ZPE* 50:287–90

(1985) 'Protection of the genitals in Greek athletics', *AncW* 11:43–52

(1987) *Sport and Recreation in Ancient Greece.* Oxford

SZASTYŃSKA-SIEMION, A. (1971) 'Le πόνος du sportif dans l'épinice grec', in *Acta Conventus XI 'Eirene'*, 81–5. Wroclaw

(1981) '*Dapana* und *ponos* bei Pindar', in E.G. Schmidt, ed., *Aischylos und Pindar*, 90–2. Berlin

TANCKE, K. (1991) 'Wagenrennen. Ein Friesthema der aristokratischen Repräsentationskunst spätklassisch-frühhellenistischer Zeit', *JDAI* 105:95–127

THEMELIS, P. (1994) 'Damophon of Messene: new evidence', in K.A. Sheedy, ed., *Archaeology in the Peloponnese. New Excavations and Research*, 1–37. Oxford

THOMAS, R. (1989) *Oral Tradition and Written Record in Classical Athens.* Cambridge

THOMPSON, W.E. (1979) 'More on the Prytaneion decree', *GRBS* 20:325–9

THUILLIER, J.-P. (1988) 'La nudité athlétique (Grèce, Etrurie, Rome)', *Nikephoros* 1:29–48

TIVERIOS, M. (1996) 'Shield devices and column-mounted statues on Panathenaic amphoras. Some remarks on iconography', in Neils (1996), 163–74

TOMLINSON, R.A. (1995) 'The stadium' (review of Romano (1993)), *CR* 45:372–3

TOO, Y.L. (1995) *The Rhetoric of Identity in Isocrates. Text, Power, Pedagogy.* Cambridge

TRACY, S.V. (1991) 'The Panathenaic festival and games: an epigraphic inquiry', *Nikephoros* 4:133–53

TRACY S.V. and HABICHT, C. (1991) 'New and old Panathenaic victor lists', *Hesperia* 60:187–236

TZACHOU-ALEXANDRI, O. (1989) ed., *Mind and Body: Athletic Contests in Ancient Greece.* Athens

ULF, C. (1991) 'Die Frage nach dem Ursprung des Sports, oder: weshalb und wie menschliches Verhalten anfängt, Sport zu sein', *Nikephoros* 4:13–30

ULF, C. and WEILER, I. (1980) 'Der Ursprung der antiken Olympischen Spiele in der Forschung', *Stadion* 6:1–38

VALAVANIS, P.D. (1986) 'Les amphores panathénaïques et le commerce athénien de l'huile', in J.-Y. Empereur and Y. Garlan, eds., *Recherches sur les amphores grecques*, 453–60. Athens and Paris. (*BCH* Supp. 13)

(1987) 'Säulen, Hähne, Niken und Archonten auf Panathenäischen Preisamphoren', *AA* 1987:467–80

VANDERPOOL, E. (1984) 'Regulations for the Herakleian games at Marathon', in *Studies Presented to Sterling Dow on His Eightieth Birthday*, 295–6. Durham NC (*GRBS* Monograph 10)

VANHOVE, D. (1992) ed., *Le sport dans la Grèce antique du jeu à la compétition.* Brussels

VEBLEN, T. (1924[1899]) *The Theory of the Leisure Class.* London

VERMAAK, P.S. (1993) 'Šulgi as sportsman in the Sumerian self-laudatory royal hymns', *Nikephoros* 6:7–21

(1994) 'The Sumerian GEŠPÚ-LIRÙM-MA', *Nikephoros* 7:65–82

VERMEULE, E.T. (1958) 'Mythology in Mycenaean art', *CJ* 54:97–108

VERTINSKY, P.A. (1994a) 'Gender relations, women's history and sport history: a decade of changing enquiry, 1983–1993', *Journal of Sport History* 21:1–24

(1994b) 'Sport history and gender relations, 1983–1993: Bibliography', *Journal of Sport History* 21:25–58

VISA, V. (1992a) 'L'image de l'athlète d'Homère à la fin du Ve siècle avant J. C., dans la littérature et l'iconographie' (Dissertation Université de Paris Sorbonne)

(1992b) 'L'image de l'athlète dans la Collection hippocratique', in J.A. López Férez, ed., *Tratados hipocráticos*. (*Estúdios acerca de su contenido, forma e influencia*). *Actas del VIIe colloque international hippocratique* (*Madrid, 24-29 de septiembre de 1990*), 273–83. Madrid

(1994a) 'Les compétitions athlétiques dans l'*Odyssée*: divertissement, mise à l'épreuve et jeux funèbres', *BAGB* 1994.1:31–40

(1994b) 'Un image cynégétique et sportive pour le triomphe de Cypris (*Hippolyte*, 1268–1271)', *REG* 107:381–99

WACHTER, R. (1995) 'Lakonisch ἀσσκονικτεί', *MH* 52:155–69

WADDELL, G. (1991) 'The Greek pentathlon', *Greek Vases in the J. Paul Getty Museum* 5:99–106

WARD-SMITH, A.J. (1995) 'The application of modern methods of biomechanics to the evaluation of jumping performance in ancient Greece', *Journal of Sports Sciences* 13:223–8

WEBSTER, T.B.L. (1967) *The Tragedies of Euripides*. London

(1972) *Potter and Patron in Classical Athens*. London

WEILER, I. (1974) *Der Agon im Mythus. Zur Einstellung der Griechen zum Wettkampf*. Darmstadt

(1983) 'Einige Bemerkungen zu Solons Olympionikengesetz', in P. Händel and W. Meid, eds., *Festschrift für Robert Muth zum 65. Geburtstag am 1. Januar 1981 dargebracht von Freunden und Kollegen*, 573–82. Innsbruck (Innsbrucker Beiträge zur Kulturwissenschaft 22)

(1985–6) 'Der "Niedergang" und das Ende der antiken Olympischen Spiele in der Forschung', *GB* 12–13:235–63 (cf. 'Problems in the discussion of the reason for the decline of the ancient Olympic games', in *International Olympic Academy. Twenty-fourth Session, 4th - 19th July 1984. Ancient Olympia*, 121–36)

(1988a) *Der Sport bei den Völkern der alten Welt*. 2nd edn. Darmstadt

(1988b) 'Zu "Krise" und "Niedergang" der Agonistik im dritten nachchristlichen Jahrhundert', in *Krise – Krisenbewusstsein – Krisenbewältigung. Ideologie und geistige Kultur im Imperium Romanum während des 3. Jahrhunderts*, 112–19. Halle (Saale) (Wissenschaftliche Beiträge der Martin-Luther-Universität Halle-Wittenberg 1986/62 (C40))

(1989) 'Langzeitperspektiven zur Genese des Sports', *Nikephoros* 2:7–26

(1991) 'Korruption in der Olympischen Agonistik und die diplomatische Mission des Hypereides in Elis', in Rizakis (1991), 87–93

(1993) 'Ursprung der antiken Olympischen Spiele – Ursprung des Sports. Ein Beitrag zum Forschungsstand', in D.P. Panagiotopoulos, ed., *The Institution of the Olympic Games: a Multidisciplinary Approach. Proceedings of the International H.C.R.S.L. Congress, Olympia, Greece, September 3–7, 1991*, 127–39. Athens

WEST, W.C. (1990) 'M. Oulpios Domestikos and the athletic synod at Ephesus', *AHB* 4:84–9

WHITEHEAD, D. (1983) 'Competitive outlay and community profit: φιλοτιμία in democratic Athens', *CetM* 34:55–74

WHITEHORNE, J. (1995) 'Women's work in Theocritus, Idyll 15', *Hermes* 123:63–75

WILHELM, A. (1908) 'Inschriften aus Halikarnassos und Theangela', *JÖAI* 11:53–75

WILL, G.F. (1990) *Men at Work. The Craft of Baseball.* New York and London

WILLCOCK, M.M. (1995) *Pindar: Victory Odes.* Olympians *2,7,11*; Nemean *4*; Isthmians *3,4,7.* Cambridge

WILLETTS, R.F. (1977) *The Civilisation of Ancient Crete.* London

WOODFORD, S. (1971) 'Cults of Heracles in Attica', in *Studies Presented to G.M.A. Hanfmann,* 211–25. Mainz

WÖRRLE, M. (1988) *Stadt und Fest in kaiserzeitlichen Kleinasien. Studien zu einer agonistischen Stiftung aus Oinoanda.* Munich (Vestigia 39)

YALOURIS, N. (1979) ed., *The Eternal Olympics. The Art and History of Sport.* New Rochelle NY

YOUNG, D.C. (1968) *Three Odes of Pindar.* Leiden (*Mnemosyne* Supp. 9)

(1983) 'Professionalism in archaic and classical Greek athletics', *AncW* 7:45–51

(1984) *The Olympic Myth of Greek Amateur Athletics.* Chicago

(1988a) 'How the amateurs won the Olympics', in Raschke (1988a), 55–75

(1988b) 'The riddle of the rings', in S.J. Bandy, ed., *Coroebus Triumphs. The Alliance of Sport and the Arts,* 257–76. San Diego

(1996) *The Modern Olympics: A Struggle for Revival.* Baltimore

YOUNGER, J.G. (1976) 'Bronze Age representations of Aegean bull-leaping', *AJA* 80:125–37

Index and glossary

Achaea, 86, 110
Achaeus, 157
Achilles, 3, 88–9, 91, 92, 93–4, 116, 119, 134, 136, 148
Acrisius, 24
Actia, 11, 35
Aegiale, 91, 93
Aegina, 78, 84, 87, 107
Aegisthus, 96, 97, 101, 102
Aegyptus, 74
Aeschines, 61, 68, 148–9, 157, 158–9
Aeschylus, 98–9, 101, 167, 168
Aetolus, 45
Africanus, Sextus Julius, 61, 63
Agamemnon, 89, 94, 96, 98, 99
Agathos Daimon, 118
age, x, xi, 5, 6, 45, 117–23, 142 n. 1, 176, 178
age classes, 104–16, 139, 177
ageneioi, 'beardless youths', 9, 83, 87, 104–16, 166
Agesilaus, 71, 106, 134, 138 n. 29, 161
Agesipolis, 71
agones, 'contests', xi, 24, 25, 102
agonothetai, 'sponsors *or* managers of contests', 94, 105, 133
Ajax, son of Oïleus, 89, 94
Ajax, son of Telamon, 89, 93
akoniti, 'without dust' (used of an uncontested victory or walkover), 49, 72, 78
Alcibiades, 74, 84, 85, 86, 99, 117, 119, 123, 161, 169–71, 173, 174
Alcimedon, 83, 113
Alcmaeon, 170
Alexander Balas, 122
Alexander the Great, 35, 160
Alexandria, 33, 87, 107
Alexidamus, 80
Aleximachus, 91
Altis, *see* Olympia
amateurs, amateurism, ix, 141–2
Amazons, 128, 137

Amphiaraeia, 108, 172
Amphion, 147
Anaxilas, 40, 41, 43
Antaeus, 59, 135, 153
Anthesteria, 95
anthippasia, 27
Anticles, 158
Antilochus, 88, 91, 94, 119–20
Antioch, 127
Antipater, 110
Antiphon, 24
Antonius Callippus Peisanus, M., 109
apenē, 'mule-cart race', 40–3, 99, 120
Aphrodisias, 39, 71
Aphrodite, 95, 136, 147
apobatēs, 'dismounting race' (an equestrian event in which a contestant, in armour, both ran and rode in a chariot), 3, 41, 43, 120
Apollo, 10, 11, 16, 34, 44, 83, 89, 96, 102, 123, 150, 152
Apollodorus, 146, 150–2, 154–6
Apollonia, 76
Apollonius of Rhodes, 147
Aratus, 119
Arcadia, 17, 28, 107
Arcesilas, 35, 83
archaeology, ix, 47, 56–7, 64–5, 93
archery, 2, 30, 31, 89, 91, 92, 93, 95, 112, 154
Archilochus, 77
Ares, 25, 44
Argos, 10, 11, 23, 34, 35, 76, 175
Arieti, John, 67
Aristagoras, 80, 81, 84, 108
Aristodemus, 63
Aristomenes, 109
Aristophanes, 124, 125, 160, 167, 169
Aristophanes of Byzantium, 81, 103
Aristotle, 10, 28, 38, 71, 114–15, 117, 143, 149, 158, 159, 163
Arrachion, 24, 85

arktoi, 'bears', 126
Arrigoni, G., 129
Artemidorus, 3, 61, 124, 144
Artemidorus (athlete), 114
Artemis, 126, 136
Asclepieia, 52, 70, 104, 105, 107, 115
associations of athletes, 145, 154
Astyanax, 157
Astylus, 37
Atalanta, 70, 76, 134–7
Athena, 76, 81, 89, 90, 91, 96
Athenaeus, 137, 157
Athenion, 110
Athens, ix, xi, 9, 16, 27, 35, 37, 41, 42, 43, 45,
    47, 48, 59, 76, 82, 83, 84, 86, 91, 96, 106,
    107, 108, 110, 117, 122, 123, 125–7, 130,
    137, 138, 143, 148–9, 157–75, 178
athletics, contrasted with equestrian events,
    x, xi, xii, 11, 34, 43–5, 118–23, 134, 170 n.
    24, 174, 178
athlothetai, 'prize setters' (officials of the
    Panathenaea), 164
Augeas, 12, 151, 155–6
Aurelius Asclepiades, M., 118
Aurelius Helix, 105, 113
Aurelius Heras, M., 35, 116
Aurelius Septimius Irenaeus, 116
Autolycus, 74, 112, 166–7
Azan, 44, 45

Babylonians, 30
Bacchylides, xi, 78, 79, 80, 107, 110
ball games, 7, 9, 25, 127
barbaroi, 'non-Greeks', 2, 4–5, 66, 87, 134,
    146, 176, 177
baseball, x n. 1, 24, 33 n. 26
Basileia, 114
Bérard, Claude, 125
Berenice II, 87–8, 133–4
Bernal, Martin, 29, 46
bibasis (jumping competition at Sparta), 128
Bilistiche, 133, 134
boat races, 8, 9, 25, 26, 34, 164
body, 7, 49, 66, 68, 71, 79, 90, 103, 106, 124,
    149, 157–8
Boeotia, 41, 43, 108
Boiscus, 28
Bourdieu, Pierre, 6, 40
boxing (*pyx*, a combat event in which
    competitors wore leather straps to
    protect their hands and fought without a
    break until one gave in or could not go
    on), 1, 28, 30, 32, 33, 37, 38, 43, 44, 46,
    49, 52, 53, 54, 55, 59–60, 65, 71, 79, 83,
    89, 90, 91, 93, 95, 105, 108, 110, 113, 114,
115–16, 118, 128, 137, 145, 153, 155, 158,
    163
Brasidas, 91
bulls, 32, 37, 127
Burckhardt, Jacob, 29
Burkert, Walter, 13–14, 18
Bybon, 55

Caillois, Roger, 18
Callias, 77
Callicrates, 153
Callimachus, 63, 84, 86–8
Callippus, 16
Capitolia, 83
Carrhotus, 83
Castricius Regulus, L., 127, 138
cavalry, 27, 122, 123, 169, 173, 174
Ceos, 77–8, 82, 107, 110, 112
Chabrias, 74, 75, 173
chariot races, 2, 33, 35, 37, 39, 40, 43–5,
    64–5, 79, 82, 87, 88–9, 92, 93, 94, 95,
    99–101, 102, 106, 119–23, 138, 153, 154,
    165, 170, 171
charioteers, 3, 44, 51, 58, 64, 65, 82–3, 91, 99,
    109, 119, 120, 139, 169
Charmides, 70
cheating, 15–16, 20, 21, 37, 44, 95, 109, 110,
    133
Chionis, 60, 61
Chios, 35, 127, 137, 153
Chloris, 129
Cicero, 68, 118
Cimon, 37, 175
class, ix, x, 5–6, 45, 141–5, 158–62, 165,
    166–9, 178. *See also* elite
Clazomenae, 110
Cleitomachus, 55, 75
Cleitor, 34
Cleombrotus, 137
Cleonae, 23
Cleopatra II, 134
Clytaemnestra, 96, 101
combat sports, ix, 18, 24, 30, 31, 32, 37–8, 73,
    83, 89, 92, 93, 94, 154
competitiveness, x, 10, 28–30, 70, 118, 119,
    125, 141
Copreus, 151
Corinth, 10, 57, 87
Cornelius Ariston, P., 113
Coroebus, 63, 143
Cos, 52, 70, 104, 105, 107, 110, 115
Coubertin, Pierre de, 131
Crete, 1, 2, 12, 13, 30, 32–3, 48, 126, 127
cricket, 72
Crison, 118

Critias, 35
criticisms, of athletics, 27–8, 157–8, 162–9; of
equestrian competition, 165–6, 169–71,
173–5, 178; *see also* athletics, contrasted
with equestrian events
Critolaus, 91, 93
Crius, 78
Cronus, 12, 44
Croton, 37, 117, 143
crown games, xi, 10–11, 33–4, 70, 76, 84, 141,
142, 146, 150, 158, 171
Crowther, Nigel, 3
Cylon, 9
Cynisca, 133, 134
Cyrene, 75, 83
Cyzicus, 114

Daedalus, 147–8
Damatrius, 116
Damiscus, 105, 115
Damonicus, 109
Damonon, 40, 119
danger, 2, 24, 100, 115–16, 120, 169–70
Davies, J.K., 171–5
Decker, Wolfgang, 30–1
dedications, 15, 21, 64–5, 76, 83, 84–6, 91,
133, 166
defeat, 9, 70, 91, 93–4, 100–1, 109, 166, 177
Deinolochus, 109
Delos, 61 n. 13, 76, 108
Delphi, xi, 10, 16, 19, 21–3, 27, 45, 54, 56, 58,
77, 84, 98, 128, 138, 150; *see also* Pythian
games
Demades, 173
Demeter, 13, 17, 132
Demosthenes, 3, 4, 61, 148–9, 158–9, 166
Diagoras, 79, 108, 109
diaitatores (earliest judges at Olympia), 15
diaulos (a foot race of two lengths of the
ancient stadium, 1200 Greek feet, about
400 m), 19, 79, 82, 87, 98, 110, 115, 116,
118, 126, 128
difference, x, 4–6, 33–45, 175–8; *see also* class,
gender, hierarchy
Dio Chrysostom, 52, 144
Diocleia, 28
Diodorus, 158
Diodorus of Sicily, 12
Diomedes, 89, 91, 93
Dionysia, 138
Dionysiades, 128
Dionysus, 8, 128, 157, 167
Dioscuri (Castor and Pollux), 98, 101, 102
discus (*diskos*, a disc-shaped metal object
thrown for distance), 2, 24, 28, 38, 38 n.

33, 43, 55, 58, 61, 62, 69, 72, 73, 90, 91,
92, 112, 127, 128, 137
Dörpfeld, Wilhelm, 57
dolikhos, 'long run' (a foot race of from seven
to twenty-four lengths of the ancient
stadium, up to about 5000 m), 1, 37, 51,
110, 112, 114, 115, 116, 126, 158
Dracontius, 1, 2, 3
draws, 73
Drees, Ludwig, 20, 23
Dunning, Eric, 7
Duris, 141
dust, 50
Dyme, 41, 42

Ebert, J., 69
egkritas (officials who assigned competitors to
age classes), 106
Egypt, 29, 30–2, 143, 145
eiselastikoi, 'games for driving in', *see* crown
games
Electra, 96, 102
Eleutheria, 49, 91
Elias, N., 7
Elis, 10, 12, 16, 17, 24, 28, 30, 36–7, 42–3, 64,
83, 91, 107, 108, 128, 129, 151, 177
elite, 5–6, 7, 8, 26, 27, 42, 43, 78, 81, 84–6,
110, 118, 145, 146, 148, 158–61, 162,
169–75, 178; finance competitions, 163–4
Enymacratidas, 119
Epaminondas, 28
Epeius, 28, 89, 90, 91, 94
ephebes (citizens, just come of age, involved
in physical and military training), 25, 26,
37, 105, 167–9
ephedroi (competitors enjoying a bye), 51, 73
Ephesia, 108
Ephesus, 114, 143
Epichares, 110
Epidaurus, 34, 52, 138
epigrams, 34, 35, 47, 48, 62, 65, 87, 128, 137
Epitaphia, 91
equestrian events, x, xi, xii, 3, 5–6, 8, 19, 27,
37, 39–45, 84; and political leadership,
169–75; older competitors in, 118–23,
139, 178; women in, 133, 134, 137–9,
177–8; *see also* chariot races, horse races
Eratosthenes, 63, 71
Erginus, 150
Erotidea, 73, 105
Etruscans, 27 n. 21, 66
euandria (a team contest demonstrating
physical fitness, perhaps a tug of war or
mock combat), 37, 162, 164
Eubotas, 75, 119

Eumelus, 89, 94
euhexia, 162
Eumeneia, 19
Eumenes, 141
Eupolis, 167
Euripides, 27–8, 38, 48, 84, 101–3, 124, 127, 147, 157, 159, 169, 177
Euryalus, 90, 95
Euryleonis, 133
Eurystheus, 150–1
Eurytus, 154
Eusebius, 61
eutaxia, 164
Euthymus, 86
Evagoras, 43
Evans, Arthur, 32

families of competitors, 77, 80, 82–3, 108, 110, 127, 145, 167, 172
fathers of competitors, 62, 83, 98, 102, 108–9, 110, 119, 139, 177, 178
festivals, 10–11, 14–15, 31–7; costs of, 54, 164–5
fines, 15–16
Finley, M.I., 93
Flamininus, 34
foals, 106, 133, 134, 177
footraces, 13, 23 n. 17, 40, 44, 57, 89, 90, 93, 95, 100, 116, 125–31, 134–6, 144, 160
foreigners, 3, 4, 166
funeral games, 3, 11, 12, 44, 88, 89, 91–3, 119, 134

Galen, 38
Gardiner, E.N., ix, 29, 33, 141–2, 145
Gelon, 37
gender, ix, x, 4, 6, 68, 70, 89, 90, 92, 123–5, 130–2, 134–7, 138–40, 177
Germanicus, 177
gerontes, 'old men', 117, 120
Glaucus, 62
Gryllus, 115
Guttmann, A., 6, 10, 19
gymnasia, 4 n. 1, 24, 25–7, 47, 54, 65, 66, 117, 125, 144, 153, 157, 158, 159, 160, 162, 167
gymnasiarchs (officials in charge of gymnasia), 50, 117, 133, 137, 162, 163–4, 168

Hadrian, 11
Hagesias, 40
Hagesidamus, 155–6
hair, 78, 101, 113, 157
halteres, 'jumping weights', 55, 57, 60
Hamilton, Richard, 126

Harris, H.A., ix, 69, 72, 73, 132, 141–2, 145
heavy events, 37–8
Hector, 3, 88, 94
Hedea, 138
Helen, 127, 128
Hellanodikai (judges at Olympia), 15, 40, 42, 106
Hephaesteia, 164, 168
Hephaestus, 147, 150
Hera, 125, 129, 131, 150
Heracleia, 153
Heracleides Ponticus, 37
Heracles, xi, 1, 4, 11, 12, 13, 38, 43, 44, 49, 54, 59, 79, 92, 111, 132, 146–57
Heraea (*Aspis*) at Argos, 11, 34, 35, 76, 142
Heraea at Olympia, 125, 127–32
heralds, xii, 24, 62, 82, 102, 170
Hermes, 26, 44, 153
Hermesianax, 138
Hermione, 34
Herodotus, 32, 146, 158
Herodotus (athlete), 110
heroes, athletes as, 18, 19, 86, 154
Hesychius, 52, 127, 167
hierarchy of events, 37–40, 71–2, 80–1, 88, 176, 178; of festivals, 33–7, 80–1, 87, 146, 155
Hierocles, 55
Hieron, 37, 78, 84, 85, 161
hippeis, 'cavalrymen', *see* cavalry
Hippias of Elis, 16, 43–5, 63–5, 104, 178
hippios (a foot-race of four lengths of the ancient stadium, 2400 Greek feet, about 800 m), 37, 41, 78, 102, 126
Hippocleas, 75
Hippodameia, 44, 125, 129
hippodromes, 23, 79 n. 4, 92, 95
Hippolytus, 2, 95
Hipposthenes, 117–18
Hittites, 31–2
hockey, 7, 72
Homer, 3, 25, 28, 65, 88–95, 118–19, 150
homosexuality, 7, 67, 74–5, 137, 174
hoplites (heavy infantry soldiers), 25–7
hoplitodromos, hoplitēs, 'hoplite race' (a foot-race in armour), 26–7, 34, 38 n. 33, 40, 49, 65, 110, 116, 153
horse races, 1, 2, 35, 44, 153
horses, 51, 59, 78, 82, 99, 102, 173 n. 27, 174
Huizinga, Johan, 24
Humphreys, Sally, 162
hunting, 17–18, 68, 126, 134, 136, 158
Hyacinthus, 24
hydrophoria, 87
Hyperides, 16
Hysmon, 71

Ibycus, 77, 78, 99
Iccus, 75
ice boxing, *see* hockey
Iliad, 3, 43, 88–9, 91, 92, 93, 94, 100, 147
infibulation, 68
initiates, initiation, 13, 32, 68, 113, 129, 132
injuries, *see* danger
inscriptions, 3, 26, 39, 40, 47, 51, 54–5, 81,
    115, 128, 138, 171
introduction of new events, 40–3, 107–10, 172,
    174
Iolaeia, 76
Iolaus, 98
Iphicrates, 107
Iphitus, 44, 111
Irus, 90
Isidorus, 118
Isocrates, 33, 159, 162, 170
Isthmia, Isthmian games, 8, 10–11, 21, 24, 33,
    34, 36, 52, 76, 78, 80, 82, 87, 91, 96, 104,
    105, 106, 107, 109, 110, 115, 119, 127, 137,
    138, 170

Jason, 69–70
javelin (*akōn*, a light spear thrown, by means
    of a thong, for distance as part of the
    pentathlon but also thrown at a target
    by mounted competitors), 2, 24, 37, 38 n.
    33, 39, 43, 52, 58, 61, 67, 69, 72, 73, 79,
    92, 112, 127, 137
jockeys, 3, 65, 82, 139
Julius Demosthenes, 11
jump (*halma*, probably a running long jump,
    at least as part of the pentathlon), x, xi,
    2, 8, 55, 60–2, 69, 72, 90, 91

kalpē, (a (?) mares' race involving
    dismounting), 40–3
Klee, T., 105
klimax, 'ladder', 52
Kurke, Leslie, 81
Kyle, Don, 15, 69, 70, 72, 73, 165, 173

Lachon, 78
Lampon, 109
Laodicea, 115
Laomedon, 152
Larissa, 37
Lee, Hugh, 69
Leonidas, 118
Leontini, 77
Lesbos, 28
Lichas, 120, 162 n. 15
light events, 37–8
Liparion, 110

Livia, 128
local games, 33–4, 35, 55, 61, 76, 80, 82, 84,
    104, 143–5
loincloth (*diazoma, perizoma, zoma*), 65–7, 91,
    128, 135
Lousoi, 34
Lucian, 124–5, 132, 146
Lucillius, 137
Lycaea, 34, 107
Lycia, 38
Lycinus, 106
Lycon, 117
Lycurgus, 170
Lysias, 4, 12

Macedon, 78, 87
Malalas, John, 127
Mallwitz, Alfred, 57, 64–5
Mandrell, Richard, 6–7
Mantinea, 34
Marathon, 76, 153
marathon (a long distance race in which
    ancient Greeks did not compete), 73
Marcianus Rufus, 115
Marxists, 7
Megacles, 86, 169, 175
Megara, 28, 76
Melancomas, 52
Melanion, 136
Meleager, 134, 136
Meleagria, 145
Melesias, 83, 109, 118
Melicertes/Palaemon, 91
Melissus, 79, 119
Melkart, 30
Menander, 83
Menelaus, 89, 94
Meuli, Karl, 18, 92
Middleton, Eric, 7
Miletus, 107, 110
Milon, 117, 118, 153, 157
Miltiades, 91
Minoans, 30, 32–3, 65
Morgan, Catherine, 65
Morris, Desmond, 18
mothers of competitors, 108–9
Mouratidis, John, 13, 68, 132
mules, 43, 46; *see also apenē*
music, xi, 17–18, 34, 60, 84, 90
Mycenaeans, 32, 33, 43, 65, 92–3, 97
Myrrhine, 137
Myrtilus, 44, 99, 102, 171

Nagy, Gregory, 13–14, 92
Naples, 11, 127, 128

Neleus, 91, 92
Nemea, Nemean games, 10–11, 21, 23, 23 n.
 17, 33, 34, 36, 52, 55, 56–7, 70, 71, 76, 80,
 82, 83, 87, 91, 104, 105, 107, 108, 109,
 110, 113, 115, 118, 119, 134, 137, 138, 151,
 153, 155, 170
Nero, 11, 33 n. 27, 177
Nessus, 152
Nestor, 88, 89, 91, 119
Newton, Isaac, 63
Nicasylus, 105
Nicegora, 127
Nicolaidas, 111–12
Nicomachus, 83
Nicomedeia, 115
Nicopolis, 11
Novak, Michael, 10
nudity, x, 9, 26, 48, 65–9, 88, 96–8, 127, 128,
 177

oaths, 14
Odysseus, 89, 90, 93, 94–5, 148, 154–5
Odyssey, 89–90, 94–5, 96, 148
Oebotas, 86, 110
Oenoanda, 11, 145
Oenomaus, 12, 44, 91, 109
oil, 3, 4 n. 1, 17, 26, 68, 76–7, 124, 133, 165
'Old Oligarch'/pseudo-Xenophon, 163–4,
 168
Olympia, 4, 10, 25, 56, 58, 84, 85, 86, 96, 102,
 125, 132, 133; Altis (sacred grove) at, 14,
 17, 21–3, 132; hippodrome at, 79 n. 4;
 stadium at, 16, 18–19, 21–3, 130–1, 139
Olympic games, x, xii, 2, 4, 9, 10, 11, 24, 30,
 37, 46, 51, 54, 55, 62, 71, 75, 76, 77, 78,
 82, 83, 86, 102, 106, 108, 110, 111, 113,
 114, 115, 117, 127, 132, 133, 134, 143, 160,
 169–75; age classes at, 104–5; and
 Heraea, 129–31; dating by, 11, 16, 39;
 foundation date of, x–xi, 63–5; history of
 programme at, x, 40–5, 109–10, 134;
 home cities of victors at, 107; mythic
 origins of, 12–14, 91, 111, 155–6;
 preeminence of, 33–7, 80–1; religion and
 sport at, 14–23; schedule at, 18–20, 27,
 55, 73, 112; training period at, 16, 108
Olympics, modern, 46, 131–2, 142
Onasiteles, 105, 106
Opheltes/Archemorus, 91
Orestes, xi, 2, 96–103, 159, 177
Oropus, 108, 116
Orsilochus, 2
Orsippus, 65–6, 68

paides, 'boys', 1, 3, 4, 9, 15, 17, 38, 40, 44, 51,

 71, 82, 83, 87, 98, 104–16, 119, 123 n. 16,
 138, 141, 142–4, 155, 165, 166, 176–8;
 paides Isthmikoi, 104–6, 107–9, 114; *paides
 Puthikoi*, 104–6, 107, 114
paidotribai, 'trainers', 144, 160
palaestrae, 3, 26 n. 20, 28, 38, 39, 54, 97–8,
 101, 124–5, 137, 153, 162, 167, 168
Panathenaea, ix, 3, 8, 9, 37, 39–40, 42, 55, 70,
 71, 74, 76, 87, 104, 105, 106, 111–12, 122,
 123, 126, 129, 134, 142, 143, 162, 164–6,
 167–9, 174
Panhellenia, 143
pankration (a combat event in which
 competitors hit, kicked and grappled,
 upright or on the ground, without a
 break until one gave in or could not go
 on), 1, 2, 24, 37, 39, 40, 54, 55, 59, 65,
 68, 71, 74, 75, 79, 84, 91, 93, 105, 108,
 110, 111, 113, 114, 115, 116, 118, 119, 124,
 128, 141, 145, 153, 154, 157, 160, 166
papyri, 47, 55–6, 78
Parmeniscus, 116
participation, 70–1, 158
Pataecus, 41
Patras, 14, 127
Patroclus, 3, 43, 88, 91, 93
patronage, 143
Pausanias, 14, 15, 36, 38, 42, 44, 58, 62, 63,
 65, 82, 86, 105, 107, 111, 124, 125, 128,
 129, 132, 133, 134
payments to athletes, 55, 143–4
Peisistratus, 37, 78, 120 n. 15
Peisodorus, 109, 132
Peleus, 48, 69–70, 91, 127, 134–6, 137
Pellene, 76, 86
Pelopion, 14
Peloponnese, 10, 34, 35, 108, 109
Pelops, 12, 13–14, 44, 57, 91, 99, 101, 102, 125,
 129, 171
pentathlon (a five-part event including
 stadion, wrestling, jump, discus, javelin),
 x, xi, 16, 17, 19, 21, 24, 38, 42, 55, 60, 61,
 69–73, 79, 82, 91, 109, 110, 111–12, 115,
 116, 119
Pentathlus, 71
periodonikēs (a winner at each of the games of
 the *periodos*), 11, 108, 116 n. 10
periodos (the 'circuit' of crown games), 10–11,
 16, 25–6, 34, 129
Phayllus, 60–2, 160
Pheidippides, 120
Pherenice/Callipateira, 109
Pherenicus, 78, 82
Pherias, 105
Philammon, 61

Philip II of Macedon, 4, 35, 122, 141
Philo of Alexandria, 95
Philopoemen, 28, 50, 91
Philostratus, 18–19, 36, 38, 48–50, 54, 70, 72, 108, 111, 113, 117
Phlegon, 63
Phocis, 107
Phoenicians, 29, 30
Phoenix, 88, 91
Pindar, xi, 24, 43, 44, 52, 70, 74, 79–84, 86, 87, 107, 108, 109, 113, 119, 120, 144, 146, 155–6
Pisa, 12, 17, 129
Pisidia, 4, 38
Pisus, 12
Plataea, 49, 91
Plato, 28, 35, 47, 50, 66, 74, 76, 112 n. 6, 117, 126, 160, 174
Plutarch, 27, 44, 50–2, 54, 63, 117, 127, 141, 158
Pleket, H.W., 144–5
Polybius, 63, 117
Polycles, 87
Polyclitus, 71
Polycrates, 134
Polynicus, 110–11
Polypoites, 89, 93
Polyxenus, 110
ponos, 'effort', 77, 80, 156
Poseidon, 10, 21, 152
presbuteroi, 'elders', 117
prizes, 3, 6, 11, 18, 33, 35, 39, 50, 54, 64, 71–2, 76–7, 89, 90, 91, 94, 111–12, 122, 141–3, 146, 155, 156–7, 165–6; for second place and lower, 70, 89, 93, 111–12, 136, 165
professionals, professionalism, 20, 21, 107, 141–2
Prolaus, sons of, 24
Promachus, 75
Prometheia, 164
Propertius, 127–8
Protagoras, 26
Psaumis, 40, 120
Ptolemaieia, 33
Ptolemy II, 134
Ptolemy VI, 122
Pulydamas, 153
Pylades, 96, 98, 101, 102, 103
pyrrhic dancing, 27, 51, 111, 126
Pythagoras, 113
Pytheas, 83, 105
Pythian games, xi, 4, 10–11, 27, 33, 34, 36, 51, 54, 62, 74, 75, 76, 78, 79, 80, 81, 82, 83, 91, 98, 99–100, 108, 110, 115, 138, 172–3, 175; age classes at, 104–6; history of

programme at, 45, 110; home cities of victors at, 107; schedule at, 99–100, 112
Python, 91

quantification, 6, 61

records, 6, 31 n. 25, 61–2, 139, 177
referees, 53, 91, 120, 162, 163, 169
religion, ix, x, 2, 10–23, 43, 54, 85–6, 91, 112, 126, 127, 128, 129, 133, 153, 162, 176
rewards for victors, 76–7, 98, 111, 142, 171, 177
Rhodes, 55, 81
Rhodes, P.J., 172
ritual, 17–18
rhabdoi, 'rods', 50, 53, 120, 162, 163, 169
Rome, Romans, 11, 21, 32, 34, 177

sacrifice, 2, 13–14, 17–19, 49, 91, 112, 125, 130, 176
Salmoneus, 45 n. 40
Samos, 117
Sansone, David, 17–19, 23, 68
Scanlon, Thomas, 126, 128
Schliemann, Heinrich, 93
sculpture, 37, 38 n. 33, 57–8, 59–60, 71, 84–6, 103, 109, 110, 111, 128, 129, 132
Seaford, Richard, 95
Sebasta, 11
Sebasteia, 138
Seia Spes, 127, 128
Sekunda, N.V., 168
Seneca, 54
Serwint, Nancy, 132
sex, 74–5, 117, 124–5, 129, 137; abstinence from, 75
Shulgi, 31
Sicily, 41, 84
Sicyon, 34, 76, 77, 81, 138, 145
Simonides, xi, 43, 66, 77–8, 80, 84, 85, 161
Sinn, Ulrich, 54
slaves, 2, 3–4, 54, 82, 134, 145, 149
Smyrna, 114
Socrates, 48, 70, 75, 113, 117, 118, 157, 159, 162, 171
Socrates (athlete), 108
Solon, 3, 51, 76, 85
Sophocles, 44, 99–101, 102, 171
Sosibius, 86–8, 119
Sostratus, 86, 110
Sotades, 2
Sparta, 1, 3, 9, 19, 24, 26, 35, 40, 48, 54, 59, 71, 76, 77, 78, 81, 106, 107, 114, 117, 119, 120, 125, 127–9, 130, 133, 134, 137, 138, 159, 166, 174
spectators, 21, 23, 34, 51, 64, 89, 91, 94, 100, 129, 137, 157, 166, 167–8

sphaireis, 'ball players', 9

sport, definition of, xi, 17, 29; origins of, ix, 6–8, 12–13, 17–18, 20, 91–3

stadion (a foot race of one length of the ancient stadium, 600 Greek feet, about 200 m), 14, 16, 18–19, 37, 38, 39, 40, 43, 44, 51, 57, 61, 65, 69, 70, 71, 72, 75, 78, 82, 98, 105, 109, 111, 116, 119, 126, 127, 138, 143, 145, 158

stadium, 13, 16, 18–19, 21–3, 54, 55, 57, 125, 129–31, 139

statues, *see* sculpture

stephanitai, see crown games

Strabo, 12

Stratoniceia, 110

strigil (*stleggis*, a metal tool used by athletes to scrape off dust, oil and sweat after training or competition), 26, 97–8, 124, 125

subsidies for athletes, 143

suitors, 13, 44, 90, 92, 94–5, 135–6, 154

Sumerians, 31

sunoris, 'two-horse chariot race', 43, 45, 64, 77, 121; *see also* chariot races

swimming, 8

Sybaris, 37, 76

symposia, 60, 74, 75, 112

Syracuse, 37, 78, 110

tainiai, 'victory ribbons', 18, 95

taurotheria, 37

teams, 9, 24–5, 71, 111, 126, 162, 167–9

Tegea, 34, 76

Teisias/Diomedes, 169, 170

Telesicrates, 74

Tenedus, 28, 81, 108

tethrippon, 'four-horse chariot race', 44, 45, 64, 74, 77, 79, 82, 93; *see also* chariot races

Thasos, 11, 86

Thebes, 107

Theocritus, 127

Theogenes, 52, 86, 116, 118, 157

Theophrastus, 109

theoroi (official delegates of Greek states to the Olympic festival), 19

Theron, 83, 84

Theseia, 104–5, 110

Theseus, 38, 59, 123–4, 150

Thespiae, 76, 105, 111

Thessalonica, 114, 115

Thessaly, 78, 100, 102, 116

Thibron, 26

Thrasydaeus, 98

Thucydides, 16, 62, 66, 108, 170–1

Thucydides, son of Melesias, 109

Thuillier, J.-P., 67–8

Tiberius, 177

Timaeus, 63

Timanthes, 118

Timocrates, 173

Timoleon, 91

Timon, 82, 123 n. 16

Timositheus, 158

Tisamenus, 24

Titormus, 157

torch races, 19, 25, 105, 162, 164, 167–9

trainers, 15, 26, 50, 75, 81, 83, 91, 95, 109, 118, 132, 143, 144, 160

training, 15, 16, 38, 49, 65, 75, 108, 114–15, 157

Tralles, 76, 138

Trapezus, 1, 2, 4, 5

truces, 14, 16–17, 46

trumpeters, xiii

Tryphosa, 138–9

Tydaeus, 89, 92

Tyrtaeus, 162

vases, 38 n. 33, 52, 57, 58–60, 66–8, 74, 96–8, 125, 126, 136, 174; Panathenaic, 55, 58–9, 165, 166

Veblen, Thorstein, 24

victory, xi, 4, 6, 9, 17, 18, 19, 24, 26, 28, 70, 80, 82, 84, 85–6, 95, 101–3, 110–11, 177; in different events, 116

victory songs, xi, 48, 76–88, 100, 103, 110, 177

war, x, 2, 4, 9, 10, 23–8, 32, 37, 44, 50–1, 71, 88, 89, 92, 94–5, 96, 112, 117, 126, 176

Webster, T.B.L., 174

weight classes, lack of, 37, 73, 139

weight lifting, 31, 57

weight throwing, 25 n. 19, 31, 55, 89, 91, 93

Weiler, Ingomar, 154

women, xi, 1, 5, 13, 17, 18, 46, 47, 68, 88, 93, 104, 123–40, 176, 177–8; distinguished from girls, 128, 132–3

wreaths, 17, 25, 26, 33, 35, 37, 39, 76, 110, 125, 130, 136, 155, 156

wrestling (*palē*, a combat event in which competitors grappled until one threw the other to the ground), 1, 19, 24, 28, 30, 31, 37, 38, 39, 40, 43, 44, 46, 49, 50, 51, 52, 59, 69, 71, 72, 73, 78, 79, 87, 88, 89, 90, 91, 94, 98–9, 102, 105, 106, 108, 109, 110, 111, 113, 116, 117, 118, 124, 127, 134, 135, 136, 137, 141, 144, 145, 153, 154, 157

Xenocrates, 83

Xenophanes, 20
Xenophon, 1, 2, 4, 5, 6, 29, 45, 74, 75, 117,
    120, 134, 157, 161, 162
Xenophon (athlete), 82

Young, David, 142–4, 165

Zacynthus, 110
Zanes, 15–16, 17
Zenon, 55
Zethus, 147, 151
Zeus, 1, 10, 12, 13–14, 15, 17, 18–19, 21, 23, 44,
    56, 78, 86, 98, 99, 102, 129, 132, 155

SOUTHEASTERN COMMUNITY COLLEGE LIBRARY

3 3255 00066 5803

SOUTHEASTERN COMMUNITY
COLLEGE LIBRARY
WHITEVILLE, NC 28472